DURHAM COUNTY COUNCIL
Cultural Services

Please return or renew this item by the last date shown.
Fines will be charged if the book is kept after this date.
Thank you for using *your* library

100% recycled paper.

The world is my country
All men are my brothers
And to do good is my religion

Thomas Paine

ZILLIACUS

A Life for Peace and Socialism

Archie Potts

The Merlin Press

First published 2002 by The Merlin Press Ltd.
PO Box 30705
London WC2E 8QD
www.merlinpress.co.uk

ISBN: 0850365090

◆

British Library Cataloguing in Publication Data
is available from the British Library

◆

Printed in Great Britain by Antony Rowe, Chippenham

Contents

Illustrations

Foreword

This is a brilliant biography of a brilliant man, who devoted his life to the cause of peace and socialism and exercised great influence from his early years as an official working in the League of Nations through to his work in and out of parliament as a Labour MP until his death in 1967, highly critical of the Cold War policies being followed by his party.

There are now not many people left in active politics who will remember Zilly, and his massive contribution to an understanding of the world has been largely forgotten or deliberately omitted by those who have written about that period.

But whatever view may be taken of what Konni Zilliacus said and wrote during his long and active life, his perspective on that period of history is of the greatest interest for anyone seeking to understand the years following the Russian Revolution and also has a contemporary relevance in the new circumstances facing the world after the end of the Soviet Union.

Zilly was an internationalist above all else, a man who spoke many languages who had an immense knowledge of many countries and their leaders through his travels and discussions with figures ranging from Stalin, Tito, Khrushchev and Castro to Attlee, Dalton, Morrison and Bevan.

Indeed he was seen as a valued adviser to the Labour leadership during the nineteen thirties and, though later expelled from the party because of his left-wing campaigns as a Labour MP, was subsequently re-admitted and re-elected, dying in 1967 as Labour MP for Gorton, active to the end in the cause of peace.

His greatest commitment as an internationalist and a socialist was to the League, where he worked with Phil Noel-Baker and later to the United Nations to which he was absolutely committed.

Through the pages of this beautifully researched and intensely readable book it is possible to understand the nature of the long Cold War which began with the war of intervention launched by the West to destroy the new Soviet Union, through the years when appeasement was just a cover for those who really supported Hitler and Mussolini, and the Hiroshima bomb, which was intended as a warning to Stalin, up to the formation of NATO and the witch-hunting of the Left.

Though often falsely accused of being a Communist sympathizer Zilly was for cooperation rather than confrontation and during the notorious Slansky show trial in Czechoslovakia he was scandalously denounced as a secret agent of Western intelligence and many of his friends were executed.

Unfortunately the post-war Labour government whose record is now widely recognized as having been a brilliant story of progressive reform was marred by its subservience to Washington and its deep hostility to the USSR for which Ernie Bevin must take some responsibility, and criticism of this policy in the House of Commons led to Zilly's own expulsion.

If his advice had been taken the tragic failure to make a lasting peace after 1945 might have been averted, along with the wasteful and dangerous nuclear arms race, which is now set to escalate again.

I served in the House of Commons for many years with Konni Zilliacus, attending committees at which he spoke, and knew of his many books, which were powerfully written and won a wide readership. But I now regret that I did not take the opportunity to listen to him more carefully and think more deeply about what he was saying.

Happily this biography fills that gap and deserves a very wide readership, not least in the ranks of New Labour, which seems to lack any knowledge of, or interest in, the history of our movement or even the history of our times.

I recommend it unreservedly to anyone who wants to understand where we have come from and wants to avoid making the same mistakes all over again.

Tony Benn

Preface

I met Konni Zilliacus, very briefly, in 1949 in the booking hall of Sunderland railway station, when he asked me to direct him to the platform for trains going to South Shields. He was then the Labour MP for Gateshead and I recognised him immediately: a portly figure in a crumpled three-piece suit, carrying a leather briefcase bulging with papers. The former League of Nations official, who spoke nine languages, was one of the most controversial figures in British politics and I followed his career with interest in the succeeding years. I heard him speak at a public meeting in Oxford ten years later. He was then sixty-five years of age and had put on weight since I had last seen him. I did not know it at the time but he had been diagnosed the previous year as suffering from leukaemia, although his illness was not apparent and he spoke with his usual fluency and vigour in his clear and accentless voice. When he died in 1967 Sydney Silverman described him as 'the greatest international socialist of my time'. This was high praise coming from a man not noted for handing out compliments. Yet in spite of his contribution to the shaping of the Labour Party's foreign policy in the 1920s and 30s, his leading role in opposition to Ernest Bevin's foreign policy after 1945, his support for Tito after 1948, his campaign against nuclear weapons in the 1950s and his opposition to the Vietnam War in the 1960s, Zilliacus's role has rarely been given the recognition it deserved.

One of the main reasons for this is that for most of his life Zilliacus was outside the syndrome and always difficult to classify in ideological terms. Although often labelled a fellow traveller or crypto-communist he never quite fitted the bill. He was certainly a left-wing socialist but he worked out his own ideas and his credo owed more to the influence of Norman Angell than it did to Karl Marx. Hence because he could not be placed neatly into any category he did not fit into the Manichaean thinking of the Cold War years and it was easy to dismiss him as a crank or even to ignore him altogether. It is time he was rescued from the footnotes of history and given his rightful place in the gallery of Labour dissenters on foreign policy, standing alongside figures such as E. D. Morel, H. N. Brailsford and Sir Charles Trevelyan – indeed, in many respects, Zilliacus was the connecting link between the Union of Democratic Control dissenters of the First World War and the New Left thinkers of the 1960s. It is also important to put the record straight on several points, for Zilliacus's views were sometimes misunderstood and frequently misrepresented.

Whenever and wherever possible I have allowed Zilliacus to speak for himself by quoting from his speeches, books, pamphlets and articles. He destroyed the bulk of his private papers before he entered hospital for the last time. These papers would have been a rich treasure trove to any biographer. What he did leave, however, was the manuscript, over 300,000 words in length, of an unpublished book called 'Challenge to Fear', which was the most autobiographical of his writings, and his wife, Jan, held some of his personal documents such as his naturalisation papers and a long run of diaries Zilliacus used as appointment and address books. After Jan Zilliacus's death in 1999 a large suitcase stuffed with papers was discovered in her flat. Among these papers was Zilliacus's correspondence with George Bernard Shaw and his files on the Nenni telegram incident, his expulsion from the Labour Party in 1949, and the suspension of his membership in 1961. These helped to fill some gaps. I should also like to thank David Clark, then the MP for South Shields, for his assistance in helping me to gain access to Zilliacus's military service record held at the Ministry of Defence.

Many of Zilliacus's letters to other people were to be found in various collections and this entailed a trawl through archives offices and libraries across the country, and I should like to thank the staffs of the following institutions for their assistance: the Bedales School Library, Petersfield; the Bodleian Library, Oxford; the British Library of Economics and Political Science, London; the British Newspaper Library, Colindale; Christ Church Library, Oxford; Churchill College Library, Cambridge; Gateshead Borough Library; the Brynmor Jones Library, University of Hull; the John Ryland Library, University of Manchester; the Marx Memorial Library, London; the National Museum of Labour History, Manchester; Newcastle City Library; the University of Newcastle upon Tyne Library; the University of Sussex Library; United Nations Library, Geneva; the Modern Records Centre, University of Warwick and the Working Class Movement Library, Salford. I should also like to thank Tim Nolan for checking out some sources held in the USA.

Oral evidence has had its part to play and I owe a huge debt to three people who showed great patience in putting up with my interminable questioning: Zilliacus's widow, Jan; his daughter, Linden Empson; and his step-daughter, Dawn Harris Stanford. Jean Mortimer Molloy, a close friend of Jan's, also provided useful information, as did another family friend, Anne Swingler. Len Edmondson provided much useful local background on Gateshead in the 1930s and '40s, and Stanley Carter did the same for Gorton in the 1950s and '60s. Tom Hadaway recounted his memories of Zilliacus's 1950 election campaign, John Platts-Mills talked about backbench activities in the House of Commons 1945-50, Stan Newens was kind enough to extract entries from his diaries for the 1960s, and Basil Davidson and Jim Mortimer clarified some points. Michael Foot, in spite of his poor state of health and recent bereavement, found time to write me several letters and to arrange for me to consult the *Tribune* files. I should also like to thank Linden Empson and Caroline Wallinger for allowing me to use photographs from their family collections.

I am grateful to Ray Challinor for his encouragement over several years and for giving me access to his unique collection of left-wing books and pamphlets, and to Maureen Callcott for reading early drafts and making useful suggestions.

I should like to say how much I have appreciated their interest and support. Finally, I should like to thank Leigh Clarke for her work in preparing the manuscript for publication and to acknowledge the award of a grant by the Lipman-Miliband Trust.

I once heard the late C. V. Wedgwood say that in her writing she tried to achieve accuracy, readability and objectivity. These seem to me admirable guidelines and I have followed them, to the best of my ability, in the writing of this biography while, at the same time, accepting sole responsibility for any failure to match Dame Veronica's high standards.

Lilian and Konni Zilliacus Sr.with Konni Jr.
Japan, 1894

Primary school class, Brooklyn c.1900. Zilliacus is
third from left in front row

Chapter 1

Early Life

Konni Zilliacus was born on 13 September 1894 in Kobe, Japan. He was named after his father, a thirty-nine-year-old Swedo-Finn living in exile in Japan. Konni Zilliacus Senior was described by *The Times* at the time of his death, in 1924, as the most remarkable figure in the struggle of Finland against Russia at the turn of the last century,[1] and Zilliacus Junior's birthplace was determined by his father's efforts to win Finnish independence.

The Zilliacus family were the descendants of Swedes who had settled in Finland when that country was under Swedish rule. The family name was originally 'Ziliaks' but this had been Latinised in the eighteenth century to 'Zilliacus'. In many ways, the Swedo-Finns were like the Anglo-Irish in pre-independence Ireland. They constituted an originally alien elite who had been absorbed into their adopted country, yet remaining to a considerable extent different from the native families of their adopted land. Again, like Anglo-Irish figures such as Charles Stewart Parnell and Sir Roger Casement, many Swedo-Finns became ardent nationalists, passionately devoted to securing Finnish independence from Russia. Konni Zilliacus Senior was such a man.[2]

He came from a middle-class background and was educated for the law. At twenty-one, however, he abandoned his legal career, married a wealthy widow, and settled into the role of gentleman farmer. He fathered three children but after ten years of married life he abandoned his family and went to America in search of adventure. He worked as the foreman of a railway construction gang in Costa Rica and then became a trainee journalist in Chicago. As a cub reporter he came into contact with a group of Finnish-Americans, whose influence turned him into a fierce Finnish nationalist. In 1892, he decided to return to his native land and join its struggle for independence.[3]

While travelling home, he met a very attractive, nineteen-year-old American woman, Lilian McLaurin Grafe. Although she had been born in the USA her parents were immigrants. Her father was a German-speaking wine merchant from Alsace-Lorraine, who had settled in America and been very successful in business. Her mother, of Scottish descent, died when Lilian was a child. Lilian had grown up in Brooklyn and was accompanying her father on a trip to Europe when she met Konni Zilliacus Senior.

Zilliacus's first marriage was over and after a whirlwind romance on board ship he swept young Lilian off her feet and into matrimony. The newly-married couple decided to settle in Finland where Zilliacus began writing anti-Russian tracts demanding Finnish independence. The young bride hoped for a more conventional marriage, however, and she persuaded her husband to take her to Japan where her sister was living as the wife of a successful merchant. Lilian hoped that her husband might be persuaded to join the family business. Zilliacus Senior agreed to the change but he had his own reasons for leaving Finland. The Russian secret police were becoming interested in his activities in Finland, and Japan was then a haven for anti-Russian exiles. Zilliacus accompanied his wife to Japan, where to her dismay he continued his anti-Russian activities which included working with the Japanese authorities on plans to undermine the Czarist regime.

Thus, on 13 September 1894, Zilliacus Junior was born in Kobe, Japan, and thirteen months later his brother, Laurin, was born. The two boys were close throughout their lives, although they were different in almost every way: Konni was passionate, chubby and careless of his appearance, whereas Laurin was small, dapper and very methodical by nature. Their mother loved them very much and was devoted to their welfare. It was probably concern for the education of her sons which persuaded her that their family should return to Europe, and in 1898 they moved back to Finland.

Once home, Zilliacus Senior resumed his political activities, which included bringing out a newspaper. The paper was soon banned by the Russian authorities and Zilliacus decided to move with his family to Stockholm where he brought out an underground paper called *Fria Ord* (Free Words). Copies of the newspaper were smuggled into Finland, some of them in the skirts of Finnish women travelling from Sweden to Finland. However, the number of copies which could be slipped into Finland in this way was very limited so Zilliacus Senior built a large yacht. This boat was used to smuggle in not only copies of his own paper but also publications of the Social Democratic Party and other groups in opposition to the rule of the Czar. The Russian authorities were very keen to catch the Finnish smuggler of 'subversive' literature but Zilliacus beat the blockade for three years before he decided that it was becoming too risky and he sold the yacht.

Lilian Zilliacus was not happy with her domestic life and the disruption of her sons' education by constant moves. The boys attended schools in Sweden, Finland and the USA and had a series of private tutors. It was not what she wanted for her boys, nor the kind of life she increasingly felt she wanted for herself.

With the outbreak of the Russo-Japanese War, Zilliacus Senior became even more heavily involved in politics. In Stockholm, he met the Japanese military attaché in St Petersburg, Colonel Motohiro Akashi, and they attempted to co-ordinate the activities of all political groups and parties hostile to the Czarist regime. With Akashi's backing, Zilliacus Senior helped to organise two anti-

Czarist congresses, the first in Paris in 1904 and the second in Geneva a year later. There was much discussion at these meetings but little agreement on what action should be taken and the frustrated Zilliacus Senior decided to form a new party, the Finnish Party of Active Resistance, with a policy of armed struggle against Czarist rule. Zilliacus was a Finnish nationalist who had come to support physical force, but he was no socialist although Lenin once stayed at the Zilliacus home in Finland. Politically, Zilliacus was closest to the Social Revolutionary Party which was largely peasant-based and less socialistic than some of the other parties. In 1905, as Russia struggled in its war against Japan, Zilliacus Senior, financed by Colonel Akashi, arranged for a large shipload of arms to be sent from Finland to St Petersburg. Unfortunately for the revolutionaries the enterprise was bungled, the ship was damaged by an explosion and only a few rifles got through.

After the Russo-Japanese War, Zilliacus Senior and family returned to Finland, during the period when the Czarist repression was relaxed, and his eleven-year-old son always carried memories of this brief stay in the family home. It was while the Zilliacus family were resident in Finland that the young Konni was involved in an accident at a railway station. He was waiting at the side of the track for the arrival of a train, when he carelessly put his right foot too far out and when the locomotive arrived it sliced off some of his toes. He was with his brother, Laurin, who fainted when he looked down and saw Konni's mangled foot. Young Konni was in hospital several weeks while his foot healed and it left him for the rest of his life with a slightly loping gait.

When the Russian authorities resumed their crackdown on anti-Czarist elements, Zilliacus Senior took his family back to Sweden. He was living in Stockholm when war broke out in 1914 but his health had deteriorated and he was no longer able to play an active part in political affairs. After the Russian Revolution of 1917, he returned to a Finland free at last of Russian rule where he lived in honoured retirement until his death in 1924. In the words of *The Times*: 'He will always be remembered as one of those who laid the foundations of Finnish independence'.[4]

What influence did this chequered childhood have on Konni Zilliacus Junior? The constant moves between different countries must have helped to develop the youngster's remarkable aptitude for learning foreign languages and given him a broad view of the world. Any other psychological effects can only be a matter of guesswork. Zilliacus himself wrote:

> I emerged from this childhood background with two ideas and a piece of unconscious knowledge lodged firmly in my mind: first, that some day there was going to be a revolution in Russia, and this would be something great and good to which all liberal and civilised people looked forward. Second, that the Russians were a backward, barbarous and semi-Asiatic people, from whom the rest of the world had nothing to learn politically, although the Revolution should free the Finns and

the Poles and enable the Russians to start catching up with the West.[5]

Young Konni's life was about to suffer another radical change. In 1908, after sixteen years of marriage, his mother decided to leave her husband. She longed for a more settled domestic life than her husband could provide and she had finally had enough of her husband's philandering. Throughout his life, Zilliacus Senior was extremely attractive to women and he fully exploited his masculine charms: it was rumoured that he kept several mistresses. Lilian Zilliacus moved to England and found places for her two sons at Bedales School. They started at the school in January 1909.

Bedales School lay in the heart of the Hampshire countryside, overlooking the Rother Valley. The school had been founded in 1893 at a country house called 'Bedales' in Sussex and had moved to its 120 acre site, two miles from the small town of Petersfield, in 1900. The school was founded by J.H.Badley, its first headmaster.[6] Badley had been a pupil at Arnold's Rugby and his aim in creating Bedales was to preserve what he believed was good in the public school system while avoiding some of its negative features.

Instead of the authoritarian rule of masters and prefects, Badley sought the cooperation of pupils in the running of the school, and in place of the so-called 'character building' of the public schools he encouraged self-reliance and individual development among his pupils. Service to the community was not neglected, for Badley wanted his pupils to become aware of social problems outside the school. For example, some Bedales pupils helped to run clubs for working-class children in the surrounding towns and villages.

Badley believed the educational programmes of the public schools with their emphasis on the classics to be too narrow and he planned a different curriculum at Bedales. He offered a wider choice of academic subjects, with time allowed for arts, crafts and rural skills. Bedales was non-denominational and pupils were encouraged to work out their own religious beliefs and ethical systems. Badley also believed strongly in the equality of the sexes and the school was co-educational, with women teachers on the staff as well as girls as pupils. Bedales, therefore, was very much a progressive school.

Konni Zilliacus's major interest at Bedales was in ornithology and entomology, for which he received numerous awards and prizes.[7] He loved nature and animals, and briefly flirted with the idea of becoming a forest ranger. He displayed no interest in music but appeared briefly as Third Citizen in a skit on *Julius Caesar* in one of the school's not-so-serious theatrical productions. He enjoyed swimming and was awarded a bronze medallion for life saving. He also liked boxing and the missing toes on his right foot do not seem to have handicapped him in the ring. At the school's sports day held in the summer term of 1911, Zilliacus threw a cricket ball 83 yards 10 inches, creating a new school record. Otherwise he did not distinguish himself on the sports field. In the following year, in his final term at Bedales, Zilliacus got into the school cricket team for a single game, but he batted low down in the order, made a poor score, and did not bowl. He was probably selected from among the senior boys to make up the number in the team.

Bedales held regular debates on topics of current interest, and in his last year at the school Zilliacus proposed the motion: 'That war is justifiable at present'. The year 1912 was one of international tension and the threat of war loomed over Europe.

Zilliacus began his speech by pointing out that the motion did not say 'war is justifiable and always will be' but that 'war is at the present time justifiable'. He went on: 'Is war natural or unnatural? Surely everything points to the fact that it is one of the most deeply-rooted instincts we have ... If we turn to history to such wars as those between Rome and Carthage, and between England and Spain, we must agree that they were almost inevitable. Here were two nations each growing more and more powerful, each struggling for supremacy. How could it end but in war?' Zilliacus concluded his speech by pointing out that the effects of war were not entirely negative: it 'stimulated nations' and 'built fine men and great civilisations'. Whether he was arguing a case for the purposes of a debate or really believed what he said we do not know, but the motion was lost by twenty-three votes to twenty-seven.

On the academic side, Zilliacus left Bedales with a school certificate: in 1911 he passed in German, Mathematics, English and History, and failed in Mechanics, and in his final year he passed in Latin, German, additional Mathematics, English and Botany.

Zilliacus's time at Bedales was a happy one: he obtained a good, modern education in congenial surroundings. He would later describe his mother as 'a strong liberal and supporter of women's suffrage' and there is little doubt that she made a good choice of school for her two sons. If she had chosen a traditional English public school the emphasis would have been on strict discipline, the study of classics, and compulsory games, and this would not have suited the young Konni Zilliacus. Indeed, it is interesting to speculate on how young Zilly would have responded to fagging and being caned by older boys, not to mention by begowned masters, and he might have encountered the darker side of public school life such as bullying and homosexuality. His unusual name and family background would have made him stand out as a likely target for aspiring Flashmans.

Considering that Mrs Lilian Zilliacus was immensely proud of her Scottish ancestry it is surprising that she did not entertain sending her boys to a Scottish school where they would have received an excellent education, albeit on traditional lines. In the event, it must be said that her judgement was sound. Bedales was the right school for her two boys – among other things it gave them the longest period of residence in one place they had experienced since they were born.

Zilliacus benefited from Bedales in another way. He made some good friends at the school. He was particularly friendly with the sons of Josiah Wedgwood, then a prominent Liberal MP who later moved over to the Labour Party. Zilliacus sometimes spent school vacations at the Wedgwood home, Barlaston Hall in Staffordshire, and this contact with the famous radical MP was to change his life, although Zilliacus could not have been aware of this when he left Bedales in the summer of 1912.

Chapter 2

War And Revolution

Zilliacus left Bedales at the end of the summer term of 1912 and he was very sorry to leave. He had hoped to go on to Cambridge University but domestic developments intervened. His mother had remarried and decided to move to the United States with her husband, an industrial chemist who worked for the Lederle Laboratory in Connecticut. She wanted her sons to be near her and both Konni and Laurin reluctantly agreed to study in the USA. They both enrolled at American universities: Konni went to Yale, while Laurin attended Cornell followed by the Massachusetts Institute of Technology. Laurin was as sad as his brother to leave Bedales, however he returned to teach at the school, from 1917 to 1924, before moving to Finland where he established his own school modelled along the lines of Bedales.

Zilliacus studied at Yale from 1912 until he graduated, first in his class, with a Ph.B. in 1915.[1] His love of nature led him to concentrate on science during his first two years at Yale, but in his third year he switched to social sciences and history. This change was probably prompted by the outbreak of the First World War and the desire to learn more about the great events then unfolding in Europe.

In a college questionnaire he completed in 1915 he wrote that his future goals included working in the British civil service. Zilliacus was a Finn but he had a great affection for England. He not only loved the countryside and way of life but was fascinated by the world of politics and ideas he had briefly experienced at the Wedgwood home. He did not like the United States very much and he was certainly not very happy at Yale. He was always something of a loner and he took little part in student activities, being openly contemptuous of the student fraternities and social clubs. It was a convention that the academically abler students helped members of the football team with their work, so that the sportsmen could devote more time to training. Zilliacus refused to write essays for other students to submit as their own work, and the boxing skills he had acquired at Bedales came in useful when he was forced to defend his position. He was not always successful in avoiding retribution and on one occasion some members of the football team held him down while another shaved off his moustache.[2] Zilliacus complained that he was not fully stretched at Yale and he taught himself Italian in his spare time so that he could read Dante in the original.

After graduation at Yale, Zilliacus returned to Britain determined to do his bit for the war effort of his adopted country. As he remembered it later in life:

> At the core of things I shared that mystic sense of dedication of one's own country being something immortal and beyond price, and one's own life a grain of dust, if only England and all she stood for in the world went on and on and in the end triumphed and did not die. But, at the same time, I was too much of a cosmopolitan and a rationalist to feel mentally cosy and inert in any religious or patriotic cocoon. My capacity for taking things on trust was abnormally limited.[3]

This mixture of idealism, some would say naivety, and realism was to be a characteristic of Zilliacus's political thinking throughout his life. In future years he was to hold an idealised view of the League of Nations, although he knew better than most of the shabby dealings that went on behind the scenes at Geneva. Similarly, he was well informed about Stalinist crimes in the 1930s and '40s and disapproved of them yet he never lost his sympathy for the Soviet Union as the world's first socialist state. Some accused him of woolly thinking but this dualism made good sense to him.

On his return to Britain Zilliacus tried to enlist in the Royal Flying Corps and his choice of service is interesting: he did not want to be a member of a crew in the Navy or join the massed ranks of the Army, he wanted to be a pilot in the RFC where the emphasis was on individual skill and courage. He would be operating in the cockpit of one of the flying machines of early aviation. Zilliacus, however, was rejected for military service. He was not a British citizen and he had toes missing on his right foot. Zilliacus thereupon enlisted as a civilian medical orderly and served in a military hospital in France, stationed near the front line.

Philip Mairet, later the editor of the *New English Weekly*, was stationed in the same hospital and he left a record of the work of the hospital staff.[4] On most nights the big guns were in action 'like the rolling of distant thunder' and during the day the orderlies would meet the trainloads of wounded coming from the front, many of them 'double amputee victims'. If Zilliacus had any romantic illusions about modern war they were shattered by what he witnessed on the Western Front. He worked in the field hospital for almost a year, until he contracted diphtheria. He was brought back to Britain and after his recovery he left for the United States to enjoy a period of convalescence at his mother's home. The USA was still neutral and his mother, who was, after all, American by birth and by her second marriage, wanted Zilliacus to stay on. However, after a three months break and feeling fully recovered, he returned to Britain, determined to join the fight against German militarism, for he still saw the war in these terms.

Zilliacus remained set on enlistment in the RFC but he took on temporary posts in London, first as an aide to the Liberal MP, Noel Buxton, and then as Norman Angell's private secretary, until he could find a way of joining the air force. He also found employment in journalism, working as an assistant editor of the foreign press supplement of *The Nation* where his boss was G. Lowes Dickinson. Both Angell and Dickinson were at the heart of the British dissenting movement against the war.

Angell was the author of *The Great Illusion,* the immensely influential book published in 1909, which exposed the irrationality of modern war. Modern war was so expensive to wage and destructive in its effects that no one gained anything from it, not even the victors. Angell even challenged the view that imperialism was profitable. War, according to Angell, was not only immoral it was economic folly.

Lowes Dickinson was a Cambridge don who was passionately interested in international relations and he is now chiefly remembered as the man who coined the phrases 'League of Nations' and 'international anarchy'. He played a major part in popularising the idea of a League of Nations, and part of Zilliacus's job as his assistant was handling the massive correspondence Lowes Dickinson received from various continental League of Nations societies.

Both Angell and Dickinson were prominent members of the Union of Democratic Control (UDC) founded soon after the outbreak of war. The membership of the UDC was extremely diverse, some were pacifists and some members served in the armed forces, but all felt able to support the UDC's cardinal points: no transfer of territory without a plebiscite; the democratic control of foreign policy; opposition to balance of power politics; the creation of an international organisation for settling disputes; the reduction of armaments and the nationalisation of the arms industry. Zilliacus found no difficulty in working for the UDC programme at the same time as he was trying to get into the forces. He believed that the defeat of German militarism was essential, to be followed by the creation of a League of Nations and the adoption of any other means necessary to prevent future wars.

Zilliacus spent five months working for these two leaders of British dissent and he gained a valuable insight into how to campaign for a political programme. Furthermore, his work on *The Nation* introduced him to journalism, and for the remainder of his life Zilliacus was a prolific writer.

UDC members were often vilified for being 'pro-German', 'defeatist' or supporters of 'peace at any price', but they stuck to what they believed was right and had the satisfaction of seeing most of their ideas become widely accepted in the 1920s. This was another useful lesson for Zilliacus. He was never afraid of being unpopular when he believed that he was in the right and this trait was reinforced by his firsthand observation of the moral courage shown by the UDC leadership during the war. Given time, unpopularity would fade as people were converted to the truth, and throughout his life Zilliacus shared the liberal belief that education and debate would win over the majority of people to what he regarded as the right policies.

While working for Angell and Dickinson, Zilliacus had contacted his school

friend's father, the Liberal MP, Josiah Wedgwood, to solicit his help in gaining entry to the RFC, and on 11 October 1917 Wedgwood had written to Lord
Derby, Secretary of State for War, recommending Zilliacus for enlistment in the
RFC. Within a fortnight Lord Derby had arranged for Zilliacus to be interviewed
by the Air Board. His interview was successful and Zilliacus was promptly enlisted as a cadet in the RFC and posted to flying school.[5] His address on enlistment
was 34 Tavistock Square, Bloomsbury, and his civilian occupation was given as
private secretary.

Zilliacus never completed his training due to the intervention of his patron,
Josiah Wedgwood, who had pulled strings to get him on the course in the first
place. Wedgwood now had more important work for Zilliacus and this new mission was to put Zilliacus in direct contact with some of the most momentous
events in the twentieth century.

In March 1917, the Czarist regime had collapsed and been replaced by a
Provisional Government under Alexander Kerensky. The Kerensky Government
struggled to keep Russia in the war, until it was overthrown by the Bolsheviks
in October 1917. One of the first acts of the new government was to urge all the
warring powers to agree to an armistice. Only Germany replied affirmatively,
although laying down certain conditions. In late November Lenin informed the
Allies that unless they agreed to immediate peace negotiations as Germany had
done, the new Soviet Government would sign a separate peace with Germany.
The Allies refused and, beginning in early December and continuing until March,
the German and Soviet governments discussed truce terms at Brest-Litovsk. The
Bolsheviks also published the Allied secret treaties they had found in the Czarist
archives which exposed the imperialist aims of the Entente powers.

These developments threatened to undermine the Allied war effort. The collapse of the Russian front meant that the Germans could transfer men and resources to the Western Front and break the Allied blockade by gaining access to
supplies of food and raw materials from the eastern territories. The emergence
of the Bolsheviks also created additional problems for the Allies on their home
fronts. Talk of peace and the publicity given to the secret treaties caused unrest
among their own people. War weariness began to show itself and there were
outbreaks of strikes and anti-war protests in Britain and France. Western states-
men were well aware that this was how the Russian Revolution had started and
they were determined to head it off. Unfortunately for them there were sharp
divisions of opinion between Allied governments and between individuals and
groups inside those governments. Some wanted a conciliatory approach to the
Bolsheviks in an attempt to keep them in the war or at least prevent them becoming allies or partners of the Germans. At the other extreme there were those
who favoured a tough anti-Bolshevik policy, and, as always, there were various
shades of opinion between the two extremes. In spite of these divisions, on 1
January 1918 the Supreme Allied Council agreed that at some time and at some

place Allied intervention in Russia would be necessary. An important factor inhibiting more decisive action was a lack of reliable information on conditions inside Russia. For example, there were rumours that Kerensky's writ still ran in the Far Eastern provinces of the former Czarist Empire: but were these reports true? This was the background to the launching of the Wedgwood mission.

Josiah Wedgwood claimed that the mission was his idea and he persuaded Lord Robert Cecil, Under Secretary of State for Foreign Affairs, to support it.[6] Cecil in turn convinced the War Office that it was a worthwhile project and within a week Wedgwood was sailing for New York on the first stage of his journey. According to official orders, dated January 1918, the purpose of the mission was: to gather intelligence concerning Bolshevik power and influence in Siberia; to discover the scope and depth of the German presence in the region; to institute steps to counteract whatever German influence existed; and to try to get Russia back into the war. As to the last point, the Foreign and War Offices specifically instructed Wedgwood to enlist the aid of the anti-Bolshevik forces.[7] According to Wedgwood, Winston Churchill, then Minister of Munitions, was present at a verbal briefing at the War Office when he advised Wedgwood: 'Get on to a locomotive at Vladivostok, go as far as you can, and then retire blowing up every bridge behind you'.[8]

Captain Berg of the Grenadier Guards was to accompany Wedgwood as his Military Attaché and at Wedgwood's request Konni Zilliacus was to serve as his ADC. On 3 January 1918 Cadet Zilliacus received orders at his flying school to proceed on ten days leave and afterwards report to Commander J.C. Wedgwood at the War Office. Five days later – during his leave period – he was naturalised a British subject,[9] and the following day he was commissioned as a Second Lieutenant in the RFC.[10] The Home and War Offices, with the Foreign Office at their heels, could move quickly when the occasion required it.

When Zilliacus reported to Wedgwood he found that the swashbuckling MP for Newcastle-under-Lyme had been made a Colonel in the British Army. In earlier years of the war Wedgwood had served in Flanders, Gallipoli and East Africa as an officer in the Royal Naval Volunteer Reserve but on his new mission he came under the orders of the War Office and this entailed a change of service for him.

The Wedgwood party left London on 9 January 1918, before the completion of Zilliacus's official leave, most of which, in any case, had been taken up with naturalisation and commissioning procedures plus other preparations for the trip. The mission was under orders to proceed as discreetly as possible, therefore the three men packed their uniforms in trunks and travelled in mufti.

They crossed the Atlantic to New York and travelled by train to San Francisco, by sea to Hawaii, stopping for a swim at Waikiki beach, and then on to Yokohama. After an official reception in Tokyo the mission travelled through Korea to China. Following a brief stay in Pekin, the three men moved north to

Mukden and then farther north to Harbin.

At Harbin, Wedgwood discovered that the Kerensky Government had been replaced by Bolshevik rule and he cabled London to this effect. He received orders to proceed to Vladivostok which he found 'swarmed with every variety of exile' and was firmly under the control of the Bolsheviks. In March, Wedgwood cabled home his conclusions: that the Japanese would not fight the Germans; money spent on bribing robber chiefs and Cossack bands would be 'stupid and criminal'; Siberia feared the Japanese more than the Germans; and that British military stores in Vladivostok could and should be recovered. His views were not to the liking of the British Government, which had decided to support Japanese intervention in the area, and he was promptly recalled by the War Office.[11]

Wedgwood's young ADC was not so fortunate. Lieutenant Zilliacus received no orders to return home and he was to be stuck in Siberia for another two years. Zilliacus was keen to complete his flying course and after Wedgwood's departure he applied to the Air Ministry for permission to return to Britain and resume his training. The War Office had no objection but the British Foreign Secretary, A.J. Balfour, intervened and ordered that if Ralph Hodgson, the Consul-General in Vladivostok, needed Zilliacus then the young officer must remain there.

Zilliacus had proved to be a very useful member of the British staff in Vladivostok, for in addition to his ability to speak French, German, Italian and Swedish he had also mastered Russian. Furthermore, he was very good at writing reports and analysing information. Hodgson wanted to hold on to him and Zilliacus was duly seconded from the War Office to the British Consulate at Vladivostok where he was appointed Hodgson's cipher officer. As cipher officer Zilliacus gained an inside view of the evolution of British policy concerning intervention in Russia. Zilliacus agreed with Wedgwood's conclusions, however he was only a junior officer and in no position to influence any major decisions. He carried out his duties but with increasing reluctance as the full implications of British intervention became clearer to him. Zilliacus read the reports of Bruce Lockhart and other British consuls and agents in Russia who warned against intervention. Lockhart, among others, believed that the Bolsheviks would emerge as the victors in the civil war and it would therefore be unwise to antagonise them. Ralph Hodgson took the opposite view, which was in line with that of the British Government.[12]

The Japanese were the first to land troops in Siberia, ostensibly to protect their consulate in Vladivostok, and Britain, the USA and France followed suit. There were also 14,000 troops of the Czech Legion in the area, who were recruited to the Allied cause and used against the Bolsheviks. Zilliacus viewed these developments with dismay and he re-applied for permission to return to flying school in Britain. The answer was the same: he was too useful where he was and would have to remain in Siberia. Indeed, he was soon to be drawn deeper into the web of intervention. When General Alfred Knox arrived in Vladivostok in the summer of 1918 to take charge of Britain's interventionist forces, Zilliacus was appointed his intelligence and cipher officer. Zilliacus saw all the communications passing between Knox and London, including those in special cipher from Winston Churchill, who was the main driving force behind Britain's hardline interventionist policy in Russia. Zilliacus would later observe 'I had a ringside seat from start to finish'. [13]

From the official start of British intervention in July to the end of the war in November 1918, Zilliacus was able to convince himself that intervention was part of the British war effort and therefore it was his duty to assist it, but after the defeat of the Central Powers it was no longer possible for him to believe this. He began to have trouble in getting to sleep at night and he took to wandering about in the dark often ending up sitting on one of the small extinct volcanoes that ringed Vladivostok, staring at the harbour lights. [14] He applied for his discharge so that he could take up a place at King's College, Cambridge, and once again his application was blocked by Knox and Hodgson. Although he disagreed with their views on intervention, Zilliacus got on extremely well at a personal level with both General Knox and Consul Hodgson and in turn they liked the affable, young cipher officer who had his own opinions but did his duty. Zilliacus began to wonder, however, how much longer he could continue to carry out orders in support of a policy he believed to be misguided and immoral. Two events helped to resolve his doubts and hesitations.

Firstly, he was shocked when General Knox helped to organise a *coup d'état* in Omsk on 18 November 1918, which placed the White Admiral Kolchak in power at the head of a military government. It became clear to Zilliacus that British intervention in support of the war effort had been replaced by a policy of intervention in support of counter-revolution. Britain was now openly backing the Whites against the Reds.

The second shock came when in the late Spring of 1919 he deciphered a highly confidential message from Churchill – since January 1919 Secretary of State for War – to General Knox relaying plans for a joint White Russian-British Army offensive designed to thrust towards Petrograd and Moscow. [15] The attack, it was hoped, would deliver a 'knockout blow' to Bolshevik forces. This offensive – like Churchill's earlier strategic concept, the ill-fated Gallipoli campaign – was badly flawed. The basic weakness of intervention was succinctly stated by Douglas Young, the British Consul in Archangel 1917-1918:

Russia cannot be invaded and conquered by a few thousand men. The distances are enormous: the difficulties are great: the Bolsheviks are strong and growing stronger. It is not a question of 'restoring order' in Murmansk or the Crimea. It is a question of at least penetrating to Moscow. That means war on a large scale – it may be years of war. That means the sacrifice of thousands of lives and millions of pounds of money with them. [16]

The message in itself did not shock Zilliacus – he was well aware of Churchill's anti-Bolshevik activities – however, in June 1919, he picked up a copy of a Siberian newspaper which reported a speech Churchill had made in the House of Commons denying that any offensive by British troops had been planned and stating that any troop movements in Siberia were to facilitate British withdrawal from the area.[17] Churchill had lied to the House of Commons and deceived the British people.

After much soul searching, Zilliacus reasoned that he had joined up to fight the Germans, the war was now over and he had not agreed to fight a new enemy, therefore the oath of allegiance he had sworn on becoming an officer was null and void. This left him free to follow the dictates of his conscience and he knew what he would do: he would tell the British people the truth about intervention in Russia, and few people were better placed to do this.

He began to send press cuttings from Siberian newspapers, reports on the local situation and even extracts from some military orders to contacts in Britain. Josiah Wedgwood used some of Zilliacus's material to attack Winston Churchill in the House of Commons, Lowes Dickinson passed Zilliacus's reports of White atrocities to C.P. Scott at the *Manchester Guardian,* and Leonard Woolf briefed the editor of the *Herald.* The British public was largely ignorant of what was happening in Siberia or relied for information on the reports of Robert Wilson, *The Times* correspondent in the region, who was quite blatantly pro-White in his sympathies. Zilliacus's leaks helped to inform the public of facts they would otherwise not have known and hence he played a part in creating the climate of opinion in Britain that demanded an end to intervention in Russia.

In their turn, Wedgwood and Dickinson kept Zilliacus informed about progress on the creation of a League of Nations, and he learned from an old copy of the *Manchester Guardian* that the seat of the League was to be in Geneva and recruitment for the Secretariat had begun.[18] Zilliacus was resolved to seek employment with the League, but by being in Siberia he had missed the opportunity of being in the first wave of appointments. As intervention was being wound up by the withdrawal of British troops he was allowed to return to Britain in December 1919.

Zilliacus returned to London with a young wife. In the summer of 1918 he had met an attractive Polish woman, Eugenia Nowicka. She came from a Roman Catholic middle-class family who were strongly nationalistic and hence had incurred the attention of the Czarist police. The Nowicka family had been exiled to Vladivostok when Eugenia was fifteen. Although the family lived in political exile their social life was not too restricted and Eugenia first met Zilliacus on a tennis court. After a short courtship they were married in October 1918.

Chapter 3

Geneva

When Zilliacus returned to London in December 1918 one of his first acts was to join the Labour Party 'because it was fighting intervention in Russia and stood for a sane peace settlement and a strong League of Nations'.[1] Thus he was one of a number of Liberal Radicals who joined the Labour Party on foreign policy issues.[2] He also joined the Fabian Society, attracted by its emphasis on political education and the dissemination of information.

He outlined his post-war credo:

> I have occasionally been called a Bolshevik because I always predicted the failure of intervention, because I sometimes find it difficult to speak with moderation of the moral aspects and practical results of the Allies' Russian policy, and because I belong to the Labour Party. I am not however a communist, or even a Socialist except in a very vague and unorthodox way, and I am not a believer in direct action, let alone the 'dictatorship of the proletariat' or a bloody revolution. In general, I do not think Russian political experience can afford any but very indirect lessons to England. The war was the death struggle of our civilisation. Just as the final result of the French Revolution and the Napoleonic wars was the rise of the middle class, the Russian Revolution will be the rise of Labour and internationalism.[3]

Zilliacus was determined to find employment with the League of Nations. However this was not so easy to achieve, mainly because the League Secretariat had already recruited a fair number of British citizens and there was a danger that its staffing would appear over-weighted in Britain's favour. His first application was rejected and in the meantime he had to earn a living, especially as he had a wife and newly-born daughter, Stella, to support.

Zilliacus found part-time employment working as a translator for the foreign press department of the *Manchester Guardian*, and he applied to the paper's editor, C.P. Scott, for a job as its correspondent in Russia. Scott and his son, Edward, discussed Zilliacus's application.[4] They agreed that he was a strong candidate and his appointment would fill a gap in their foreign news staff, yet they also knew that Zilliacus's heart lay in finding employment with the League of Nations and they rejected his application. Shortly afterwards, Zilliacus was given a part-time job working for the League in London, swiftly followed by the offer of a full-time appointment in Geneva.

As he made preparations for a move to Switzerland, he informed C.P. Scott of his appointment to the League Secretariat and offered to act as the *Manchester Guardian*'s unofficial correspondent in Geneva. Under his conditions of service he was debarred from undertaking any work outside of his League duties, nevertheless Zilliacus saw no reason why he should not contribute unsigned reports or articles written under a pen-name. Scott agreed to this arrangement and for the next eighteen years that he worked at Geneva, Zilliacus made full use of his pipeline to the *Manchester Guardian*.

Indeed, in the 1920s and '30s he wrote several books and pamphlets, and numerous articles under a series of *noms de plume* such as *Roth Williams, C. Howard-Ellis, A Student of the League, A Believer in World Union, Vigilantes, Ex-Serviceman, A Socialist* and *Covenanter*. In doing this Zilliacus was knowingly breaking the League's rules. He justified it on the grounds that the public had a right to be kept informed. Furthermore, as a former UDC member he held that secret diplomacy had been a major cause of the First World War and he was determined that he would do anything in his power to prevent this happening again. He also believed that he had a duty to propagate on behalf of the League, to explain to people what it stood for and what it was trying to achieve. Because he was paid a salary by the League and used the League's library facilities in Geneva to research his books and articles, Zilliacus did not accept any payment for his reports and articles or if a fee was offered he requested that it be devoted to a charity of his choice. He wrote to educate and inform not to make money.

Zilliacus was a member of the Information Section of the League Secretariat. The Section's main function was the collection and publication of information concerning the League. It had one of the best stocked libraries in the world, including newspapers and magazines as well as books, and it published regular bulletins on the League's activities. Zilliacus's main task was to serve as a liaison officer with Britain and the Dominions (minus Canada), the Baltic States, Finland and the Soviet Union. He was also the League's link with the Labour and Socialist International (LSI) or Second International and he extended his role to cover liaison with the various political parties affiliated to the LSI.

The League Secretariat's strong links with the LSI after 1925 were due almost entirely to the efforts of Zilliacus who had to convince, first his own Head of Section, Pierre Comert, and then the Secretary-General, Sir Eric Drummond, that such contacts were likely to prove beneficial to the League's work. Zilliacus argued that the LSI's traditions of international goodwill and cooperation were in harmony with the League's aims and functions, and he admitted that he had already attended a couple of LSI meetings as an observer and had found the experience very valuable in gaining an insight into the workings of the international socialist movement. He felt that the LSI was a natural ally of the League of Nations, and he requested that he be given official approval to continue and develop this aspect of his work. After much discussion at the highest levels, the Secretariat gave its approval, although Secretary-General Drummond urged that the work be performed 'with discretion'.[5]

Zilliacus was also responsible for keeping in touch with the newly established International Health Organisation and he served as its information officer.[6] In 1921, he acted as interpreter for Professor I. Tarasovich of the Soviet Commissariat of Health, who visited Geneva to plead with the League for financial assistance to help counter the typhus epidemic then sweeping Soviet Russia, and Zilliacus attended the League-sponsored Warsaw Health Conference in the following year. The outcome of the conference was the setting up of an Epidemic Commission with a small budget to check the spread of typhus in Eastern Europe; however, to Zilliacus's disgust, no money was voted for use inside Soviet Russia. Zilliacus believed that medical aid or financial assistance should have been offered to the Soviet people out of a feeling of common humanity, but he also felt that such support would have helped to open up some sort of contact between the League and the young Soviet state. Zilliacus saw no merit in keeping Soviet Russia isolated and impoverished.

Zilliacus was a prolific letter writer.[7] He corresponded with a wide range of people, exchanging information and arguing the case for the Covenant of the League of Nations. In particular, he carried on a regular correspondence with Lord Robert Cecil,[8] Norman Angell[9] and Fritz Adler.[10] Cecil had helped to draft the Covenant of the League and was President of the League of Nations Union. Angell was an author and journalist whose writings were mainly on international affairs. Fritz Adler was an Austrian Social Democrat and Secretary of the LSI, based in Zurich.

Zilliacus also remained in close touch with leading figures in the Labour Party. It was part of his duties to liaise with the Labour Party, supply it with information on the work of the League, and to provide the League Secretariat with feedback on the Labour Party's attitude to the League. In the early 1920s the Labour Party was by no means solidly behind the League of Nations. Many Labour Party members regarded the League as part of the reviled Versailles settlement: a 'league of the victors'. Two of the Labour Party's pro-League figures in the 1920s were Philip Noel-Baker and Hugh Dalton who, together with the much respected Labour veteran Arthur Henderson, were to play an important role in persuading the party to adopt a pro-League foreign policy. Up to a point, Zilliacus's close relations with Noel-Baker and Dalton could be justified by his need to 'liaise' with the parties of the LSI. Zilliacus's intimacy with Noel-Baker and Dalton, however, went beyond this: he became to all intents and purposes a foreign policy 'backroom boy' of the Labour Party.

Noel-Baker and Zilliacus were both members of the League Secretariat in the early 1920s and therefore came to know each other very well.[11] Noel-Baker was a Quaker and during the First World War he had served with the Friends' Ambulance Unit in France and Italy. He had worked as assistant to Lord Robert Cecil in the League of Nations Section of the Versailles Conference, before joining the newly-formed League Secretariat in 1920. Under the first Labour Government he was private secretary to Lord Parmoor, the minister responsible for League of Nations affairs. He left Geneva in 1924 to become Professor of International Relations at the London School of Economics. In 1929 he was elected to the House of Commons and appointed Parliamentary Private Secretary to Arthur Henderson at the Foreign Office.[12]

Hugh Dalton was the son of Canon J. N. Dalton, who was domestic chaplain to the Royal Family. He was educated at Eton and Cambridge and, after serving with an artillery unit on the Italian front in the First World War, had joined the Labour Party in 1919. He was a lecturer in economics at the London School of Economics in the 1920s and was elected to Parliament in 1924. He developed a keen interest in foreign affairs and favoured a pro-League foreign policy. In the 1929 Labour Government he was appointed Under-Secretary of State for Foreign Affairs.[13]

Dalton first met Zilliacus at Ludwig Rajchman's house at Geneva in 1925.[14] Rajchman was at this time head of the Health Section of the League Secretariat. Dalton was impressed by Zilliacus's knowledge and intelligence, and the two men became friends as well as collaborators in the task of converting the Labour Party to collective security. When, in 1928, Dalton published his book *Towards the Peace of Nations* he sent a signed copy to Zilliacus describing him on the title page as 'the source of most of what I have learned about foreign affairs'.[15]

Zilliacus usually paid three fortnightly liaison visits to Britain every year, when he attended the Labour Party and TUC annual conferences, and arranged interviews with leading figures in the Labour Movement. Whenever possible he always tried to fit a meeting with Hugh Dalton into his schedule, these contacts often taking the form of a discussion group held at Dalton's Carlisle Mansions flat in Victoria, when Zilliacus would deliver a report on League affairs to Dalton and others. Zilliacus was also Dalton's guest on several occasions at the Daltons' West Leaze home in Wiltshire. In turn, Dalton stayed at the Zilliacus home at 112, Route de Chêne in Geneva on several occasions.[16] Zilliacus was the owner of a big, powerful car and on Sundays he would drive Dalton and other visitors, such as Labour MP Molly Hamilton, out into the Swiss countryside where they would get out and go for a long walk.[17] It was a strict rule on these occasions that no one 'talked shop'. In 1927, Zilliacus and his wife Eugenia teamed up with Hugh Dalton and his wife Ruth to enjoy a motoring holiday in France.

In the last years of his life Zilliacus paid a generous tribute to Hugh Dalton:

> I believe that the Labour Party even now does not realise how much disinterested devotion, brains, knowledge, energy and sheer hard work Hugh Dalton put into its service for many years. And I do it all the more willingly because in later years our paths diverged widely.[18]

He was less kind to his old friend Noel-Baker when, writing in the 1960s, he observed:

> I doubt whether Phil's mind has moved, in essentials, even today, beyond 1928.[19]

The Labour Party fought the general election of May 1929 on its manifesto *Labour and the Nation*, in which it promised to work for world peace by means of conciliation, arbitration, disarmament and cooperation with the League of Nations. Labour's foreign policy proposals had been shown to have considerable appeal to many electors and played a part in making Labour the largest single party in the House of Commons, without giving them an overall majority.

When the second minority Labour Government was formed by Ramsay MacDonald in June 1929, Zilliacus recalled:

> I still remember the thrill when I opened the telegram saying: 'Henderson Foreign Secretary, Dalton Parliamentary Secretary, Baker Henderson's PPS, come over'[20]

In response to Noel-Baker's invitation, Zilliacus immediately made his way to London, where he attended a meeting at Arthur Henderson's flat in Artillery Mansions near Victoria station. Those present were: Henderson or 'Uncle Arthur' as he was affectionately known, Hugh and Ruth Dalton, and Philip Noel-Baker. The group discussed how they were going to implement Labour's election pledges. The outcome of their efforts was pithily summed up by Hugh Dalton in his memoirs:

> The Second Labour Government's record abroad is a moderate success story, not lacking courage and skill. Its record at home is a hard-luck story, with failure almost unredeemed by courage or skill.[21]

The Labour Government took office when international goodwill was at a peak and the incoming government built on this. The Kellogg Pact had recently been signed by sixty-five states, renouncing war as an instrument of policy. This was followed, in 1929, by a new settlement of German reparations under the Young Plan, and by the evacuation of the Rhineland by the occupying forces, including the British troops, completed by June 1930. In September 1929, the Labour Government signed the Optional Clause of the Statute of the Court of International Justice, binding itself to submit all disputes (with certain reservations) to the Court's arbitration. This was followed, in 1931, by adherence to the General Act for the Pacific Settlement of Disputes. Diplomatic relations with the Soviet Union were resumed in October 1929, and a commercial agreement signed in April 1930. The London Naval Conference of 1930 resulted in the signing of the Three Power Pact between Britain, the USA and Japan placing agreed limits on the size of their navies. Finally a World Disarmament Conference was arranged to be opened in February 1932 under the chairmanship of Arthur

Henderson.

The Labour Government succeeded in implementing all its foreign policy manifesto commitments in spite of opposition from the permanent officials inside the Foreign Office, and Zilliacus attributed this success to the strength of Labour's foreign policy team led by Arthur Henderson. Zilliacus worked closely with the team. When Henderson came to Geneva he went to discuss League business with Zilliacus, even allowing him access to the contents of the red despatch boxes. As Zilliacus observed, the Foreign Office officials did not approve of this but they obeyed orders.[22] Similarly, Dalton used to consult Zilliacus on technical points relating to the treaties and rehearse the arguments he was going to use to overcome the objections of the permanent officials at the Foreign Office.

The 1920s were, on the whole, a happy time for Zilliacus. He enjoyed a settled domestic life in Geneva, his son Joseph was born in 1924, he published two substantial books on the League of Nations,[23] and he liked his work. Not that everything had gone smoothly for the infant League of Nations.[24]

Zilliacus believed that an opportunity had been missed at the Genoa Conference of April 1922. This meeting of all European countries had been convened by Lloyd George, in one of his last acts as Prime Minister. He wished to use it to bring Germany and Soviet Russia back into the fold, but it came too soon after the war for France, which was in no mood to be generous to either Germany or Soviet Russia, and the conference ended in failure. A week later Germany and Russia, Europe's outcasts, had signed a treaty of friendship at Rapallo. Zilliacus believed that if the League Secretariat had been allowed to organise the conference and host it at Geneva, as it offered to do, treating all participants as equal members, working to a carefully prepared agenda, then something useful could have been achieved. The burden of reparations could have been lifted from Germany, and Soviet Russia's status recognised by the rest of Europe. The path would then have been smoothed for both states to become members of the League of Nations.

The League of Nations took a hefty knock in January 1923 when France, using Germany's default on reparation payments as a pretext, occupied the Ruhr. In doing so, the French had completely ignored League procedures and resorted to a military solution. Zilliacus was delighted when Hjalmar Branting, the Swedish representative on the League's Council, criticised the French action and invited Britain to give a lead. The 1922-23 Conservative governments of Bonar Law and then Stanley Baldwin, which had succeeded Lloyd George's Coalition Government after the 'Chanak incident' had brought Britain close to war with Turkey, were in no mood to take on the French. The French also hinted that if they were charged with aggression at the League they would withdraw their membership of the body. The League thereupon lapsed into silence and the French continued their occupation of the Ruhr.

In August of the same year Mussolini's Italy bombarded and occupied the

Greek island of Corfu in retaliation for the killing, allegedly by Greek bandits, of an Italian diplomat. The League's Council discussed the incident, prompting Italy to threaten to withdraw from the League.[25] A compromise was eventually botched together, outside the League, which favoured Italy at the expense of Greece. Zilliacus wrote to his friend and mentor, Norman Angell: 'I feel depressed and fed up. Who could have imagined things would turn out as badly as this?'[26]

Zilliacus was also disappointed with Britain's failure to ratify the so-called Geneva Protocol of 1924, which he helped to draft. The Protocol, in effect a tightening up of some provisions in the Covenant of the League of Nations, would have pledged signatories to accept arbitration in international disputes and offer support in cases of unprovoked aggression. The Protocol was supported by Arthur Henderson, who led the first Labour Government's delegation to the Geneva Assembly in 1924, with the lukewarm backing of Prime Minister and Foreign Secretary, Ramsay MacDonald, but it was rejected by the incoming Conservative Government.[27] Instead the new Conservative Foreign Secretary, Austen Chamberlain, negotiated the Locarno Treaty of 1925. This was in essence a non-aggression pact between France and Germany, guaranteed by Britain and Italy. Although the Locarno Treaty increased the feeling of goodwill in Europe and paved the way for German membership of the League, Zilliacus saw it as a return to Great Power diplomacy and he would have much preferred the use of the League's machinery to achieve the same ends.[28]

The League had some success in averting wars in the cases of the Iraqi-Turkish border dispute of 1925-26, the Bulgarian-Greek border clashes of 1925 and the Polish-Lithuanian frontier disputes of 1927. The League also scored signal successes in the areas of drugs control, refugee work and famine relief, although Zilliacus was very critical of Britain's tardy support for the League's efforts to relieve the post-civil war famine in Soviet Russia.[29]

In the early 1920s Britain and France still tended to conduct most of their foreign policy outside the League, as Zilliacus put it: 'The League is being gradually ignored to death by the Allies.'[30] However this began to change. Prior to 1924 member states had been normally represented at the League by delegates who were not ministers responsible for the foreign policies of their countries. When MacDonald and Herriot came in person to Geneva for the Assembly of 1924, they set a precedent of far-reaching importance. Thereafter the foreign ministers of leading countries began to attend on a regular basis, and Geneva in September came to be a recognised meeting place for the leaders of Europe. In 1929, the Assembly was attended by every European foreign minister. Most member states were beginning to work through the League or at least to give it a greater role in the conduct of their foreign policy.

Hugh Dalton recalled of the September 1929 meeting of the League's Assembly:

In those weeks we had the sensation that the moral leadership of the world had returned to this country, as when Mr MacDonald and Mr Henderson had first gone to Geneva in 1924. The League seemed to have come to life again, and to have gained a new significance.[31]

And, as Molly Hamilton, a Labour MP who was a member of the British delegation to the League of Nations observed:

Geneva in 1929 and 1930 was a genuine International clearing-house of ideas.... Was it all illusion, the Geneva atmosphere? It need not have been. There was hard work, and there was goodwill.[32]

The autumn of 1929 marked the zenith of the League of Nations. Although the 'spirit of Geneva' lingered on into 1930, after this it was difficult to feel anything but pessimistic about the international situation. In the words of a League official: 'From 1931 onwards one felt that the sun had departed from Geneva and that the cold shadows were creeping on the League'.[33] On 24 October 1929 share prices began to plummet on the New York Stock Exchange, signalling the start of the world depression 1929-33. The 'magic house of paper'[34] built with so many good intentions in the 1920s was swept away as the Labour Government fell and the Japanese marched into Manchuria in 1931, followed seventeen crisis-ridden months later by the coming to power of the Nazis in Germany.

Chapter 4

The Manchurian Crisis

On 23 August 1931 the second Labour Government broke up in disagreement over budget economies and the Prime Minister, Ramsay MacDonald, tendered his resignation to the King. The next day MacDonald emerged as Prime Minister of a National Government enjoying the support of Conservative and Liberal MPs plus ten Labour members. The remaining Labour MPs went into opposition under the leadership of Arthur Henderson. On 27 October 1931 the National Government went to the polls and was returned with a huge majority. Among Labour's leading figures only George Lansbury retained his seat and among ministers of second rank only C.R. Attlee and Stafford Cripps managed to scrape back. Zilliacus's friends Arthur Henderson, Hugh Dalton, Philip Noel-Baker and Norman Angell all lost their seats in Labour's electoral débâcle.

At his home in Geneva Zilliacus stayed up late to listen to the election results broadcast on the BBC's long wave band and he later recalled:

> Almost every result seemed to be 'Conservative gain'. Labour had been not only defeated but routed. I went to bed in such utter despair that I could not go to sleep and ended by weeping in the dark. [1]

Next morning a weary and dispirited Zilliacus dragged himself into his office in the former *Hotel National* building, now the home of the League Secretariat, where he met his friend and colleague, Hilary St George Saunders.

> 'Oh, Zilly', said Saunders. 'Isn't it wonderful - everyone rallied and went to the polls. This is national unity.'

Zilliacus replied:

> 'OK, St. G, you asked for it so I'll tell you what I think. This is the greatest disaster that has fallen the world since the war. It means the triumph of black reaction. After this, if we don't have another war within ten years we'll be lucky'.

A month before the general election the Manchurian Crisis, as it came to be called, was provoked by the actions of the Japanese army in Manchuria. [2] Zilliacus was very well informed about the situation in the Far East. He had spent six months in China 1930-31 on a League of Nations mission with Dr Ludwig Rajchman and Robert Haas to provide assistance to the Chinese

National Reconstruction Commission. During this visit Zilliacus observed the growth of Chinese nationalism, with its desire to unify the country and free itself from foreign commercial interests that had established themselves on Chinese territory. He was sympathetic to those aspirations and foresaw a future clash between Chinese nationalism and Japanese imperialism.

On 18 September 1931 Japanese troops occupied Mukden, following an explosion on a length of railway track, and in a carefully prepared campaign the Japanese army rapidly occupied large areas of Manchuria. Whether by chance or design, the Japanese army had timed its intervention to perfection. The attention of most of the world's governments was focused on the effects of the slump: it was with some reluctance that they turned their minds to consider events in a remote part of the Far East.

Manchuria was a province of China, although the Japanese owned the main railway line running through the territory and had the right by treaty to police it. The Chinese Government appealed to the League of Nations under Article 11 of the Covenant 'to take immediate steps to prevent further development of a situation endangering the peace of nations; to re-establish the *status quo ante*; and to determine the amounts and character of such reparations as may be found due to the Republic of China'. [3] China also appealed to the USA as a signatory of the Nine Power Pact and the Kellogg Treaty. The matter was debated by the Council of the League on 22 September. The Japanese representative was conciliatory. Lord Cecil, speaking for Britain, proposed an inquiry and persuaded the Council to appeal to both Japan and China to stop fighting and return their forces to their previous positions. The suggestion of an inquiry was abandoned by the Council when H.L. Stimson, the US Secretary of State, advised against it on the grounds that it would upset the Japanese. The USA, however, requested, and was allowed, to attend the next meeting of the Council. Meanwhile the Japanese army under the command of General Honjo continued to consolidate its position in Manchuria and, in an escalation of hostilities, Japanese aircraft bombed the town of Chinchow.

On 24 October 1931 the Council passed a resolution asking Japan to withdraw her troops to the railway zone, but according to League rules such resolutions under Article 11 had to be unanimous and Japan voted against thus rendering it void. In effect Japan had cast a veto. The Japanese representative in Geneva then proposed an inquiry and this was approved by the Council and a commission established under the chairmanship of Lord Lytton.

In a separate dispute a thousand miles away, fighting broke out between Japanese and Chinese troops in Shanghai, and the Chapei district of the city was bombed by Japanese aircraft. Chinese resistance proved to be much stronger than expected and Japanese attacks were repelled. Britain reinforced its garrison in Shanghai and the Americans despatched a naval squadron to the area. After a month of fighting a ceasefire was negotiated and the Japanese withdrew to their coastal settlements.

On 7 January 1932 the US Government announced it would not recognise any territorial changes that infringed the Kellogg Pact. Whereupon the British Foreign Office issued a statement saying that Japan had promised to protect British trading interests in Manchuria and therefore there was no necessity for it to support the American lead on non-recognition. Hence a possible joint Anglo-American approach to the crisis was rejected.

The Chinese Government then changed tack at Geneva and invoked Articles 10 and 15 of the Covenant, which would normally have led to the application of sanctions against Japan. The Chinese also requested the convocation of a special Assembly of the League in order to present their case. The Assembly duly met in March 1932 and after many fine speeches it supported the principle of non-recognition put forward by the USA, but otherwise chose to wait until members received the Lytton Report.

Sir John Simon, the British Foreign Secretary, spoke in the debate and warned: 'We should be abandoning our first duty if we did not persist in pursuing the procedures of conciliation by every means possible'. Zilliacus likened Sir John Simon, an eminent barrister, to the shyster lawyers who defended gangsters in the American courts.[4] Be that as it may, there is little doubt that the British Government throughout the crisis viewed the League as an instrument of conciliation not coercion; and the American Government, with the country in the grip of the slump and isolationist feeling very strong, never contemplated support for military or economic sanctions against Japan.

The Japanese were by now so sure that they had nothing to fear from the League or from either of the world's major naval powers, Britain and the USA, who had the means to check them, that they proclaimed Manchuria to be a Japanese protectorate called Manchukao.

The Lytton Report was eventually presented to the League in October 1932. The report acknowledged Japan's economic and strategic interests in Manchuria and admitted that Japan had legitimate grievances against the Chinese Government. Nevertheless the Report condemned the Japanese invasion of Manchuria and refused to recognise Manchukao as an independent state.

When the League adopted the report, Japan resigned from the organisation. Apart from some border skirmishes the next four years were relatively quiet in the Far East, until July 1937 when Japan launched a full-scale invasion of China inaugurating 'the most terrible, the most inhuman, the most brutal, the most devastating war in all Asia's history'.[5]

On Zilliacus's return from China in April 1931 he was appointed secretary of the inter-departmental committee responsible for technical cooperation between the League and China. In this capacity he came into contact with the diplomats and officials who formed the Chinese delegation to the League of Nations, men such as Alfred Sze, Wellington Koo and Quo Tai-chi. When the

Manchurian Crisis developed later in the year Dr Sze sought Zilliacus's help in presenting China's case and the League's Secretary-General seconded Zilliacus to the Chinese delegation at Geneva to assist them in any way he could. Zilliacus wrote most of the Chinese party's notes and speeches, and he claimed to have coined the famous phrase 'the skies are dark with chickens coming home to roost' used by Quo Tai-chi in one of his speeches. After the crisis Dr Sze said: 'Zilly, if it hadn't been for you we could not have done this job'.

As Zilliacus later observed:

> We could not, of course, stop the British Government appeasing the Japanese ag-
> gressors. But at least we did show clearly to world opinion on which side right and
> justice lay and who were the villains in the piece. And for a time we succeeded in
> saving the principles at stake. [6]

Throughout the crisis, Zilliacus kept closely in touch with his friend, the editor of the *Manchester Guardian*, Edward Scott, who had succeeded his father in the post. In one letter, Zilliacus wrote that he could 'find no words to describe the abjectness and the shifty dishonesty of our Government throughout this matter. I have never felt such contempt, rage and despair since the war,' and Scott shared his sentiments.[7]

Zilliacus began to send reports to Scott, sometimes containing confidential information gleaned by Zilliacus from his membership of the Chinese delegation, and the editor used these scoops in his newspaper. The *Manchester Guardian's* reporting on the Manchurian Crisis must have been the best informed in the country. Scott refused to print some of Zilliacus's articles on the grounds that the League Secretariat would be able to trace them back to Zilly, however several of Zilliacus's articles did appear in the *Manchester Guardian* under the pseudonym 'A Student of the League'. When Edward Scott was drowned in a sailing accident in April 1932 his successor as editor of the *Manchester Guardian*, W.P. Crozier, asked Zilliacus to continue to send him his reports and Zilliacus agreed to do so.[8] Although Zilliacus was breaking League rules in leaking information, his conscience was clear on this point. He felt his first loyalty was to the Covenant of the League of Nations and he saw it as being betrayed by those who should have upheld it. In these circumstances he believed that he was justified in acting the way he did.

Zilliacus was also extremely critical of the League of Nations Union in Britain which throughout the Manchurian Crisis supported the British Government's policy. He was especially critical of Gilbert Murray, the eminent classicist who chaired the executive committee of the LNU, and Zilliacus wrote to Norman Angell, who also sat on the executive committee, urging him to ginger up its members to get them to support League of Nations action in support of the Covenant. [9] Zilliacus underestimated the support there was among many pro-League Conservatives and Liberals for the policy of conciliation (the word appeasement was not then in use) pursued by the British Government. After all, the Prime Minister was the former pacifist Ramsay MacDonald and the Foreign Minister, Sir John Simon, was a Liberal member of the National Government. Stanley Baldwin, the Conservative leader, was equally opposed to any form of action by Britain which could lead to war with Japan. Zilliacus saw things differently and wanted all League countries to condemn Japan without equivocation and he believed that if this were done there was a good chance that the USA and the USSR would follow suit. The whole world would then be ranged against Japan. Would Japan have been deterred by such action? We do not know because it was never tried. However the British policy of appeasement that was followed turned out to be calamitous; it failed to maintain peace and opened the way to the Japanese military conquest of the Far East.

Zilliacus was an international civil servant, but he was never a soulless bureaucrat. He cared passionately about the League of Nations and its role in the world, and he was deeply upset by the run of events in the Manchurian Crisis. Japanese aggression angered and shocked him, and the British Government's evasion of its commitments under the Covenant disgusted him. His daughter, Stella, recalled that on the evening of the day the Japanese had vetoed League action under Article 11, her father had come home in tears, patted her and her young brother Joe on the head and said 'These children will be at war by the time they're grown up and the same thing will happen to them as happened to us'.[10] Like many of his generation who had served at the front, the horrors of the 1914-18 war weighed heavily with Zilliacus and indeed never left him, for as late as the 1960s he could not bear to watch a BBC television series covering the events of the First World War. [11] Furthermore, the development of aerial bombardment in the 1920s, and its possible use against civilian targets, meant that a second world conflict could prove even more terrible than the first had been. Yet, unlike some others of his generation, Zilliacus never became a pacifist: he put his faith in the creation of a world peace system embodied in the League of Nations. During the Manchurian Crisis he believed that the Covenant should have been enforced against Japan and failure to do so represented a betrayal of the League.

Zilliacus in Geneva, 1924

Eugenia Zilliacus (née Nowicka)

Chapter 5

Disarmament

In Zilliacus's words 'the Disarmament Conference opened on 2 February 1932 to the thunder of Japanese guns'[1] as representatives from sixty-one states assembled in Geneva in the shadow cast by the Far Eastern crisis. Indeed, the first session of the Conference was delayed for an hour while the League Council met to discuss the Japanese bombardment of Shanghai. It was hardly the most propitious opening to such a conference. Yet there was still an expectation that some measure of disarmament might be achieved or at least a new arms race could be averted.

As Zilliacus saw it:

> In February 1932, there was still a hope that the Covenant might be applied in the Far East. Germany was still democratic and a member of the League, Italy was putting forward drastic disarmament proposals, and the United States had come closer to the League than ever before. At that time a wise and strong British policy could have secured the framing of a genuine disarmament and collective security convention that would have reconciled Germany with the Western Powers, established close relations between the League on one hand and the USA and the USSR on the other, isolated Japan and so have cleared the way for a real settlement in the Far East, followed by the carrying out of the Disarmament Conference.[2]

It is hardly necessary to observe that none of these things happened. The dominoes of history did not fall this way.

The Labour Government 1929-31 had played such a prominent part in arranging the Disarmament Conference that Arthur Henderson had been chosen as its President. The choice was maintained even after the fall of the Labour Government, although it meant that Henderson presided without the authority of being British Foreign Secretary. Indeed the National Government now in power in Britain was composed of Henderson's political opponents. His task was not an easy one and made no lighter by his poor state of health. Yet Henderson was determined to make a supreme effort to achieve some measure of general disarmament, and in this he had considerable support from public opinion in Britain.

When Henderson took up the Presidency of the Disarmament Conference Zilliacus was seconded from the Information Section to act as his private secretary and serve as a liaison officer between the League Secretariat and the

Disarmament Conference. The first thing to be decided, two days before the opening of the Conference, was what Henderson should say in his opening speech. Henderson consulted his two closest aides, Zilliacus and Noel-Baker.

Zilliacus proposed that Henderson should take a tough line:

> Tell them that you propose adjourning the Conference 'sine die' until such time as the Covenant has been successfully applied to stop Japanese aggression. All members of the League have agreed, in Assembly resolution after resolution, let alone the preparatory documents of the Disarmament Conference, there can be no disarmament without security. There cannot be any security so long as aggression is not curbed and the Covenant is treated as a scrap of paper. If you tell them that, the whole volume and power of public opinion, now focused on disarmament, will or at least may, be turned into channels that will generate a politically effective demand for applying the Covenant against Japan. If that isn't done there is no hope, for we are in for another arms race and heading for a new war. [3]

Noel-Baker tendered different advice to Henderson. He urged him to start proceedings as soon as possible, and this was also the advice offered by Thanassis Aghnides, an able Greek who had served in the League Secretariat since its earliest days and had risen to be Director of its Disarmament Section. Arthur Henderson chose to follow the advice of Noel-Baker and Aghnides, and in his presidential address he urged the countries of the world to cooperate in the interests of peace and work for general disarmament. Henderson was not a great orator but in his plain and sincere style he made an effective speech telling the assembled delegates:

> The world wants disarmament. The world needs disarmament. We have it in our power to help fashion the pattern of future history. Behind all the technical complexities regarding manpower, gun power, tonnage, categories, and the like, is the well-being of mankind, the future of our developing civilisation. [4]

Zilliacus, however, after Sir John Simon's handling of the Manchurian Crisis, had little faith in the British Government's good intentions. He believed that the British Government was lukewarm towards disarmament, and he was right in so thinking because its main concern was the security of the British Empire. Britain was reluctant to strip down its defences unless other countries were prepared to do the same, and for the first ten months of the Disarmament Conference – perhaps the crucial period in the life of the Conference – Britain played a negative role, with Sir John Simon subjecting the various disarmament schemes submitted by other countries to sharp and searching scrutiny. Matters were not helped by Simon's unlikable personality.[5] Not that Britain was uniquely wicked in putting its national or imperial interests to the fore. Other major countries had their reservations about disarmament. France, as always, sought security against a future German attack, and Weimar Germany demanded equality in armaments with France, either by French disarmament or by German rearmament to the level of equality with France. Britain attempted a mediating role between the two countries but failed to reconcile their conflicting positions.

Arthur Henderson blamed the British Government for the slow progress of the Disarmament Conference and Zilliacus agreed with him. However, the Conference did not fail because of the machinations of the British Government – although its tardy approach, especially in the opening months, did not help – but because of a deteriorating world situation. The slump had spread from Wall Street to every part of the USA and then across the world, bringing the collapse of international trade and mass unemployment in its wake. The effects of this had political repercussions throughout the world.

In May 1932, the moderate Brüning was replaced as German Chancellor by the more reactionary von Papen, who in turn was succeeded in January 1933 by Adolf Hitler. The coming to power of the Nazis made the French even less inclined to consider proposals for disarmament. In October 1933 Germany announced its withdrawal from the Disarmament Conference and the League of Nations, and Hitler launched a programme of rearmament. In 1934, Japan gave notice that it would not renew the Washington Naval Treaty of 1921, limiting the size of fleets, and the USA responded by announcing it would strengthen its naval forces in the Pacific. Mussolini began planning for a military conquest of Abyssinia. The French pressed on with the building of the Maginot Line, and the British Government in its 1935 White Paper gave notice of an increase in its defence budget. A new arms race was underway.

Arthur Henderson did not allow himself to be discouraged by these developments: he kept plodding on in his search for some plan or formula for disarmament which would be acceptable to the major powers. He never found such a formula but as Maxim Litvinov, Soviet delegate to the League of Nations, observed, speaking after Henderson's death: 'If the Conference has failed, one may say, it was in spite of the great effort accomplished by Mr. Henderson'. [6] The Disarmament Conference held its last meeting in 1934, although it was never formally wound up.

In Zilliacus's words:

> The Disarmament Conference, like the old soldier, kept fading away without officially dying. No Government had the cynical courage to put it out of its misery. Most found it convenient to keep its ghost walking or at least not to lay it, in order to distract public opinion while it got on with the arms race.[7]

Zilliacus, as Henderson's private secretary, was in close and regular contact with the man everyone knew as 'Uncle Arthur', and he observed: 'The better I came to know Arthur Henderson the greater grew my admiration and affection for him' and Henderson 'in turn came to give me his entire confidence and honoured me with his friendship'. [8] This was in spite of a warning given to Henderson, presumably by the British security service, that Zilliacus was a 'Bolshevik agent'. [9] Of course the two men discussed Disarmament Conference business but Henderson, who was still Secretary of the Labour Party, would also talk over Party matters with Zilliacus, knowing him to be a fellow member of the Labour Party. 'More and more', recalled Zilliacus, 'he entrusted me with drafting his speeches and notes on Party as well as Disarmament Conference matters'. [10]

The defection of Ramsay MacDonald, followed by Labour's massive general election defeat in 1931, had left many rank and file Labour Party members confused and distrustful of 'strong leadership', and the Socialist League, led by Sir Stafford Cripps, emerged as the main left-wing opposition group to the essentially moderate Labour leadership and its middle-of-the-road policies.

On foreign policy questions there were three broad streams of opinion. First, there were those who supported Labour's official policy, which was to put its trust in a strong League of Nations linked with efforts to secure general disarmament. This policy had the backing of the Party's Deputy Leader, Clement Attlee, supported by Arthur Henderson, Hugh Dalton, Philip Noel-Baker, plus leading trade unionists such as Ernest Bevin and Walter Citrine. This was Zilliacus's own preference. Secondly, there was the pacifist position represented by the venerable George Lansbury, who became the Party's Leader in 1932, and, thirdly, a left-wing view represented by the Socialist League, which regarded the League of Nations with deep suspicion as a capitalist tool and favoured the use of a general strike in Britain – supported, hopefully, by workers in other countries – as the best way of preventing the outbreak of another large-scale war. [11]

These three streams found their way into Labour's policy in 1933. Without abandoning its settled policy of support for the League of Nations and the Geneva Disarmament Conference, the Labour Party at its Annual Conference held at Hastings in October 1933 unanimously passed two resolutions on foreign affairs. The first one called for 'the total disarmament of all nations throughout the world and the creation of an international police force', and the second committed the Labour Party to all-out resistance to war, including the use of a general strike in Britain, with the hope that this would encourage similar action in other countries.

Zilliacus attended the Conference in the company of Arthur Henderson, and both were dismayed by the lack of realism shown by the passing of the two resolutions. A few days later Zilliacus met Henderson in the lounge of Henderson's suite at the *Hotel des Bergues* in Geneva. Henderson had a pile of documents on a table in front of him and looked worried.

'Transport House has sent me all this Hastings Conference stuff,' he said, 'and told me to draft a policy from it. How can I make a policy out of resolutions that are in flat opposition to each other?' 'Will you let me try?' asked Zilliacus.

Henderson pushed the mass of papers towards Zilliacus saying: 'Go ahead,

Zilly, see what you can do.'[12]

Zilliacus went to work and the result was the *War and Peace* Memorandum, a document of 3,000 words which skilfully attempted to weave together the various policy statements and conference resolutions into a coherent whole. World disarmament remained the goal but collective security was still at the heart of Labour's policy, while war resistance could be supported if the British Government acted against the authority of the League of Nations. The memorandum recognised that under certain circumstances Britain might have to use its military forces in support of the League of Nations in order to check an aggressor state. It was important that the Soviet Union be encouraged to join the League and the USA persuaded to cooperate closely with it. Support for a general strike was rejected because it placed an undue burden on the trade union movement, when efforts for maintaining peace should be the responsibility of all sections of the community. Furthermore, there were many countries where all strikes were illegal, hence it was unrealistic to expect a widespread response to any strike move by Britain.

Henderson did not change a word of Zilliacus's draft and the memorandum was approved, with only minor alterations, by the National Executive Committee of the Labour Party, the TUC General Council, and the National Council of Labour. After its passage through the NEC, Hugh Dalton wrote to Zilliacus: 'I seem to detect your fine Italian hand in this, Zilly, but keep it up, it's good stuff'.[13]

Zilliacus was proud of his skill at drafting reports and policy statements, but he knew that this particular exercise was largely irrelevant to the new international situation. Labour's problem was not how to restrain the British Government from going to war when it ought not to, but how to push it into standing up to a fascist aggressor, even at the risk of war if collective economic action did not suffice.[14]

Arthur Henderson presented *War and Peace* to the Labour Party's Annual Conference held at Southport in October 1934, where it did not escape criticism from the Socialist League but was nevertheless approved by a comfortable majority. It formed the basis of the foreign policy section of Labour's 1935 election manifesto *For Socialism and Peace*, which was also drafted by Zilliacus on behalf of Arthur Henderson.

In the winter of 1934 Zilliacus, with the assistance of Philip Noel-Baker, ghosted for Henderson *Labour's Way to Peace*, one of a series of books covering aspects of Labour Party policy published by Methuen. Arthur Henderson was now a sick and exhausted man, and he was glad of the loyal support of Zilliacus, indeed he could hardly have carried on without it.

The 1931 general election had decimated the Parliamentary Labour Party, leaving the burden of leadership on a triumvirate of front bench survivors: George Lansbury, who became Leader of the Party, Clement Attlee the new

Deputy Leader, and Sir Stafford Cripps, formerly Solicitor-General. The day-to-day work of opposition in the House of Commons fell on the shoulders of these three men, and they enjoyed little back-up in the way of secretarial and research services. Foreign affairs began to assume a greater importance and William Gillies, Secretary of the Labour Party's International Department, did his best to keep them fully briefed. He was ably assisted in this task by Zilliacus, who provided the three leaders with a steady stream of background papers and memoranda. [15] This was particularly helpful to Attlee who spoke frequently on foreign affairs and liked his speeches to be carefully structured and well stocked with facts. Indeed, Zilliacus drafted some of his speeches and Parliamentary questions. Zilliacus recalled that his influence with the Labour Party's leadership was at its peak from 1931 to 1935. After this, leading Party figures such as A.V. Alexander, Hugh Dalton, Herbert Morrison, and Emanuel Shinwell were returned to the House of Commons in the 1935 general election, restoring some strength to the Parliamentary Labour Party. Furthermore, the League of Nations counted for much less after 1935 as the world returned to naked power politics. Geneva ceased to be the main centre of diplomatic activity, consequently far fewer people were interested in what happened there.

In 1934 Zilliacus was struggling with the problem of how fascist aggression could be countered without accelerating general rearmament. He also wanted to see the League of Nations playing a major role in checking aggressor states and wished to avoid a return to any system of alliances. His solution was to suggest the creation of an 'inner ring' of states within the League of Nations, led initially by Britain and France, to be joined later by the Soviet Union (who entered the League in September 1934). These states would 'pool' their security and act together against aggression. Zilliacus, in fact, was putting forward a precursor of the Security Council of the United Nations. Zilliacus put the idea to Attlee, who liked it, and Zilliacus included the proposal in a lecture he drafted for Labour's Deputy Leader, which Attlee delivered to the Geneva Institute of International Relations in the summer of 1934.[16]

Attlee and Zilliacus were in broad agreement on all the major foreign policy issues of the 1930s, while a rift began to open up between Zilliacus and Hugh Dalton in 1934 and continued to widen until the end of the decade. In the winter of 1932 Dalton had visited Fascist Italy. He spent several weeks touring the country and was accorded an interview with Mussolini. Dalton had served in Italy during the First World War and he made no secret of the fact that he liked Italians and disliked Germans. Dalton was impressed with several features of Mussolini's Italy, notably its public works schemes, and he got on very well with the *Duce* at a personal level.[17]

Dalton saw Nazi Germany as the main threat to peace in Europe and he favoured drawing Italy into an alliance with Britain and France against a resurgent Germany. To Zilliacus this was a return to power politics and he still held the view that the machinery of the League of Nations should be used to check aggression. Nor did Zilliacus put any trust in Mussolini, who he believed had his own aggressive designs, and he was to be proved right when Mussolini's forces invaded Abyssinia in 1935.

After 1935, in the face of growing German military strength linked to an aggressive foreign policy, Hugh Dalton, together with Ernest Bevin and Walter Citrine, began to urge support for the British Government's rearmament programme. Zilliacus was opposed to this proposed shift in Labour's policy. He believed that if the member states of the League of Nations could act together – 'pooled security' – they had sufficient armed strength between them to match the fascist aggressors. There was no need for massive rearmament measures. Furthermore, Zilliacus did not have too much faith in the National Government's willingness to use any arms increase in support of collective security measures against aggressor states.

Zilliacus's other policy differences with Hugh Dalton emerged after the outbreak of the Spanish Civil War in the summer of 1936. Dalton was cool and detached towards the struggle between the Spanish Republic and the rebels led by Franco, and he backed the policy of non-intervention. As Zilliacus put it in a letter to Noel-Baker: 'I know Hugh has never cared a damn about Spain, and thinks the Spanish campaign is all rot'.[18] Zilliacus passionately supported the right of the Republican Government to purchase arms and he regarded the non-intervention policy as the height of hypocrisy in the face of open intervention by German and Italian forces, and he was incensed by the Labour Movement's initial support for the policy of non-intervention. As he later wrote: 'I thought that Labour's behaviour over Spain was the greatest mistake of the Labour Party since the war, and denoted not only a political but a moral and intellectual failure on the part of its leaders'.[19]

Zilliacus recalled that he remained on good personal terms with Hugh Dalton, in spite of the fact that they differed on several aspects of policy, and he continued to visit Dalton at his flat in Carlisle Mansions on his periodic visits to London. However, the close social contacts between the Zilliacus and Dalton families of the 1920s were not carried over into the 1930s, although this could have been due to growing strains in Zilliacus's marriage. Zilliacus's wife, Eugenia, is believed to have developed an illness known as petit mal (a mild form of epilepsy), which sometimes made her behave rather oddly in the company of other people. This affliction would not have made her the ideal holiday companion.

Zilliacus was still on cordial terms and kept regular contact with his old friend and former League of Nations colleague, Philip Noel-Baker, who remained loyal to Labour's League policy, although Zilliacus felt that Noel-Baker had not fully recognised the foreign policy implications of the rise of fascism in Europe.

Zilliacus was also friendly with Herbert Morrison, who was trying to broaden his outlook beyond municipal affairs, and Zilliacus was happy to provide him with background papers on foreign policy matters in the same way as he did for Attlee. In August 1936, Zilliacus arranged for Morrison to deliver a lecture to the Geneva Institute for International Affairs on the topic 'A new start with the League of Nations'. The lecture was drafted by Zilliacus and it contained his proposals for the creation of an 'inner ring' of states inside the League of Nations, and the election by proportional representation of a new international debating chamber of the League of Nations. Herbert Morrison and his wife stayed with the Zilliacus family during their visit to Geneva and Zilliacus took the opportunity to brief Morrison on the background to the Spanish Civil War. On his return to Britain Morrison took a stand against the non-intervention policy and Zilliacus believed that he had helped Morrison to arrive at this position.[20]

Henderson in Geneva and Attlee, Dalton, Morrison and Noel-Baker in London were numbered among Labour's leaders, and Zilliacus was glad to assist them by providing advice and information. In doing so he never disguised the fact that he tried to influence them. Zilliacus believed in the enforcement of the Covenant of the League of Nations and everyone knew where he stood. The Labour leaders were not fools and if they followed Zilliacus's advice or tapped his expertise it was because they broadly agreed with his views on foreign policy. In the 1930s Zilliacus was part of Labour's mainstream thinking on international affairs and from his base in Geneva he exercised considerable influence behind the scenes.

He also worked to inform and educate a new crop of rising Labour politicians. Arthur Henderson was instrumental in persuading a wealthy British socialist to finance the holding of an annual Labour Party summer school in international affairs at Geneva. Over two dozen students were chosen to attend the school every year, and they were accommodated in a rambling house, with most of the lectures being held in the open air. Konni Zilliacus was the director of studies at these schools and, with the permission of the Secretary-General of the League of Nations, he was allowed to take two weeks of his annual leave in order to run each school. There were lectures on the work of the League of Nations and the International Labour Organisation, and Zilliacus usually gave some lectures on current topics. He was, by all accounts, a stimulating lecturer, who impressed everyone by his knowledge of foreign affairs.

The summer school of 1935 was something of a vintage year. Among the twenty-eight students were thirteen future Labour MPs and six Ministers, including a Chancellor of the Exchequer, Hugh Gaitskell, and two Foreign Secretaries, George Brown and Michael Stewart. Also in attendance was Ted Willis, a future television scriptwriter and peer, then a left-wing activist.[21]

In addition to the Labour Party summer schools, Zilliacus also used another fortnight of his annual leave entitlement to run an annual summer course for the Scandinavian Folk High School, where the students were young Danish, Finnish, Norwegian and Swedish Social Democrats and trade unionists. The programme was similar to that followed by the British students except that

Zilliacus lectured to them in Swedish. He also did some lecturing on international affairs for Professor Alfred Zimmern's School of International Studies and the Geneva Institute of International Relations, as well as acting as host for parties of visiting students from several American universities.

After 1935 Zilliacus's lecturing work became more important to him as the League of Nations' role in world affairs began to decline, accompanied by a run-down in the League Secretariat's workload. As Zilliacus remembered his educational efforts:

> It was all rather drop-in-the-ocean work while the world was galloping to the devil, but I went on, mostly out of sheer obstinacy I think, but also because I felt I could not look my children in the face if I did not go on fighting even if there was no hope left.[22]

Arthur Henderson

Chapter 6

The Italo-Abyssinian War

On 3 October 1935 Italian troops crossed the River Mareb and started to advance from their Eritrean colony into Abyssinia.[1] On the following day a southern Italian army launched a second offensive from bases in Italian Somaliland. After a seven month military campaign in which tanks, armoured cars, aeroplanes and poison gas were used against bare-footed tribesmen armed with spears, Italian forces entered the Abyssinian capital, Addis Ababa, on 5 May 1936, and five days later their northern and southern armies linked up at Dire Wawa, bringing the war to an end. Four days afterwards, official victory celebrations were held in Rome, when Mussolini addressed a huge crowd packed into the Palazzo Venezia and declared: 'Italy finally has her empire.'[2]

Italy had harboured imperial ambitions in East Africa since the 1880s when she had carved out coastal colonies in Eritrea and Somaliland. Abyssinia was at this time the only remaining African territory to have escaped European control and was recognised by other European powers as an Italian 'sphere of interest'. Italian forces began to penetrate Abyssinian territory until, at Adowa in 1896, 20,000 Italians were routed by 90,000 Abyssinian warriors, ending this Italian attempt to conquer an African empire. The victory also consolidated the power of the Abyssinian Emperor Menelek, and gave the peoples of Abyssinia enormous self confidence in their ability to safeguard their independence. After his triumph at Adowa, Menelek could have carried on and swept the Italians out of their Eritrean colony, but he was content to rule within his traditional borders. In 1923 Abyssinia was admitted to membership of the League of Nations: a far-sighted move initiated by Ras Tafari, then Regent to the Abyssinian throne, who was crowned Haile Selassie in 1930. In an attempt at improving relations between the two countries, Italy and Abyssinia had signed a treaty of friendship in 1928, under which both were pledged to settle all disputes by 'processes of conciliation and arbitration'.

The Italian military campaign of 1935-36 had been long in preparation. As early as the spring of 1933 Mussolini had despatched General de Bono to Eritrea and Italian Somaliland to prepare the ground for a military campaign against Abyssinia. New ports, roads and barracks were built in the colonies to cope with the expected influx of troops and military equipment. Mussolini left his generals to prepare for the invasion while he kept the making of political decisions in his own hands. He would decide when the time was right to strike.

The political situation looked promising to the Italian dictator. Many countries were still preoccupied with economic problems created by the world slump. The Manchurian crisis had demonstrated the weakness of the League of Nations. Britain and France were powerful enough to block Italian ambitions if they chose to do so, however Mussolini was hopeful that they could be persuaded to give him a free hand in Abyssinia. Meanwhile, the Italian military build-up in East Africa continued.

Then, on 5 December 1934, it was reported that Italian and Abyssinian troops had clashed at Wal Wal waterhole in the Ogaden desert. The border between Abyssinia and Italian Somaliland was not clearly delineated, nevertheless Wal Wal was usually regarded as lying well inside the Abyssinian border. Frontier skirmishes were not uncommon in many parts of the world and were usually settled by some form of face-saving compromise. The Wal Wal incident was obviously not going to be resolved in this way. The government-controlled Italian press put forward its version of events and Mussolini demanded an apology plus compensation from the Abyssinian government. Haile Selassie refused to accede to the *Duce*'s demands and instead proposed arbitration under the terms of the 1928 Amity Treaty. When Mussolini rejected this offer Haile Selassie submitted the dispute to the League of Nations.

The Manchurian Crisis had severely damaged the credibility of the League of Nations, but it had not destroyed it completely. Indeed support for the League in Britain reached a new peak in the 1930s. Its perceived failure over Manchuria could be explained by the fact that the crisis had coincided with a worsening of the world depression, and that Manchuria was a remote and little known area to many Europeans. In addition, American support would have been required to deter Japan and such assistance was by no means certain, and, after all, the Japanese did have grounds for complaint against a Chinese Government which had lost control over one of its provinces.

There was also something of a time-lag between the ending of the First World War and the development of strong anti-war feeling in Britain. Anti-war memoirs, plays, novels and poems of the 1920s gradually built up an anti-war climate, reinforced by the publication of several books exposing the profitability of the arms trade. Only a minority of people became out-and-out pacifists, but even amongst those who did not there was a strong revulsion 'against war' and this overlapped with support for the League of Nations, which appeared to offer a means of avoiding war. In February 1933 the Oxford Union passed its famous resolution that 'this House will not fight for King and Country'; and later in the same year a Conservative candidate advocating rearmament was heavily defeated in the Fulham East by-election. In June 1935 the results of the Peace Ballot, organised by the League of Nations Union, were announced. The ballot was supported by 11.5 million people, 10.5 million of whom declared their faith in the League of Nations and the use of non-military sanctions against aggressor states. A large majority also voted in favour of disarmament.

Unfortunately for Haile Selassie the British Government did not share its own people's faith in the League of Nations and the cause of collective security. The coming to power of Hitler and his rearmament programme had convinced Sir Robert Vansittart and other officials inside the British Foreign Office that Nazi Germany posed the main threat to the country's security. Accordingly they favoured the creation of a new triple alliance of Britain, France and Italy to check a resurgent Germany, and Mussolini's designs on Abyssinia cut across this policy. The British Government attempted to pursue a pro-League policy to meet the demands of its electorate at the same time as it tried to avoid alienating Mussolini in order to maintain the so-called Stresa Front.

When the Abyssinian appeal came before the League Council in January 1935, the Italian delegate deprecated discussion of the Wal Wal incident under Article 11 of the Covenant since he did not regard it as likely to affect peaceful relations between the two countries and professed a willingness to settle the dispute by arbitration under the 1928 Amity Treaty. On this understanding the Council adjourned the question.

For the next three months the Italian Government delayed the appointment of arbitrators while it continued to send troops and war supplies into its East African colonies. Frustrated by this delay, on 16 March 1935 the Abyssinian Government invoked Article 15 of the Covenant, putting the dispute in the hands of the League Council. Three weeks later British, French and Italian ministers met at Stresa in order to form a common front against Germany. No mention of Abyssinia was made at this meeting.

In June, Britain offered to give Abyssinia the port of Zeila in British Somaliland if Abyssinia in return ceded the Ogaden province to Italy. However this proposal was dismissed by Mussolini as totally inadequate. Britain's attempt to buy off the *Duce* had failed.

After five months of deliberation, on 3 September, the arbitrators over the Wal Wal incident ruled that no party was to blame for the armed clash at the waterhole. On the following day Count Alosai, the Italian delegate to the League, declared that Wal Wal was no longer important. He denounced Abyssinia's forty years of hostility towards Italy and declared the African state to be unworthy of League membership. Italy therefore reserved the right to deal with Abyssinia in its own way. An Italian invasion of Abyssinia looked imminent.

When, on 11 September, the new British Foreign Secretary, Sir Samuel Hoare, addressed the League Assembly, he surprised everyone by declaring that Britain would carry out its obligations under the Covenant. What was not widely known at the time was that the day before Hoare had met Pierre Laval, then Prime Minister and Foreign Minister of France, and assured him that in no circumstances would the British Government agree to any form of action against Italy that might involve any danger of war with that country. Laval promptly reported this information to Mussolini, who received it with great satisfaction. The *Duce* now knew he had little to fear from Britain and France, and three weeks later he ordered Fascist Italy's long expected attack on Abyssinina.

Few people were better informed than Zilliacus on the events leading up to the Italo-Abyssinian war, and although he wanted to believe that the British Government would meet its commitments under the Covenant, after the Manchurian Crisis he had little faith that it would do so. He was remarkably prescient about what would happen. Zilliacus forecast that the British Government would deceive its electorate into believing that it meant business over Abyssinia, while at the same time trying to do a deal with Mussolini which would give the Fascist dictator most of what he wanted, although he was perceptive enough to see that Mussolini would not settle for anything less than the whole of Abyssinia.[3]

Although filled with reservations about the National Government's real intentions, Zilliacus had no doubts that it was his duty to do everything he could to get the League to act against Italian aggression. Firstly, Zilliacus decided to prod the Labour Party into action. In March 1935 the Party's Advisory Committee on International Questions (ACIQ) had advised the National Executive Committee (NEC) to support Abyssinia's case, but for two months the Labour Party had remained mute as the crisis deepened. In May Zilliacus wrote to Clement Attlee, the Deputy Leader, briefing him on the current situation, and Attlee incorporated most of Zilliacus's suggestions in a speech he made to the House of Commons on 7 June 1935. Attlee's speech included a proposal that, in the event of an Italian attack on Abyssinia, Britain should close the Suez Canal to Italian traffic, a move that would have brought Mussolini swiftly to heel.[4]

Zilliacus continued to supply Attlee with information and suggestions throughout June and July, including advice gleaned from French sources that if Britain led the way in imposing sanctions against Italy, France would follow her lead. Attlee was able to include this point in a speech he made to the House of Commons on 11 July.

After lobbying Attlee Zilliacus turned his attention to Hugh Dalton, an influential member of the NEC, urging him to initiate a national campaign in support of Abyssinia. Dalton, however, did not respond positively to the suggestion, accusing Zilliacus of over-dramatising the situation and arguing that 'no-one in England cared a damn about Abyssinia'.[5]

Zilliacus also tackled Stafford Cripps in an attempt to line up the Socialist League behind the NEC's policy of support for collective security. Zilliacus pointed out to Cripps that the entry of the Soviet Union into the League had transformed it from a purely capitalist organisation. Zilliacus argued that an Italian attack on Abyssinia would be an imperialist war, but to the Abyssinians it would be an anti-imperialist struggle in which they would be fighting for their independence and it was surely right to support them. He concluded that in his view the Conservatives were hand-in-glove with Mussolini and did not intend to press sanctions. Zilliacus failed to convince Cripps and observed: 'I might have saved my breath to cool my porridge'.[6]

Zilliacus had better luck with Noel-Baker who, when approached by Zilliacus, agreed to get the ACIQ to re-state its support for Abyssinia. Zilliacus also felt that the League of Nations Union (LNU) in Britain was too passive in the face of the developing crisis. The LNU contained many Conservative and Liberal supporters who were reluctant to criticise the National Government, especially with a general election in the offing, however Zilliacus was able to persuade Noel-Baker to use his influence to get the LNU's executive committee to come out in support of upholding the Covenant.[7]

In the run-up to the Labour Party's Annual Conference opening on 27 September 1935 Zilliacus and Noel-Baker assisted William Gillies in the drafting, on behalf of the NEC, of a strong pro-League motion with support for sanctions in the event of an Italian attack on Abyssinia. The motion was moved at the Conference by Hugh Dalton, who had now fallen into line on the policy, and it was opposed by George Lansbury, the Party's Leader, on pacifist grounds, and by Stafford Cripps, who argued that if accepted the Labour Party would be committed to supporting an imperialist war. Ernest Bevin weighed in with a blistering attack on Lansbury, and Herbert Morrison wound up on behalf of the NEC. After a dramatic two days' debate the NEC's motion was approved by 2,168,000 votes to 102,000. Zilliacus was well satisfied with the result.

On the following day Italian troops invaded Abyssinia.

In the meantime Zilliacus had been busy with his pen. He drafted a six page supplement on 'The Abyssinian Dispute' for the *New Statesman and Nation*. It was published on 7 September 1935 under the pen-name 'Vigilantes'. He had used this pseudonym two years before in an earlier pamphlet he had written for the *New Statesman and Nation* called *The Dying Peace*. In a publisher's note to *The Dying Peace* 'Vigilantes' was described as the cover-name for 'a small group of expert students of international affairs, who by virtue of their position are able to speak with unusual knowledge of the diplomacy of recent years', and in a later publication 'Vigilantes' was described as 'the pooled mental resources of three people'. [8]

There is no doubt that the books and pamphlets published under the authorship of 'Vigilantes' were drafted by Zilliacus. Who, then, were the other two people who assisted Zilliacus in the preparation of these publications? They were two of Zilliacus's colleagues in the League Secretariat: the Frenchmen Pierre Comert and Henri Vigier.[9] The three men met on a regular basis in connection with their work at Geneva, and they often held out-of-work discussions on world affairs. In 1935 Pierre Comert left the League Secretariat and moved to a post in the Quai d'Orsay, thereafter 'Vigilantes' was reduced to two people.[10] Books and pamphlets written by 'Vigilantes' are now credited to Zilliacus. This is justified because the writing of them was entirely his work and much of the analysis contained in them can be attributed to him. Furthermore, it was his drive and energy that resulted in their publication. The contributions of Comert and Vigier should not be overlooked, however. Although neither of them ever pressed a claim to joint authorship, they provided Zilliacus with much useful information and helped to sharpen up his ideas. Hence he was anxious to give them credit for their assistance by making the pseudonym 'Vigilantes' plural not singular.

The *New Statesman and Nation*'s supplement on Abyssinia sold 25,000 copies in Britain, and the Carnegie Endowment for International Peace reprinted it at its own expense for distribution in the USA. The demand for the supplement outstripped the supply, but rather than reprint another run of the first edition, Zilliacus took the opportunity of expanding the supplement into a pamphlet, which reached the market before the end of September, retailing at six pence a copy.[11]

It was obvious that Stanley Baldwin, who had taken over from MacDonald as Prime Minister, in a reconstructed government in which Sir Samuel Hoare had replaced Sir John Simon at the Foreign Office, would not delay too long before he called a general election. In anticipation of this, the publisher Victor Gollancz commissioned Zilliacus to write a critique of the National Government's foreign policy. Zilliacus got straight to work and *Inquest on Peace* by 'Vigilantes' was in the bookshops by the end of October. Kingsley Martin, writing in the *New Statesman and Nation*, believed the book to possess 'knowledge, expertise, vigour and wit'.[12] Zilliacus began with the Manchurian Crisis, continued with an account of the failed Disarmament Conference, described the rearmament of Nazi Germany, and ended with Mussolini's invasion of Abyssinia. The National Government, argued Zilliacus, had consistently failed to support the Covenant of the League and stated his conviction that they would behave the same way over the invasion of Abyssinia. Finally, he criticised the National Government's proposals to increase spending on armaments, which he believed would help to fuel another international arms race.

Four days after the launching of the Italian invasion of Abyssinia the Council of the League declared that Italy 'had resorted to war in disregard of the covenants under Article 12 of the Covenant of the League of Nations', and within days the Assembly had approved the Council's resolution and set up a committee to organise the imposition of sanctions against Italy: credits to Italy were stopped and some trade restrictions were imposed. There was widespread satisfaction across the world that the League was taking action against Italy, although it was significant that steel, coal and oil were omitted from the list of banned commodities on the grounds that these could continue to be supplied by non-sanctionist states.

Zilliacus was delighted that the League was imposing sanctions, however limited, although he feared that the British and French governments still hankered after a deal with Italy. 'The last thing our Tories and some of our Foreign Office officials want', he wrote in a letter to London based League official H.R. Cummings, 'is the defeat of Mussolini for they want to keep Italian Fascism as a bulwark against communism'.[13]

Stanley Baldwin judged the time was right to call a general election: he dissolved Parliament on 25 October with polling day on 14 November. In its election manifesto the Conservative-led National Government promised that the League of Nations would 'remain, as heretofore, the keystone of British foreign policy'; the Government would 'do all in our power to uphold the Covenant and to maintain and increase the efficiency of the League'. In the dispute over Abyssinia 'there will be no wavering in the policy we have hitherto pursued'. This did not remove the need for some measure of rearmament: gaps in the nation's defences would be filled, but at the same time the Government would work for a general limitation of arms.

Baldwin had outflanked his political opponents by taking over much of Labour's foreign policy while, at the same time, Labour could be castigated as a bunch of woolly pacifists or bloodthirsty warmongers according to the requirements of the election campaign. The Conservative-led 'Nationals' won the election, returning 425 MPs, giving them an overwhelming majority in the new House of Commons and a renewed lease of power.[14] Zilliacus was disappointed but hardly surprised by the result, however he was pleased to see Hugh Dalton regain his seat in the Commons.

After the general election the Italo-Abyssinian War continued to dominate the world's headlines. The first three months of the conflict had gone less well than had been expected for Italy. Italian forces had penetrated deep into Abyssinian territory, but Haile Selassie's main armies remained intact, and it appeared improbable that Italy would be able to subdue them before the start of the rainy season in June. The bulk of the Italian army and airforce, therefore, looked likely to be tied down in Africa for over a year. Both Britain and France resisted any tightening of sanctions against Italy: an oil embargo, in particular, would have had a devastating effect on the *Duce's* war machine. Neither country had any desire to topple Mussolini. On the contrary they hoped that once the Abyssinian dispute was settled the Stresa Front could be patched up. It was against this background that Sir Samuel Hoare and Pierre Laval put together a deal which they believed would be acceptable to Mussolini. Under the Hoare-Laval plan Abyssinia would cede two-thirds of its territory to Italy and receive in return an outlet to the sea at Assab. This was a straightforward imperialist deal at Abyssinia's expense, which Hoare and Laval intended to keep secret until the agreement of Mussolini and Haile Selassie had been secured. The deal would then have been presented to the League of Nations as a peace settlement secured by Britain and France acting as conciliators. Unfortunately for Hoare and Laval their plan was leaked to the press in Paris, according to Zilliacus by his former League colleague Pierre Comert.[15] Comert had recently moved from the Information Section of the League to the Press Bureau at the Quai d'Orsay. He had been disgusted when he had learned the full details of the Hoare-Laval plan and felt it his duty to leak them to the press.

The publication of the Hoare-Laval plan provoked an enormous rumpus in Britain. The National Government had promised to pursue a pro-League policy with support for sanctions against Italy, yet within a month of being returned to office it proposed to reward the aggressor at the expense of the victim. Baldwin was badly shaken by the outburst of indignation that swept the country. Hoare resigned as Foreign Secretary and was replaced by Anthony Eden. The National Government, with its large majority, weathered the storm and the British and French governments continued to block the imposition of oil sanctions against Italy. In Abyssinia, Mussolini replaced de Bono by the more ruthless Badoglio, who used poison gas against Abyssinian forces and brought the Italian campaign to a successful conclusion by early May. In the following month, the Chancellor of the Exchequer, Neville Chamberlain, called the continuance of sanctions against Italy 'the very midsummer of madness', and the Assembly of the League voted for their abandonment on 6 July 1936.

Italy had been allowed to conquer Abyssinia. Sanctions had not been applied in sufficient strength to deter Mussolini but they were strong enough to alienate him from Britain and France. The Stresa Front was broken beyond repair and Mussolini moved Italy into an alliance with Germany and Japan. The foreign policies of Britain and France were not only morally dubious, they were also spectacularly unsuccessful. In the process the League of Nations had been dealt a fatal blow. This was evident to Zilliacus when he wrote to W.P. Crozier, in his regular correspondence with the editor of the *Manchester Guardian* : 'We are witnessing the end of the great experiment of the League as conceived in 1919'.[16]

Chapter 7

Angell Plus Marx

Writing in 1939, Zilliacus stated that 'Norman Angell has had more to do with the shaping of my mind on international affairs than any other person', although he went on to say that since 1931 he had turned from being a disciple of Angell to a 'partial heretic'.[1]

What prompted this revision of Zilliacus's views was the Manchurian Crisis. In his own words:

> I started by loathing Sir John Simon in the Sino-Japanese conflict. Then, thinking about it, I began to realise not only that he was doing his best according to his lights, but represented the views of the whole Cabinet and the Government and Party behind them, who were doing their best according to their conception of their public duty and the national interest. The trouble was that their conception of the national interest was warped and their minds were conditioned by their way of life, by the section of the community in which they lived and moved and had their being, and whose interests they identified with the interests of the nation as a whole. They regarded the rest of the community as, in some sense, outsiders, almost enemies, who had to be kept quiet by being fooled.[2]

Zilliacus came to believe that what was missing from Norman Angell's analysis of international affairs was greater consideration of the economic factor.[3] Angell assumed that a smoothly functioning capitalist world economy would underpin the work of the League of Nations. The world slump had rudely shattered this assumption and Zilliacus believed that a global economy organised along socialist lines had become a necessary condition of world peace. He came to view Japan's invasion of Manchuria as a response to the effects of the world slump. The lower middle-class junior officers of the Japanese army stationed in Manchuria had been particularly hard hit by the depression, and they forced the pace in mounting the attack on the Chinese. What was emerging in Japan, argued Zilliacus, was a 'sort of militarist Oriental version of Fascism'.[4]

Zilliacus said that he did not know where this line of thought was leading him until one day in a discussion on this subject with Philip Noel-Baker his friend had observed: 'Zilly, you're talking like a Marxist'.

'Oh!' replied Zilliacus, 'if that's what old whiskers has been saying he must be right. I'd better have a look at it'.

Zilliacus had use of the League of Nations' library and what books it lacked he went out and bought. He soaked himself in the words of Marx, Engels, Lenin, Stalin and Trotsky, plus Brailsford, Cole, Dutt and Laski. He read Max Eastman's *Marxism: Is it a science?* and concluded that it was not.[5]

In this way, he gained his knowledge of Marxism. He was never a 'trained Marxist' as Communist Party theoreticians Palme Dutt or Emile Burns would have understood the term. In his own words:

> As for being a Marxist, I am at best an empirical pragmatic self-made semi-Marxist, for such reading I have done has been to eke out experience and first-hand impressions, and to help arrive at an understanding of intimately apprehended events.[6]

And in another context he said:

> I am no more a Marxist than I am a Darwinian or a Freudian. But it seems to me that the work of all three should be regarded as part of the history of civilisation and of our intellectual heritage, and as casting light on much that we recognise as true today.[7]

Zilliacus's conversion to some kind of Marxism did not mean that he abandoned the body of ideas associated with the Union of Democratic Control. To the end of his life Zilliacus remained opposed to power politics, secret diplomacy and arms races, and in favour of the democratic control of foreign policy plus some form of world organisation designed to keep the peace. His Marxism was superimposed upon his Angellism, it did not replace it. The outcome of this combination, as A.J.P. Taylor wittily observed, was that Zilliacus's books appeared to have been written by a partnership of Ramsay MacDonald and Lenin.[8]

An uneasy merging of old Liberal-Radical views on foreign policy with his newly found Marxism was certainly apparent in 'Vigilantes' earlier books *The Dying Peace* (1933) and *Inquest on Peace* (1935), but in his next three books on international affairs, *The Road to War* (1937), *Why the League Has Failed* (1938), and *Why We Are Losing the Peace* (1939), all published by the Left Book Club, Zilliacus had worked out a synthesis which he held for the remainder of his life. He had found his own voice or rather his own style and line of argument.

The world slump had convinced Zilliacus that capitalism was defunct and needed to be replaced by some form of socialism. In countries with a tradition of constitutional government, such as Britain and France, he believed the transition could be achieved by parliamentary means, in countries with no experience of democracy, for example Czarist Russia, then revolutionary methods would be used. Fascism, however, had emerged to frustrate the transition to socialism. It was, according to Zilliacus, the most extreme form of counter-revolution. Thus after the collapse of the German economy 1929-33, German capitalists in alliance with the big landowners, the military caste, the state bureaucracy and with the support of many in the middle class, had turned to the Nazis to block any movement towards a socialist solution to Germany's problems. Once in power, Hitler proceeded to rearm and carry out his expansionist foreign policy. In this he was aided, or at least not prevented, by the governments of Britain and France, who preferred to see the Nazis in power rather than face the alternative of a German socialist government. Furthermore, a strong Nazi Germany would serve as a useful check on the Soviet Union. Thus, Zilliacus argued, the governments of Britain and France, through their appeasement of Nazi Germany and Fascist Italy, were putting their class interests before their national interests, because a rearmed Germany in alliance with Italy would, in time, threaten the leading world positions of both Britain and France. The same class attitudes also ruled out any serious attempt at drawing the Soviet Union into a defensive alliance with Britain and France.

Zilliacus's books were densely written and supported by impressive documentation of sources. Above all, they were remarkably accurate in forecasting future events. From a different viewpoint, he was as prescient as Winston Churchill in his warnings of the most likely outcome of Chamberlain's appeasement policy.

For example, in May 1938 Zilliacus wrote:

The Liberal Government of 1906-14 helped to make the World War inevitable by its power politics and Imperialism. But it did play power politics well enough to ensure that when war came we had a united nation, a united Europe, half the world on our side, and a cause that at least looked good. Whereas the 'National' Government are playing power politics with such crass incompetence that they are not only making the next war inevitable, but losing it before it has begun. They are rapidly producing a situation where we shall find ourselves at war almost single-handed against all three Fascist dictatorships.[9]

This is not a bad forecast of Britain's position in 1940, except that Japan did not enter the war until 1941, although its hostility towards the British Empire was never in doubt.

In March 1937 membership of the Left Book Club stood at 39,400, reaching a peak of 57,000 in August 1939.[10] Thus the works of 'Vigilantes' enjoyed a wide readership, mainly among left-wing activists or sympathisers, and one can assume that many were influenced by what they read. In the words of A.J.P. Taylor 'the books which K. Zilliacus wrote under the name of "Vigilantes" were of great contemporary significance'.[11] *Guilty Men* was published under the pseudonym of 'Cato' in July 1940 and sold 200,000 copies. Written by three Beaverbrook journalists – Michael Foot, Peter Howard and Frank Owen – in four days, at the time of Dunkirk, it pilloried Britain's leaders of the 1930s, holding them responsible for the country's military unpreparedness. *Guilty Men* was a brilliant piece of polemical journalism whose publication was perfectly timed to make a major impact on public opinion.[12] Zilliacus spent the 1930s criticising the foreign policy of the same 'guilty men' – MacDonald, Baldwin, Chamberlain, Simon,

Hoare and Halifax: 'Vigilantes' ploughed the ground from which 'Cato' was to reap a rich harvest in the 1940s.

The military uprising in Spain, which began on 18 July 1936, soon developed into a full-scale civil war between those who supported the Spanish Republic and those who sought to overthrow it. Zilliacus saw the struggle as 'a further development of the international Fascist offensive against Socialism and democracy'.[13] From his post in Geneva he kept in close touch with events in Spain and knew at an early stage that the rebels were receiving military assistance from Italy. He was appalled by the non-intervention policy pursued by the British and French governments, which deprived the Republic of its right under international law to purchase arms from foreign suppliers while Italy, and later Germany, openly supported Franco's forces. Zilliacus was not too shocked by the behaviour of the National Government, however he was deeply upset when on the first day of its Annual Conference in October 1936 the Labour Party endorsed the Government's non-intervention policy. Two days later two Spanish fraternal delegates addressed the Conference and after their speeches the Labour Party effectively reversed its earlier decision. Nonetheless much damage had been done to the credibility of Labour's policy, and with Bevin and Dalton at best lukewarm to the Republican cause, Labour Party support for the Spanish Republic was never wholehearted.

Zilliacus was on close personal terms with Salvador de Madariaga, the Spanish delegate to the League of Nations and a former member of the League Secretariat and with Pablo de Azcarate, another former member of the League Secretariat, who succeeded de Madariaga at Geneva. He was also friendly with the Spanish Foreign Minister, Alvarez del Vayo, who often visited Geneva to canvass support for his government.

Zilliacus was a passionate supporter of the Republicans in their struggle. As he put it: 'the Spanish Republic represented the freeing of the Spanish people from the heritage of a semi-feudal past, the dawn of hope in Spain',[14] and he was disgusted by the Labour Party's vacillation over what its policy towards the Spanish Civil War should be.

Zilliacus was also deeply disappointed with the editorial policy of the *Manchester Guardian* which backed the British Government's non-intervention policy. In its leader of 10 August 1936 the newspaper had equated communism with fascism as part of its argument for supporting non-intervention in the Spanish Civil War.

Zilliacus wrote to the editor, W.P.Crozier:

> Can't you Liberals really see that the Communists are trying – by violent, wasteful and if you like mistaken means – to bring about social and economic changes that must come, and that Fascism is an attempt by violence to hold back the forces of social change?… We Socialists care as much as you Liberals for democracy and freedom, but we realise that today, in the face of terrible danger of Fascist aggres-

sion, the Communists are allies and not enemies, as is being shown in Spain.[15]

Zilliacus disapproved so strongly of the *Manchester Guardian*'s position on Spain that he broke off all communications with Crozier. Fortunately for him he remained on cordial terms with Kingsley Martin, and for the next couple of years, usually writing under the *nom de plume* 'A Socialist', the *New Statesman and Nation* became the main outlet for his articles and letters on international affairs.

Support for Republican Spain in Britain helped to push various left-wing parties and groups into common action. Socialists, communists and many non-party 'progressives' campaigned for 'Arms for Spain' and worked together to raise money in order to send food and medical supplies to the beleaguered Republic. In January 1937 the Socialist League, the Independent Labour Party and the Communist Party of Great Britain issued a 'Unity Manifesto' calling for working-class solidarity to defeat fascism and the National Government. It called on workers to mobilise to save the peace, protect the Soviet Union from fascist aggression, and create a bloc of states willing to resist fascism. It also called for opposition to the National Government's rearmament programme and for the nationalisation of the arms industry. Zilliacus, under his pseudonym 'A Socialist', wrote a letter of support for the Unity Campaign in the new left-wing weekly *Tribune* on the 19 February 1937 – a further indication of his move to the left.

Zilliacus outlined his new position in a letter to Norman Angell dated 3 April 1937, for although they disagreed on important aspects of international affairs, Zilliacus and Angell continued to correspond on a friendly basis. Indeed, they planned to write a book together in which they would discuss their conflicting views on the importance of the economic factor in international relations.[16] Zilliacus wrote from Geneva:

> I have been through the mill here from the beginning and took part in the endless discussions and negotiations during the many years of attempts to build up treaties of non-aggression, arbitration and mutual assistance, to interpret the Covenant, apply it to disputes etc. As a result of all that I have gradually and reluctantly come to the conviction that the only thing that really matters in the world today is the class struggle and that the only way to peace is to get a working class Government into power, which in England means to help the United Front Movement to victory within the Labour Party, and then extend that movement into a popular front.[17]

In the summer of the same year Dalton, with the backing of Bevin, changed the Labour Party's policy on rearmament. In July 1937, Dalton persuaded the Parliamentary Labour Party to abstain from voting on the Defence Estimates instead of voting against as was the Party's previous practice; and in the same

month, again with Bevin's support, he gained approval for a revised policy statement, issued under the title *International Policy and Defence*, which accepted
the need for British rearmament. The policy was then approved at the Party's
Annual Conference in October 1937. The disaffiliation of the Socialist League
and the rejection of a United Front Policy were also approved at the same
Conference.[18]

Zilliacus not only disagreed with these changes but it was an indication of how
far he had become marginalised on foreign policy matters inside the Labour
Party that he was not consulted or in any way involved in these far-reaching
policy moves. His old Labour Party friends – Attlee, Morrison and Noel-Baker
– accepted the policy shift engineered by the Bevin-Dalton axis, and the Party's
leadership closed ranks behind the new policy. By the end of 1937 Zilliacus
found himself closer to the left-wing rebels – Stafford Cripps, Aneurin Bevan
and George Strauss – on policy questions than he did to his old friends and colleagues on the centre-right of the Labour Party.

Chapter 8

Annus Miserabilis

Neville Chamberlain succeeded Baldwin as Prime Minister in May 1937, with Anthony Eden remaining at the Foreign Office. Chamberlain was determined to put his own stamp on foreign policy and to end what he considered to be the drift of the Baldwin years. Chamberlain wished to avoid Britain's involvement in another European war and he favoured removing sources of grievance by negotiation with the dictator-states of Germany and Italy: in other words he intended to pursue a policy of appeasement. He was confident he could do business with Hitler and Mussolini, and secure a new European settlement. Anthony Eden was equally anxious to avoid another European war, but whereas Chamberlain saw greater scope for personal contacts between himself and the dictators, Eden preferred the methods of conventional diplomacy, with a role for the League of Nations. The policy differences between the two men were more those of method and timing than of substance.

On 1 January 1938, Sir Robert Vansittart was moved from his post of Permanent Under Secretary at the Foreign Office to the newly established position of Chief Diplomatic Adviser. Vansittart favoured the creation of a European coalition to check the growing power of Nazi Germany, and his views ran counter to Chamberlain's appeasement policy. Vansittart's new appointment had the appearance of promotion but in effect he was being sidelined inside the Foreign Office hierarchy.

Ten days later President Roosevelt proposed to Neville Chamberlain the holding of a world conference to discuss points of dispute between various countries. Eden was on holiday at the time and Chamberlain sent a discouraging reply to the President's letter. Eden believed that some good might have come out of Roosevelt's proposal and he was piqued that Chamberlain had replied without consulting him. In the following month the two men clashed over reaching an accommodation with Italy: Chamberlain wished to move faster than Eden in improving relations with Mussolini. Eden resigned and was replaced by Lord Halifax.[1]

Zilliacus interpreted these events in Marxian terms. He saw the dispute between Chamberlain and Eden as a clash between 'the power-politics of the Foreign Office and the class-war politics of the City'.[2] Vansittart viewed Germany as the main threat to the British Empire and he wished to build up a counter balance to the Nazis. An alliance with France would not be strong enough in itself to deter Hitler, therefore a second ally must be sought. Soviet Russia was beyond the pale, therefore Italy would have to be courted. 'The blood of Abysinnia and the scraps of paper of the Covenant were to seal this alliance',[3] except that the Hoare-Laval deal misfired. Undeterred by this failure Vansittart hoped to appease Mussolini in Spain by turning a blind eye to Italian intervention in the Spanish Civil War. Only when it became obvious that Mussolini would not be wooed into breaking his growing friendship with Hitler did Eden wish to put a brake on this policy.

Chamberlain, on the other hand, according to Zilliacus, was motivated by class-politics. He represented the interests of the City and British industry and he wished to buy a place for Britain in the Berlin-Rome Axis. The price would be paid by sacrificing small countries such as Austria and Czechoslovakia, and handing over some colonies to Germany and Italy. The fascist states represented a 'bulwark against Communism' which must be preserved at almost any cost, even if it meant that Britain's national interests were sacrificed in the process.

Winston Churchill in *The Gathering Storm* has described his response to Eden's resignation:

> Late on the night of February 20 a telephone message reached me as I sat in my old room at Chartwell … that Eden had resigned. I must confess that my heart sank, and for a while the dark waters of despair overwhelmed me …. From midnight till dawn I lay in my bed consumed by emotions of sorrow and fear. There seemed one strong young figure standing up against the long, dismal, drawling tides of drift and surrender, of wrong measurements and feeble impulses …. Now he has gone.[4]

Zilliacus's remembrance of Eden in the 1930s was rather different. He wrote:

> Eden in those days was a high-minded, well-meaning young man, very much in earnest about peace. But he was correct and tame, wholly a product of the Establishment and a scion of the upper classes. From start to finish he was the embodiment of the Foreign Office tradition and the obedient servant of the Tory party machine. The idea of challenging either was literally unthinkable to him.[5]

Zilliacus had first observed Eden when the young politician was serving as a junior minister under Sir John Simon and Lord Londonderry, during the period of the Disarmament Conference. In Zilliacus's words:

> He did all the dirty work at Geneva and hated it, deplored it, bewailed his fate, wore his wounded heart on his sleeve to an admiring little coterie of diplomatic correspondents, like W. N. Ewer of the 'Daily Herald' and Vernon Bartlett, with whom he was soon on first name terms and to whom he kept confiding that it was all really too awful, he could not stand it any longer, he thought he must resign etc.

At first I was impressed by the accounts of his Laöcoon-like wrestling with his conscience. But as time passed without a decision, whilst the world went on rattling to hell, I began to realise that the exercises were Eden's way of letting off steam, easing the ache of his conscience, a substitute and not a preparation for action. And so when Vernon Bartlett came rushing in one day starry-eyed to give me another sob story of Eden's sufferings and desire to resign, I gave him a bit of a shock by replying: 'I wish to hell the beggar would resign. But he won't. After all he wants to be leader of the Tory Party some day, so he'll choke his conscience with his old school tie …' to us in the Secretariat he seemed a well-meaning, correct young man, who believed in hastening slowly enough not to lose his place and his chance of promotion in the Tory team.[6]

After getting his promotion to the Foreign Secretaryship, in the wake of the ignominious failure of the Hoare-Laval deal, Zilliacus recalled 'Eden helped to assassinate the Spanish Republic.'

In September 1936 del Vayo had appealed to the League under Article 10 of the Covenant to provide the Spanish Government with the arms it needed to defend its territorial integrity and political independence against Hitler's and Mussolini's aggression. I can still remember that black day in the Assembly, listening to Eden droning away from the rostrum, explaining why it was contrary to the Covenant of the League to interfere in an ideological conflict.
What cunning bastards they are, the damned hypocrites, thought I, standing there with death in my heart, light-headed from the stench of catastrophe, feeling a little sick with the "steely taste of defeat" in my mouth.[7]

In the space of two months Chamberlain had removed Vansittart and then Eden from positions of power and influence in the Foreign Office, and he could proceed to implement what Zilliacus termed a policy of all-in appeasement.[8]

Chamberlain's intentions were soon put to the test when Hitler annexed Austria on 13 March 1938. The *Anschluss* or union of Germany and Austria had long been part of the policy of the Nazi Party. In the opening months of 1938 Hitler felt strong enough to do something about it. On 12 February he had met the Austrian Chancellor, Kurt von Schuschnigg, at Berchtesgaden, where he had browbeaten him into agreeing to Nazi participation in his government and the lifting of the ban on Nazi Party activity in Austria. On his return to Vienna Schuschnigg decided to fight back by announcing the holding of a referendum on the question of Austrian independence. Hitler was furious and faced with the threat of a German invasion Schuschnigg cancelled the referendum and resigned in favour of the Nazi, Artur Seyss-Inquart. On 12 March German troops marched into Austria and the next day Hitler declared its annexation. There was no resistance to the German invasion, indeed in some places ecstatic crowds greeted the German troops. The Austrian Government did not appeal to the League of Nations, nor did any other country on her behalf. An independent

state and member of the League of Nations had been absorbed by its more powerful neighbour. Mussolini, the former 'protector' of Austria, gave his approval
to the Nazi takeover. Britain and France voiced their protests, but it was clear
that they would acquiesce in Hitler's action.[9]

Chamberlain's response to Hitler's seizure of Austria was not to put a brake on
the appeasement of the dictators but to speed it up. He was determined to take
the initiative and remove points of dispute before they developed into major
international crises. He pressed on with the appeasement of Mussolini and on
16 April Britain agreed to recognise Italian sovereignty over Abysinnia. In return
Mussolini promised to phase out the force of Italian troops fighting in Spain.

The agreement was followed by 'one of the most discreditable episodes in the
history of the League of Nations',[10] when at the meeting of the League Assembly
on 12 May 1938 Lord Halifax moved that each member of the League should
be free to recognise Italian dominion over Abysinnia. 'Nothing is gained, and
much may be lost, by the refusal to face facts', he argued, and Italian control over Abysinnia was a fact. Speaking immediately after Lord Halifax, the
Emperor Haile Selassie, a man of immense dignity, asked 'that Ethiopia shall be
allowed to remain among you as an image of violated rights'. After the debate
no vote was taken and none was considered necessary because the Chairman of
the Assembly ruled that there was a clear majority in favour. Haile Selassie then
walked slowly out of the magnificent council chamber of the Palais des Nations
and into exile.

It was evident that Hitler's next victim would be Czechoslovakia, a small
democratic state of 15 million people, strategically situated in the heart of
Europe, whose integrity was secured by mutual defence pacts with France and
the Soviet Union. The presence of 3.5 million Sudeten Germans living as citizens
inside Czechoslovakia gave Hitler the lever he needed to destabilise the state as
a prelude to its destruction. In April 1938 Hitler ordered Henlein, the leader of
the Sudeten Germans, to agitate for autonomy inside Czechoslovakia. The new
French Premier, Edouard Daladier, met Chamberlain on 28 April in London.
He told Chamberlain that France was ready to meet its treaty commitments to
Czechoslovakia and proposed joint action with Britain. Chamberlain was cool
towards the French proposal and let it be known that he favoured a negotiated solution. At the same time Chamberlain rejected Soviet overtures for the
creation of a four power defence pact embracing Britain, France, the USSR and
Czechoslovakia.

On 19 May Hitler began to mobilise troops on the Czech border and the Czech
Government responded with a partial mobilisation of its own. France and the
Soviet Union promised to honour their treaty obligations to Czechoslovakia,
and Lord Halifax warned that a German attack on Czechoslovakia would probably draw in Britain.

Hitler held back and this gave Chamberlain the time he needed. He appointed Lord Runciman to act as a mediator between the Czech Government and the Sudeten Germans, but with Henlein encouraging mob violence in the Sudetenland the situation grew worse. Chamberlain judged the time was right for his personal intervention and on 15 September he met Hitler at Berchtesgaden, on 22 September at Godesberg, and on 29 and 30 September there took place the meeting at Munich attended by Chamberlain, Daladier, Hitler and Mussolini, at which Czechoslovakia was stripped of the Sudetenland, and with it the militarised frontier areas which had protected her from German attack.

Chamberlain was pleased with the outcome and claimed to have secured 'peace with honour'. Hitler should have been satisfied because he had got the Sudetenland without a fight, yet, curiously, he was disgruntled by the way things had turned out. His main aim had been the destruction of Czechoslovakia and this had not been achieved, although, as events proved, its dismemberment had only been postponed for six months.[11]

At Geneva the officials of the League Secretariat could only watch as these events unfolded. At least the Manchurian Crisis and the Italo-Abysinnian War had involved the League. Throughout 1938, however, the League had been sidelined as Europe's leaders indulged in secret diplomacy and power politics. Zilliacus was depressed and concentrated his mind, as well as he was able, on his writing and lecturing work. Finally, on 9 August 1938 he tendered his resignation to the Secretary-General of the League of Nations, Joseph Avenol, to take effect from 15 October. In his letter of resignation he pointed out to Avenol that since 1933 the League Secretariat had 'adjusted itself to the prevailing moral and political standards of the chief Government Members of the League, instead of sticking to the standards imposed by the Covenant'. Hence, Zilliacus went on, principles, treaty obligations and ideals had been abandoned in the name of realism, resulting in 'humiliation, defeat and disaster'.[12]

Joseph Avenol had succeeded Sir Eric Drummond as Secretary-General of the League of Nations in 1933. He was a Frenchman who had worked in France's Ministry of Finance before joining the League Secretariat as Deputy Secretary-General in 1923. Behind a mask of civil service impartiality, Avenol had been an ardent, though discreet, supporter of the appeasement policies, including non-intervention in the Spanish Civil War, pursued by Britain and France in the 1930s, and had done what he could to ease their passage through the League. He was a man of right-wing views and after the fall of France in June 1940 pledged his allegiance to Petain and offered to resign his post if the Marshal so wished. The Vichy Government duly instructed him to do so and he tendered his resignation as Secretary-General of the League of Nations on 25 July 1940. He then sought a post with the Vichy Government and after rejection – mainly due to his poor personal relationship with Pierre Laval – he retired to Haute-Savoie, moving to Switzerland in December 1943.

Although Zilliacus had great respect for most of his colleagues in the League

Secretariat he must have had Avenol's views and activities in mind when he penned his resignation letter. This was not the only reason, however, for he recalled: 'I resigned from the Secretariat because the League was dead and the fight was now at home. I knew there was no hope any longer, that no power on earth could avert war.'[13]

The year was also a miserable one for Zilliacus at a personal level. In the spring of 1938 his mother had died at her home in the USA. There were strong bonds between her and both her sons, and her death hit Konni and Laurin Zilliacus very hard. She was a wealthy woman and left a substantial estate to her two sons. This made Konni Zilliacus financially independent, enabling him to contemplate resignation from his post in the League Secretariat. He also separated from his wife, Eugenia, in 1938. Personal differences between them were exacerbated by Zilliacus's move to the left. Eugenia was a devout Roman Catholic and Zilliacus's flirtation with Marxism did not meet with her approval. Zilliacus gave half of his inheritance to his wife, who moved to a house in Guildford. In the same year, their daughter, Stella, left Bedales to take up a place at Cambridge, and their son, Joseph, left his school in Geneva to complete his education at Bedales. After he had wound up his affairs in Geneva, Zilliacus moved to a rented flat in Albany Street, in the St Pancras area of London.[14]

Chapter 9

Raising Hell

When Zilliacus moved into his flat in St Pancras in January 1939 he was free to play a more active role in British politics and he plunged into a spurt of left-wing activity. Looking back twenty years later he considered this to have been a mistake:

> When I came home I should, of course, have looked up my old friends among the Labour leaders, and taken counsel with them. I was wrong not to do it. But I was fed up. 'I know what they will say', I thought. 'They'll tell me to do nothing just like they are doing'. And that's one thing I refused to do.[1]

At that time Zilliacus still remained on cordial terms with Attlee, Morrison and even Dalton, although, as described earlier, he had moved away from them on policy matters and closer to the position taken up by Cripps and Bevan. Would a chat with Attlee or Morrison have made much difference? Zilliacus was never a trimmer nor was he a careerist. They may have advised him to take his bearings before he took any precipitate action, but it is doubtful if he would have heeded their advice. Nevertheless this was an important turning-point in his life, for if he had thrown in his lot with Attlee or Morrison at this juncture he might have been given a position in the post-war Labour Government or succeeded William Gillies as head of the Labour Party's International Department at Transport House, when the post became vacant in 1945. However, this is speculation; Zilliacus did not seek their advice much less follow it, and events took a different course.

As he observed to W.P. Crozier in March 1939, resuming his correspondence with the editor of the *Manchester Guardian* after a gap of two years:

> I resigned and came home to raise hell about the National Government's drift to Fascism and war, and the Labour Party's failure to oppose it vigorously – and I'm only just beginning.[2]

For the twelve months following his resignation from the League, Zilliacus campaigned in support of war resistance, ousting the National Government, and the building of an alliance with the Soviet Union. He had supported war resistance since the early thirties when he had been largely instrumental in getting it accepted as part of Labour's policy. Zilliacus did not believe in the dictum 'my country right or wrong'. He held that every citizen had the right to withhold his or her support from a government if it became engaged in an unjust war, such a war being defined by Zilliacus as one which was fought in breach of the Covenant of the League of Nations. He feared that the National Government might lead Britain into such a war and if it did then its citizens, he argued, should refuse to fight. Zilliacus thought the National Government's foreign policy had been disastrous and he favoured the creation of a Popular Front in order to remove it from office and replace it with a People's Government. Such a government would be well placed to establish a Peace Bloc with France and the Soviet Union, and, hopefully, win the support of Roosevelt's USA. Zilliacus believed that this way lay the only hope of defeating fascism in a war he was convinced was now inevitable.

These policies were being supported by Cripps and Bevan in the pages of *Tribune*, and from September 1938 until the outbreak of war Zilliacus wrote a series of articles for the paper, mainly on foreign policy issues. Because he was no longer an employee of the League of Nations he was able to publish these articles under his own name, and he could draw upon his considerable knowledge of foreign affairs plus his many international contacts.

In his articles he exposed further attempts at appeasing Italy[3] and Japan[4]. He wa-rned that Poland would not prove to be a 'strong ally' and considered the USSR a much better military proposition.[5] He went on to accuse Chamberlain of sabotaging a possible alliance with the Soviet Union.[6] He was against the introduction of conscription – 'Chamberlain cannot be trusted with the lives of Britain's young men';[7] and when conscription was brought in on 26 April 1939 Zilliacus described it as 'taking the high road to Fascism'.[8] He was critical of the Labour Party leadership for confining their efforts to Parliament: he wanted to see more political campaigning across the country.[9] Zilliacus did not condone the signing of the Nazi-Soviet Pact but he dismissed the 'tales of a secret Nazi-Soviet alliance for the partition of Poland' as 'mere propaganda'.[10] Three weeks later he took a benign view of the expropriation of Polish landowners and capitalists as the Red Army secured the Soviet slice of newly partitioned Poland.[11]

Zilliacus also contributed a long article, 'Appeasement and Armageddon', to Palme Dutt's *Labour Monthly* in April 1939, in which he attacked Chamberlain's appeasement policy and the National Government's rearmament programme. 'Rearmament for what purpose?' asked Zilliacus, and he answered: the defence of imperial interests. He saw the moves to introduce industrial and military conscription, together with the possibility of increased censorship, as a form of creeping fascism and urged maximum opposition from Labour's leaders.[12]

Zilliacus completed two books in the early months of the year. *Why We Are Losing the Peace* was published by the Left Book Club in March 1939, under the pseudonym 'Vigilantes' but this time with Zilliacus's name printed in brackets after the pseudonym. In his new book he updated his critique of the National Government's foreign policy into the post-Munich period. His book, *Between*

Two Wars?, published as a Penguin Special, was completed after Munich but before the fall of the Spanish Republic, and a large section of it was devoted to the war in Spain, with a plea that it was still not too late to save the Republic from defeat. Unfortunately the publication of the book was overtaken by events: Madrid fell in March 1939, bringing the Spanish Civil War to an end. Like his previous book its authorship was given as 'Vigilantes' (K.Zilliacus). What added to the book's interest was the introduction by Norman Angell, in which he criticised Zilliacus's Marxist approach to international affairs but nevertheless concluded that the book was 'worthy of the closest examination'.[13]

In addition to his writing, Zilliacus did a three months speaking tour of Britain on behalf of the Left Book Club. These meetings enabled him to put over his views on foreign policy and at the same time they helped to publicise his books. He was already an accomplished lecturer but he valued the experience he gained by travelling the country and addressing the political meetings organised by the Left Book Club.[14] In August he was the main speaker at the Left Book Club's summer school held at Matlock in Derbyshire, where he lectured on 'The present international situation'.

On taking up residence in London, Zilliacus had joined his local constituency Labour Party, St Pancras South West, and was elected its delegate to the 38th Annual Conference of the Labour Party held at Southport in May 1939.

At the Conference, Noel-Baker introduced the NEC's resolution on foreign affairs which called for 'a return to the spirit and the principles which animated the foreign policy of the Labour Government from 1929 to 1931' as the only hope of restoring 'Britain's moral influence and power of international leadership' and of rebuilding the League of Nations. It deplored the delay in concluding defence pacts with France and the Soviet Union, and called for closer contact with the USA and other countries in 'a programme of agreed limitation of armaments' and a solution of the world's economic problems.[15]

There followed a rambling debate whose only highlight was the speech by Ernest Bevin, in which he argued that collective security was not enough, and that attention must be paid to the solution of the world's economic problems. He sketched out the desirability of greater economic cooperation between the British Empire and the USA as a prelude to the creation of a wider bloc of like-minded states.[16]

Zilliacus, attending his first Labour Party Conference as a delegate, moved a resolution on behalf of the St Pancras South West Labour Party. The resolution was in procedural terms not an amendment, although if passed it would have added to the resolution put forward by Noel-Baker on behalf of the NEC.

Zilliacus began by praising Bevin's contribution to the debate. He agreed with the trade union leader that economic factors were extremely important in foreign affairs, and went on to say that he supported the NEC's resolution but wished to strengthen it. He asked Conference to recognise the growing discontent in Britain's colonies and claimed they should be put under a system of international trusteeship, India should be granted independence, and the Labour Party should not support any war fought for colonial possessions. The second part of the resolution urged the Labour Party to resist any form of conscription, industrial or military, in peace or war – the Party should return to the policy of war resistance it had abandoned in 1936.[17]

Noel-Baker, winding up the debate on behalf of the NEC, said he was concerned about talk of resisting conscription, opposition was already being carried out by constitutional means and he hoped there would be no support for unconstitutional action. He need not have worried: the St Pancras South West resolution was lost by 286,000 votes to 1,670,000 and the NEC's resolution approved by 2,363,000 votes to 55,000.[18]

Looking back, twenty years later, on the St Pancras South West resolution, Zilliacus observed: 'It was hopelessly unreal in the circumstances and got knocked down.'[19]

Later in the week the Conference went into closed session to discuss the role of the *Daily Herald*. During the debate Zilliacus mounted the rostrum and launched an attack on the newspaper, accusing it of being an 'organ of the appeasers' and of failing to support Labour Party policy. Zilliacus then made the mistake of mentioning a particular part of the paper and saying that the author of the column was the worst of the lot.

Ernest Bevin, who tended to regard the *Daily Herald* as 'his paper', stumped his way to the rostrum to reply to Zilliacus's criticism. He denounced Zilliacus's speech as 'wicked and dastardly personal' for attacking a man who was not present to defend himself, and who, unlike Zilliacus, was a member of the National Union of Journalists. He went on to warn the delegates that he did not want Zilliacus to play the same tricks on the Conference that the former League of Nations official had tried to play on him at Geneva.

Zilliacus, by this time, was very upset. It was true that he was not a member of the NUJ but this was because he had not yet qualified for membership under the union's rules. Bevin's references to his alleged trickery at Geneva, however, roused him to fury and he started shouting: 'What tricks? Withdraw! What tricks? Withdraw!' The cry was taken up by many delegates in the hall and the uproar became so great that the Chairman closed the session for the day.

After the closure Zilliacus was surrounded by delegates who 'in the accents of every part of England, Scotland and Wales' told him what they thought of Ernest Bevin and said: 'Comrade, you wait until tomorrow – we'll raise hell'.[20]

Zilliacus requested them not to press the matter provided he was allowed to make a personal statement. He then went to see George Dallas, the Chairman of the Conference, who had frequently been a guest at Zilliacus's home when the Scot had been in Geneva attending meetings of the International Labour Organisation and said:

Look here, George, I'm awfully sorry, I didn't want to be a cause of trouble when I came as a delegate for the first time. But if you will let me make a personal explanation tomorrow, I can promise that everything will pass off quietly. What worries me is that a good many of our chaps seem to be indignant at the way I was treated and want to make a further row, but I think I can stop them if you give me a chance.[21]

Dallas listened and agreed to allow Zilliacus to return to the rostrum to make a personal statement. When the Conference reconvened in closed session the next day Dallas was as good as his word and called Zilliacus to speak, whereupon Ernest Bevin moved quickly to the rostrum ahead of Zilliacus. Bevin began to speak but he was shouted down and could not make himself heard above the din. The Chairman asked him to return to his seat and Zilliacus then took his place at the rostrum.

As Zilliacus recalled it:

When I took my turn on the rostrum there was a breathless silence. Everything in me was keyed up and taut, and I could see the skin white on my knuckles as I grasped the sides of the railing. I spoke slowly, in a dead flat voice:
"Comrades, I am desperately sorry that at my first appearance at this Conference, I should be the cause of trouble and upset. I did not want it like that. If anything I said can be construed as a personal attack on anyone, I can only say I am sorry and it was not meant that way. What I was trying to do was to criticise certain features of the 'Daily Herald', which was on the agenda for discussion. But in view of what Ernest Bevin said yesterday, about my trying to play tricks on him at Geneva, I think I am entitled to tell you that the only time I had the honour of meeting Mr Bevin in Geneva was when he was my guest at my home for luncheon. In view of the privileged nature of that occasion, I cannot of course repeat anything he said to me. But I think I may tell you that what I was trying to do during that luncheon was to persuade him that Labour's support for non-intervention in Spain was wrong and should be abandoned. With that I am content to leave it to your sense of fair play.[22]

Zilliacus was told afterwards by delegates who had attended several Annual Conferences, that they thought it unique for the redoubtable Ernest Bevin to be bested by a newcomer. Zilliacus was immediately approached by four constituency parties asking him to accept a nomination to become their Parliamentary candidate.

As Zilliacus recalled:

It had begun to dawn on me some time before that if I really meant to carry on the fight for peace, I should get into Parliament. But that seemed to me something rather remote that I wanted to think about after being at home a year or two. However, if the thing was thrust at me now, I felt I must accept, so I let my name go forward in Gateshead.[23]

Chapter 10

Gateshead

Why did Zilliacus choose Gateshead? Most probably because it was the first selection conference to be held of the four constituencies on offer to him. The selection of the Gateshead Labour Party took place five weeks after the Labour Party's Annual Conference and, if Zilliacus had failed to obtain selection at Gateshead, he could then have sought nomination at one of the others. Whatever the reason, Zilliacus opted for Gateshead, a North Eastern industrial town of 106,820 people,[1] located on the opposite side of the river to Newcastle upon Tyne.

J.B. Priestley had visited Gateshead in 1933 on his famous 'English journey', when he had described the town as a 'huge dingy dormitory' having been 'carefully planned by an enemy of the human race'.[2] Gateshead in the 1930s was certainly not a town of any architectural distinction. The old riverside districts contained some of the worst slums in Britain, and the massive housing expansion of Victorian times had been carried out to provide cheap housing for Gateshead's industrial workers. Depression had hit the town in the early 1920s, after the ending of the post-war boom, when Gateshead's remaining collieries and chemical works were closed, followed in 1932 by the closure of the local railway works. Unemployment was very high throughout the 1920s and '30s with over 25 per cent of the town's insured population being unemployed in the depression years of 1929-35. Private capital was not very interested in investing in the town but the government-sponsored Team Valley Trading Estate had opened the first factory unit in 1936, bringing some much-needed light industry to the area, and the rearmament drive of the late 1930s stimulated heavy industry on Tyneside. By 1939 Gateshead was beginning to emerge from a deep and prolonged depression.[3]

Although there was heavy unemployment and widespread social deprivation in the Gateshead of the inter-war years, the cultural life of the town was not impoverished. The Gateshead public library was well used and two branch libraries were opened in the 1930s. The Bensham Grove Settlement was founded in 1921 and became the venue for WEA courses and art classes, drama and music groups met there, and the site housed a club for the unemployed. The Gateshead ILP Dramatic Club was founded in 1920, and in 1924 the group formed itself into a company called the Progressive Players which performed plays at the ILP's Westfield Hall. Performances during the 1930s included works by Shaw, Ibsen and O'Casey, as well as new plays by local playwrights such as Ruth Dodds and Fred Chadwick. The Shipley Art Gallery was opened in the town in 1917, and in the 1920s and '30s it judiciously added to the collection of paintings left by Joseph Shipley. Open-air band contests were held in Saltwell Park in 1933 which proved particularly popular with the unemployed.

The first Jews, immigrants from Eastern Europe, had settled in Gateshead in the 1880s, and although the resident Jewish community in Gateshead remained small, consisting of only thirty families in 1938, the town became an important centre of learning for the Jewish faith. A high school for Orthodox Jews was opened in 1927, followed by a teacher training college, an institute of rabbinical studies, and a boys' boarding school. Furthermore, by 1939 the Team Valley Trading Estate had attracted twenty-one new factories owned by Jewish refugee businessmen. Events in Nazi Germany were naturally of great interest and concern to members of the Jewish community in Gateshead.

The Gateshead Labour Party was overwhelmingly working-class in its composition. Ruth Dodds, the daughter of a local printer, a Quaker and Labour councillor with a keen interest in social problems, was the only identifiably middle-class member of the twenty-two-strong Executive Committee.[4] Railwaymen were strongly represented on the EC, reflecting the importance of railways to Gateshead: the town served as a junction on the LNER and a transship station for parcels traffic in North-East England. The Gateshead Labour Party had its own monthly newspaper called the *Gateshead Herald*, edited (and largely written and financed) by Ruth Dodds, which covered international as well as local topics of news; and its own Labour Hall in the centre of the town. The Westfield Hall, owned by the ILP, could also be rented for left-wing causes, and the Gateshead branch of the Socialist League met there for several years before switching to the Labour Hall.

Labour Party members were obviously interested in the local problems of heavy unemployment and poor housing but not to the exclusion of international affairs. The progress of the Spanish Civil War was closely followed. Twelve men from the Gateshead area fought in the International Brigade and five of them died in Spain. A Gateshead Spanish Workers' Relief and Medical Aid Committee was formed in the town in February 1937 and this was transformed into the Mayor of Gateshead's Spanish Relief and Medical Aid Fund, which became the focal point for fund-raising in the town. Gateshead people also participated in Tyneside's Spain Week held in June 1937, and the sending of a food ship to Republican Spain in February 1939. Local co-operative societies also joined in the Co-op Movement's 'Milk Campaign' in which tokens could be purchased to raise money to finance the sending of powdered and condensed milk to Spain.[5] A branch of the Friends of the Soviet Union was inaugurated at the Westfield Hall in 1935, when Shapurji Saklatvala gave a talk on his recent tour of Soviet Asia. Meetings were held on Sunday evenings in the Westfield Hall and membership was drawn from the Labour Party, the ILP and the Communist Party as well as from people with no party affiliation. In May 1939, Sir Charles Trevelyan spoke at a public meeting in the Gateshead Town Hall, organised by the Congress for Peace and Friendship with Russia, when he argued that an alliance with the USSR would guarantee peace because the Soviet military and industrial machine was superior to that of Nazi Germany.[6] There was no branch of the India League in the town but several Gateshead residents were members of the Newcastle branch, which included a number of Indian students. Krishna Menon was one of several guest speakers who visited the branch.[7] The town's people and the local Labour Party were not isolated from the political currents then flowing across the wider world.[8]

Zilliacus was placed on a short-list of four. He was described in the local press as a political journalist and member of the Fabian Society. The others were: Grace Colman, a lecturer at London University and former WEA tutor with lengthy membership of the General and Municipal Workers Union; Alfred Dodds from Leeds, a national organiser for the Union of Boot and Shoe Operatives; and Alderman Joseph Toole, a former Lord Mayor of Manchester and MP for Salford for two terms – 1924 and 1929-31 – who was also a long-serving member of the General and Municipal Workers Union.[9]

The Gateshead seat was held by a Liberal National, who had won the constituency from Labour in 1931 and retained it in 1935. However, there had been three Labour candidates in the constituency since the 1935 general election. James Wilson, a Newcastle railwayman, had fought the seat in 1935 and been re-selected afterwards. He resigned the candidature in 1936 and was succeeded by Bart Kelly, chief clerk in the compensation department of the Durham Miners' Association. He was de-selected in September 1938 after some friction with certain members of the local party. After his enforced resignation he complained that 'the railwaymen have always been hostile to me' and he was 'fed up with the fossils of the Gateshead Labour Party'.[10] He was succeeded by Charles Goatcher, secretary to the Labour members of the House of Lords, who resigned for obscure reasons after only a few months as the prospective candidate. The Gateshead Labour Party was therefore trying to get a candidate who would fight the seat at the forthcoming election, widely expected to be held in 1940.

The selection conference took place in the smoke-filled meeting room of the Labour Hall in Walker Terrace, on the evening of Tuesday 18 July 1939, with a hundred delegates in attendance. Following the customary procedure each of the four candidates addressed the meeting in turn.

Zilliacus recalled:

> I started by telling the party General Management Committee that this was the first time I had ever been present at such an occasion, and probably was doing it all wrong. But I thought that I ought to begin by telling them what my disadvantages were – I was an Englishman with an international background and a jaw-break-

ing name, who had lived abroad most of his life, knew little about national affairs and nothing about local affairs. I would, of course, if selected, set to work and learn. But the only reason I felt I could go before them and ask to be selected was that I had learnt thoroughly and by many years of personal experience that you cannot separate the workers' fight for a new social order from the struggle for peace. The two are inseparable. Moreover, no one was a hero to his valet, and we of the Secretariat had been the political valets of so many Prime Ministers, Foreign Ministers, Ambassadors and other great ones of this earth, that they no longer meant anything to us. What I did feel respect for was the fact that that they might choose us as their representative in Parliament. The one thing I could promise was that if they did select me I would not change after getting into the House, and would always put first keeping faith with those who had sent me there.[11]

Zilliacus's specialist interest in international affairs was not the handicap he expected it to be. Many members of the Gateshead Labour Party followed world events with keen interest and they appreciated Zilliacus's deep knowledge of the subject. 'He knew his stuff' was a comment frequently heard from Gateshead people who had heard Zilliacus speak. Moreover, he had other factors working in his favour. First, he had joined the Labour Party in 1919, therefore he had been a member of the Party for twenty years and his close association with Arthur Henderson would have counted strongly in his favour. Secondly, he was a good speaker and he did not have a lah-de-dah accent: he spoke clear, classless English. He also treated people with respect: he never patronised or talked down to them. Zilliacus also had a strong but pleasant personality, and handled questions with courtesy and humour. Although he was financially quite well off he did not wear expensive clothes – indeed he was careless about his appearance – and usually wore baggy three-piece suits. Finally, his career as a League of Nations official and his authorship of several books was impressive. He was clearly someone out of the ordinary and there was a feeling, certainly among some delegates, that the previous three prospective Labour candidates – Wilson, Kelly and Goatcher – had been worthy but rather dull men. No one ever accused Zilliacus of being dull. Some delegates, therefore, felt it was time to try their luck with a more exotic candidate.[12] Whatever was in the minds of the hundred delegates when they voted, they selected Zilliacus to be their candidate to fight the next general election.

One of the first to congratulate Zilliacus on his success was his former patron, Josiah Wedgwood, who also wrote an open letter to the Gateshead Labour Party congratulating them on their choice of candidate. Wedgwood's missive was printed in the *Gateshead Herald* under the heading, 'Zilliacus is the Man for Gateshead'.[13]

After his selection Zilliacus paid several visits to Gateshead to get to know the layout of the town and to meet its people. It was his first close contact with ordinary members of the British working class and he found that he liked them very much. Perhaps because he was a linguist and familiar with the dialects of other countries, what J.B.Priestley called their 'uncouth accents'[14] did not upset him as they had the famous Yorkshire writer when he had visited Tyneside six years before. In turn the people of Gateshead liked what they saw of Zilliacus, even though initially they had difficulty pronouncing his name.

Stories concerning Zilliacus's name were legion in Gateshead, some true and others, no doubt, apocryphal.

Two men were watching an election poster being pasted on to a hoarding. The poster carried the words *Vote for Zilliacus the Labour candidate.*

'That's a funny name,' observed one man.

'What's your name?' asked the second man.

'James Brown', came the reply.

'Well that's a funny name where he comes from'.

A crowd was gathered at an open-air meeting to hear the Labour candidate speak. The chairman introduced the candidate as Konni Zilliacus.

'Where's he from then?' one man asked his neighbour in the crowd.

'Never mind where he's from, he's here now and we're lucky to have him', came the reply.[15]

Zilliacus was not given much time to nurse the constituency before the outbreak of war, which took place only six weeks after the selection meeting. He was in his London flat, when at 9 a.m. on 1 September 1939 he heard on the radio that German troops had invaded Poland. Two days later Britain and France declared war on Germany. The armed conflict Zilliacus had dreaded for several years had started. He put aside all thoughts of organising war resistance against the National Government, although he had little faith in Neville Chamberlain's leadership, and in an article in *Tribune* he argued that 'we must support the war without illusions'.[16]

Jan Zilliacus (nee Trimble)

Zilliacus's daughters, Linden and Stella, 1943

Chapter 11

The War Years

On the outbreak of war Zilliacus offered his services to the British Government and within a month he had been recruited to the newly established Ministry of Information. He was employed throughout the war in the Ministry's Censorship Division, located in Senate House of the new London University buildings in Bloomsbury. His main responsibility was to brief Swedish journalists based in London and to censor their dispatches in order to avoid any breaches of security. He was immensely popular with the Swedish correspondents and at the end of the war they presented him with a glass bowl suitably inscribed with words of gratitude for his services. When the Soviet Union entered the war in June 1941 Zilliacus's ability to speak Russian plus his knowledge of the Soviet Union were put to good use and he did some work for the Ministry's Soviet Relations Department.

The early months at the Ministry were not particularly arduous. There were the usual teething problems connected with building up a new ministry from scratch, but there was little sense of urgency.[1] This was the period of the phoney war and nothing much was happening on the battle fronts. France's large army and Britain's much smaller force were content to shelter behind the Maginot Line and await developments, while Hitler digested his half of conquered Poland and prepared for an assault on the West. The lull in hostilities ended in April 1940 with the German invasion of Norway and Denmark, closely followed by *blitzkrieg* campaigns against Belgium, Holland and France. Churchill replaced Chamberlain as Prime Minister. On 22 June 1940 France concluded an armistice with Germany. The summer saw the Battle of Britain and in the autumn months came the blitz on Britain's towns and cities.

Zilliacus joined the Home Guard in the summer of 1940 and he would sometimes get up at 5 o'clock in the morning to attend drill and weapon training sessions held in Hyde Park, before he reported for his normal day's work at the Ministry of Information. He now worked long hours at Senate House and in common with other London residents he had to endure the heavy bombing raids of 1940-41. After working a night shift at the Ministry of Information he would often walk back through London's shattered streets to his home in St John's Wood and arrive there covered in dust and glass particles resulting from the previous night's bombing raid on the capital.[2]

The course of the war affected Zilliacus at a deeper personal level. Early in the war his daughter, Stella, married Christopher Cadogan, the son of Sir Alexander Cadogan the Permanent Under-Secretary of State at the Foreign Office. Christopher served in the Royal Navy and was lost at sea in 1942. Zilliacus had liked his son-in-law very much and was saddened when his death was confirmed by the Admiralty. Zilliacus's son, Joe, joined the Royal Marine Commandos in 1943 and was one of the first ashore on D-Day. After the defeat of Nazi Germany he was posted to the Far East to take part in the anticipated invasion of Japan. Thus Zilliacus shared the stresses and strains suffered by most people in Britain during the war years, yet in addition to his full-time job and Home Guard duties he managed to fit in a number of additional activities.

In the early months of the war he kept in touch with friends and acquaintances who had become foreign exiles living in London. In the summer of 1940 he found time to entertain to lunch at the Savoy Dr Juan Negrin, the former Prime Minister of the Spanish Republic, and Zdenek Fierlinger, a former Czechoslovak delegate to the League of Nations, who was to become the first post-war Prime Minister of Czechoslovakia 1945-46. After the fall of France, his former League of Nations colleague, Pierre Comert, joined de Gaulle's Free French administration in London, and Zilliacus was glad to renew his friendship and take him out to lunch at the Piccadilly Hotel. Zilliacus had known these men in Geneva and was able to offer hospitality to them in war-time London. Such meetings also helped to keep him in touch with the international scene.[3]

On joining the staff of the Ministry of Information Zilliacus had become a temporary member of the civil service. Normally this would have meant that he had to sever all his political ties on appointment. However the war had brought into the civil service several people with political backgrounds and the rules were relaxed to accommodate them. For example, both Hugh Gaitskell and Christopher Mayhew had been adopted as Parliamentary Labour candidates before they became war-time members of the civil service, as had Zilliacus, but they were not forced to resign their candidatures, although they were not expected to make public statements of a political nature, which meant that they could visit their constituencies but not make speeches there. Zilliacus observed this rule in that he did not make a public speech in Gateshead during the war, although he did address local party meetings and he wrote regularly for the *Gateshead Herald* on a wide range of subjects. He also lectured at several Fabian Society schools on various international topics, without incurring any reproof from Whitehall. Presumably such activities were interpreted as educational rather than political. Zilliacus was certainly adept at stretching rules to their limits. He had done this as an official of the League of Nations and he did the same when he worked for the Ministry of Information.

Nor did employment as a civil servant prevent Zilliacus's attendance at Labour Party conferences. He attended the 1940 Annual Conference held at Bournemouth as a delegate from the Gateshead Labour Party and in 1941 he was again a Gateshead delegate when the Conference was held at the Central Hall, Westminster. At this Conference Hugh Dalton, speaking on behalf of the NEC, introduced a memorandum on post-war planning, with particular reference to measures needed to secure full employment. Zilliacus spoke in the debate seeing 'a great deal of good' in Dalton's presentation, although he thought there was some complacency in believing that society was moving in a socialist direction. He warned that big business had its own agenda for the peace.[4]

Zilliacus did not attend the 1942 Annual Conference but he was back at the Central Hall, Westminster, in the following year when he moved a motion on behalf of the Gateshead Labour Party urging the NEC to send a delegation to the USSR to discuss with the Communist Party of the Soviet Union the creation of a new International embracing all Socialist and Communist parties throughout the world. The winding up of the Communist International, he argued, opened the way for the setting up of a united international workers' organisation. Harold Laski, replying on behalf of the NEC, observed that a Labour Party delegation would be going to the USSR, as agreed at the previous year's Annual Conference, and he urged Conference not to tie the delegation's hands. The Gateshead motion was thereupon defeated.[5]

Zilliacus missed the 1944 Annual Conference but writing in the *Gateshead Herald* he observed:

> The thing that depressed me most about the Conference was the failure to come to grips with the issue of Greece. Ernest Bevin, with courage and candour, rammed home the point that Labour Ministers share responsibility for the Government's policy in Greece. That policy pretends to be one of impartiality as regards the different parties in Greece.... in point of fact they have for years supported the pro-Fascist and anti-democratic Greek King and the gang around him, and are determined to force him on the throne whether the Greek people want him or not. Those who know the history of intervention in Russia and of non-intervention in Spain know it is class war.
>
> We want, if possible, to finish the war against Nazi Germany on the basis of national unity. But we cannot do it if the Tories turn on the resistance movements.[6]

He attended the 1945 Annual Conference held at Blackpool and in the debate on the NEC's Report to Conference he again raised the idea of a new International embracing Socialists and Communists,[7] and speaking on Labour's general election manifesto *Let Us Face the Future* he was concerned about possible obstruction from the House of Lords. In reply, Herbert Morrison assured him, 'We would stand no nonsense from them'.[8]

When Zilliacus took up his appointment at the Ministry of Information *Tribune* announced that 'Vigilans' would be 'taking the place of K. Zilliacus now engaged on war work of a character which makes it impossible for him to continue his signed articles'.[9] Thus Zilliacus continued to write for *Tribune* under the *nom de plume* 'Vigilans' and also contributed articles as 'Our Diplomatic Correspondent' and 'A Labour Candidate'. Over the two years 1940-41 he was one of the weekly's most prolific writers and was invited to attend meetings of the editorial board, then consisting of Raymond Postgate (Editor), Aneurin Bevan, Victor Gollancz and George Strauss. Postgate remembers that Zilliacus invariably slept through board meetings[10] although it is necessary to point out that Zilliacus had probably been working through the night at the Ministry of Information prior to these meetings and should have been in bed catching up on his sleep.

Zilliacus used the pages of *Tribune* to support the war effort, for he had no doubts that fascism had to be fought and defeated, and he was attacked by Communists and others who supported the prevailing Communist line that the armed struggle between Britain and France on one hand and Nazi Germany on the other was an imperialist war. When the Soviet Union attacked Finland in December 1939 Zilliacus, writing as 'Vigilans', criticised the Soviet invasion as both immoral and misjudged, although he declared that he would not 'join in the wave of hysterical propaganda against the Soviet Union'.[11] He believed that it would be 'military madness' to take on the USSR as well as Germany and argued that Britain and France could act as mediators in securing a settlement between the Soviet Union and Finland. He believed that an agreement between the two countries had been very close prior to the Soviet invasion. Once again 'Vigilans' was attacked by Communists in the letter columns of *Tribune* for having the temerity to criticise the actions of the Soviet Union,[12] although a future Labour Foreign Secretary, C.A.R. Crosland, then an Oxford undergraduate, wrote to *Tribune* defending 'Vigilans' for his 'sane and realistic articles'.[13]

In January 1941 'Vigilans' examined the Communist-sponsored People's Convention then campaigning for 'a People's Government and a People's Peace' and condemned it as:

> phoney, dishonest, a fraud, a swindle, a snare and delusion from start to finish.... They (the Communists) operated as usual not only openly but also through a cloud of 'cryptos' (secret members of the Communist Party and fellow travellers who take their orders from the Party, while remaining ostensibly good Labour men, trade unionists and Co-operatives).... objectively assisting the enemy to encompass our defeat ... following the old Leninist policy of revolutionary defeatism as a prelude to seizing power.[14]

It was at this time that Zilliacus contributed to a book highly critical of the Communist position on the war. The book was *The Betrayal of the Left*. It was edited and published by Victor Gollancz in February 1941 and contained contributions from Harold Laski, John Strachey and George Orwell, who clinically dissected Communist policy since the outbreak of war in September 1939. Zilliacus contributed a chapter under the *nom de plume* 'A Labour Candidate' in which he contrasted Harry Pollitt's early statements in support of the war with those of Palme Dutt, after the CPGB's change of line, in opposition to the war. Zilliacus did not mince his words, commenting:

> Any way one looks at it, therefore, the present policy of the Communists of agitating, nominally for a People's government to make peace, actually for an anti-war revolution, puts the Communists, whether they know it or not, in the position of working for Hitler's victory.[15]

The entry of the Soviet Union into the war in June 1941 helped to heal these divisions on the left, although some unsightly scar tissue remained, and Gollancz, Laski and Strachey among others were thereafter very wary of the Communist embrace. Zilliacus, who faced no 'darkness at noon' in the period 1939-41,[16] had a well balanced view of the Soviet Union based upon twenty years of close observation of developments inside the USSR and of its external policies.

When reviewing two new books on Stalin for *Tribune* in September 1940 he wrote:

> The realistic conclusion is that the Soviet Union is not an earthly paradise and the Bolshevik Party are not the infallible and inspired leaders of the world proletariat, a model to be slavishly copied. We must stand on our own feet and think things out for ourselves. But neither is the Russian Revolution a dead loss, a total failure. The revolution has not yet said its last word. When the power and prestige of Fascism are broken in this war and a wave of revolution spreads across Europe the current in Russia will once more set towards democracy and international cooperation – but when it does it will have to break down some pretty hard obstacles.
>
> Meanwhile, Western Socialists while repudiating Russia as the Socialist fatherland and Stalin as their leader should learn to regard the USSR as a great power which is a first-class factor in world affairs and with which it is of literally vital importance to come to terms on the broadest possible basis – a commercial treaty, a non-aggression pact, a free hand for the Soviet Union in Eastern Europe and an agreement on the foreign policy to be pursued in the Far East and with regard to the anti-Fascist involvement in Europe and the peace settlement.
>
> For the rest, Western Socialists must renew their allegiance to the ways and institutions of democracy and to the values of liberal civilisation. Socialism in this view has come not to destroy but to fulfil the promise of liberalism.[17]

Zilliacus, of course, welcomed the USSR's entry into the war and was pleased when Churchill held out the hand of friendship to her. He believed the social and economic foundations of the Soviet Union to be strong and that her people would offer determined resistance to the Nazi invader. He did not expect her to collapse within a few weeks as did Sir Stafford Cripps and others. Zilliacus, however, was saddened to see Finland join the war as an ally of Germany.[18]

In August 1941, as German Panzers tore into the heartlands of Russia and after the Polish Government-in-exile and the Soviet Union had agreed to restore diplomatic relations, Zilliacus wrote an article on the future of Poland. He expressed his concern at the suffering being endured by the Polish people and supported the reconstitution of a new Polish state after the war. However he argued that Poland's eastern borders, established in 1939 in the wake of the Nazi-Soviet Pact, could not be altered and he urged the Polish Government-in-exile to recognise this fact. In other words, the eastern territories of pre-1939 Poland were likely to remain part of the Soviet Union after the war and it was unrealistic to expect otherwise. In this he was proved right, although at Yalta Poland was compensated with territory on her western border up to the Oder-Niesse line.[19]

After the Japanese attack on Pearl Harbour in December 1941 the USA entered the war, and although her entry made an Allied victory almost certain Zilliacus warned that it would be a mistake to underestimate Japanese strength.[20] His article in *Tribune* on 19 December 1941 'Form the Grand Alliance Now' proved to be his last contribution to the left-wing weekly for the next three years.[21]

In the same month Aneurin Bevan had quarrelled with Raymond Postgate on the editorial board, and the outcome was the resignation of Postgate as editor of *Tribune* and his replacement by Bevan. Bevan brought in Jon Kimche and Evelyn Anderson to assist him with the day-to-day running of the magazine and he introduced much longer and weightier editorials, leaving less space for other contributions.[22] Zilliacus was no longer invited to meetings of the editorial board and Zilliacus in the form of 'Vigilans' and the other pseudonyms he had adopted disappeared from the pages of *Tribune*. A fresh editor had brought in new people and Zilliacus was one of the victims of these changes. There is no evidence that he felt any bitterness towards Bevan – on the contrary he always admired the mercurial Welshman – and there was no loss of income involved because Zilliacus had never accepted any money for his articles.

Zilliacus was certainly not short of things to do in his off-duty hours. He had become an active member of the Union of Democratic Control and he served on its executive committee throughout the war. In the 1930s the UDC had campaigned against fascism, supported China in its struggle against Japanese aggression, and had championed Indian independence. Its name still counted for something in left-wing circles although it was chronically short of money and operated from a cramped office in the attic of a house in Victoria Street. Zilliacus together with Kingsley Martin and Dorothy Woodman helped to keep it alive during the difficult war years and the UDC was to survive for another twenty years.[23]

Zilliacus was also associated with the 1941 Committee. This Committee was formed in the wake of J.B. Priestley's famous war-time broadcasts. For nineteen weeks, between 5 June and 30 October 1940, Priestley had a regular slot at a peak listening time following the nine o'clock news on the BBC's Home Service. He proved to be a superb broadcaster and, of course, he wrote his own scripts. The subject of his first broadcast was Dunkirk, in which he had special praise for the heroism of the crews of the pleasure boats and steamers, and criticism for those whose decisions had made the evacuation necessary. The author of *The Good Companions* and *English Journey* was perfectly in tune with the mood of the times and in his *Postscripts* he began to look ahead to post-war Britain. Priestley argued that there must not be a return to the depressed conditions of the 1920s and '30s; the British people deserved better than that. The broadcasts were immensely popular, although some people in positions of influence within the Government and inside the BBC saw them as becoming too political and, moreover, biased towards the left. In spite of this criticism Priestley did a second series of *Postscripts* from January to March 1941 but he was not invited to do a third.[24]

The *Postscripts*, however, did have a political impact. They were heard by Sir Richard Acland, who had been elected to Parliament as a Liberal in 1935 but had then embraced Christian Socialism. He contacted Priestley and suggested that they cooperate in forming a ginger group devoted to social reform. The group, called the 1941 Committee, met at the home of Edward Hulton, publisher of *Picture Post*, under the chairmanship of J.B. Priestley, with Raymond Gauntlett acting as secretary.

The Committee included: David Astor of the *Observer*; Thomas Balogh, the Oxford economist; Bishop Blunt; Ritchie Calder, science correspondent; Victor Gollancz, the publisher; Lord Hinchingbrooke of the Tory Reform Committee; Tom Hopkinson, editor of *Picture Post*; Eva Hubback, Principal of Morley College; Douglas Jay, then working as a temporary civil servant at the Ministry of Supply; Francois Lafitte, the social scientist; Kingsley Martin, editor of the *New Statesman and Nation*; Christopher Mayhew, then employed as a temporary civil servant; David Owen, the social scientist; A.D. Peters, the literary agent; Lancelot Spicer, founder of Liberal Action; Peter Thorneycroft, a Conservative MP; Richard Titmuss, the social scientist; Tom Wintringham, former commander of the British battalion of the International Brigade in Spain; and Konni Zilliacus, present as a former official of the League of Nations to add his experience on foreign affairs.

The 1941 Committee produced a number of pamphlets on social security and joint consultation in industry, and in May 1942 issued a Nine Point Declaration to serve as a set of guidelines for use at by-elections. The nine points covered the taking into common ownership of industries and companies whose inefficiency was hindering the war effort, the establishment of workers' councils, the need to formulate a full employment policy for the post-war years, and support for universal free education. When Tom Driberg stood as an Independent at a by-election in Maldon in June 1942, he had the support of several members of the 1941 Committee and he won a sensational victory over the Conservative candidate. Following Driberg's triumph at Maldon the 1941 Committee announced that it was merging with a similar organisation called Forward March to form a new

political party, Common Wealth, with J.B. Priestley as the Party's chairman. By
the autumn Priestley had resigned from the chair. Although he held strong views
and liked to propagate them he had little liking for the often dull procedures
of political organisation. He was succeeded by Acland who rapidly established
himself as the undisputed leader of the Common Wealth Party.[25]

Zilliacus responded to the 1941 Committee's increasing participation in politics by distancing himself from the organisation. On 18 June 1942 he wrote a
letter to the Secretary of the 1941 Committee clarifying his position. He pointed
out that as a temporary civil servant he had to remain aloof from direct participation in party politics and he would in future confine his activities to undertaking research for the Committee. He went on to state that although he had been
adopted as a Labour candidate he was opposed to the war-time electoral truce
and in the absence of a Labour candidate he was pleased to see the Committee
supporting candidates who opposed Conservative candidates at by-elections.
However he believed that any attempt to start a new political party would prove
to be 'an up-to-date variant of the old Liberal idea that it is possible to produce
a third alternative to the conflict between left and right embodied in the Labour
and Conservative parties respectively, it will be ground between the upper and
nether millstones'.[26]

Zilliacus was not tempted to switch his allegiance from Labour to the new
Common Wealth Party, nevertheless his association with the 1941 Committee
remains an intriguing incident in his life, for the Committee was not particularly
left wing. It was a group of 'progressives' drawn from various political parties,
professions and occupations working together to draw up plans for the post-war
years. Yet it must have had some appeal for Zilliacus. He was certainly keen on
looking ahead and planning for the return of peacetime conditions, and he also
favoured 'Popular Fronts' in which socialists of various hues cooperated with
other 'progressives' to advance the socialist cause.

As the war entered its final phase attention began to be paid to what kind of
international organisation should replace the League of Nations. Zilliacus was
understandably very interested in such a question. He had served on the executive committee of the League of Nations Union throughout the war and had
taken part in discussions held under the chairmanship of Lord Robert Cecil.
However he had become dissatisfied with Cecil's chairmanship, once referring
to the aged peer as 'the old buzzard'.[27] He believed that the LNU was failing
to give a lead to public opinion and he resigned from its executive committee
in November 1944.[28] He was also a member of the executive committee of the
Federal Union and resigned from this body because he considered its proposals
to be hopelessly unrealistic.

Zilliacus was a war-time member of the executive committee of the Fabian
Society and he served on its Advisory Committee on International Affairs. He
was also part of an informal group of Labour Party members who met in the

evening at Leonard Woolf's flat in Victoria Square to discuss the future shape of the proposed United Nations Organisation. Members in attendance included Douglas Jay, Arthur Creech-Jones, Philip Noel-Baker and Ivor Thomas. Leonard Woolf was the long-serving secretary of the Labour Party's Advisory Committee on International Questions and he fed proposals from the group to the ACIQ. He also passed on ideas to Evan Durbin, at this time Attlee's personal assistant, who then communicated them to the Deputy Prime Minister. Attlee had a life-long interest in world government and took a keen interest in the creation of the UNO. The group continued in existence until the spring of 1945, when it disbanded once it had become clear that the setting up of a world organisation to replace the League of Nations would be on the agenda for approval at the San Francisco Conference.[29]

Zilliacus's own pet idea at this time was that the new world organisation should contain an inter-parliamentary body of some kind and not just be the creature of governments. He had earlier argued for an international parliament composed of delegations from national legislatures with membership propor-tionate to the size of each member state's population. Such an international parliament, as envisaged by Zilliacus, would be purely advisory yet it would pro-vide a forum for debate and establish some sort of link between the individual citizen and the world organisation.[30] The idea was not incorporated in the newly formed UNO, although something along these lines was used in the evolution of the parliamentary institutions of the European Union.

Zilliacus recognised that Britain and France were no longer so-called Great Powers, and in the post-war years would certainly be no match for the USA and USSR. In 1944 he favoured the creation of a West European Union with Britain and France at its core. Member states would have a single currency, a common tariff structure and citizenship, with joint defence arrangements and some form of central planning. Zilliacus saw the WEU working closely in partnership with the Soviet Union.[31] He did not want to see the USA return to the isolationism of the 1930s – indeed, Zilliacus hoped that it would play a major part in world af-fairs, especially in the provision of economic aid to countries devastated by war – but he believed that Europe should be allowed to resolve its own problems.

In the spring of 1945 Victor Gollancz approached Zilliacus, at the suggestion of Herbert Morrison, and asked him if he would be prepared to write a short book on foreign policy for a series he was planning to bring out in the run-up to the next general election. The book would be a companion volume to one on domestic policy to be written by Aneurin Bevan. Morrison was concerned that Labour's pre-war practice of voting against the defence estimates would be used against the Party and he wanted something to counter this criticism.[32] Zilliacus agreed to write the book which was published under the title *Can the Tories Win the Peace and How They Lost the Last One*. As Zilliacus conceded this was 'not a snappy title',[33] yet the book sold 50,000 copies and was widely used by

Labour candidates in the general election campaign. If Morrison was expecting a defensive approach to the subject, that was not what he got from Zilliacus, who described the theme of his book as 'a full-blooded attack on the whole of Tory foreign and defence policy between the wars, and a vindication of the line taken by the Labour Party'.[34] Be that as it may, Herbert Morrison could only have been highly satisfied with the results of his initiative for the book played its part in securing the landslide Labour victory of 1945.

In May 1945 German forces surrendered to the Allies, bringing the war in Europe to an end, and at the Labour Party's Annual Conference later in the month the Party gave notice that it intended to leave the war-time Coalition Government. Churchill then formed a 'caretaker administration' without Labour members and announced that Parliament would be dissolved on 5 June 1945 and a general election held on 5 July. Zilliacus agreed wholeheartedly with Labour's decision to leave the Churchill Coalition and he looked forward to the forthcoming election campaign. He spent the first week of June clearing his desk at the Ministry of Information and then travelled to Gateshead, where he would remain until polling day.[35]

Chapter 12

Jan

A few weeks after taking up his job at the Ministry of Information Zilliacus was invited to a meal that was to have a major impact on his life. One of his colleagues at the Ministry of Information had organised a luncheon party at the Café Royal and found himself a man short. Would Zilliacus fill the vacancy at very short notice? Zilliacus had worked through the previous night and given a press briefing to Swedish correspondents in the mid-morning, so the rest of the day was his own, and he was able and willing to accept.[1]

At the luncheon he found himself seated next to a twenty-seven-year-old American woman named Janet Harris, who on being introduced to him said: 'So you are Konni Zilliacus. I have a bone to pick with you'. In best Hollywood fashion this unpropitious start was to develop into a life-long relationship.

The bone Janet – usually known as 'Jan' and sometimes as 'Jannie' – wished to pick with Zilliacus concerned his daughter Stella. Jan Harris had been going out with a young South African who was a Rhodes Scholar at Oxford. All was going well between them until the South African attended one of Zilliacus's summer schools at Geneva and there he had met Stella. The result of this meeting was that he had then switched his affections from Jan to Stella. Jan was still smarting from this brush off when she met Konni Zilliacus at the Café Royal. In reply Zilliacus could only say that it would be wrong to hold him responsible for his daughter's actions on such matters and to this Jan was forced to agree.

Jan's former beau had been impressed by Zilliacus's lectures at Geneva and had urged Jan to read the former League official's latest book. She had done so and Konni was gratified to find himself talking to someone who was familiar with his views on the international situation. The two had got on extremely well and when the luncheon party began to break up they were still engaged in animated conversation. Zilliacus wondered if they might not continue their talk over a cup of tea. Jan agreed and said she could offer him tea at her home in St John's Wood. Zilliacus accepted the invitation and within a few weeks of this first meeting their relationship had developed to the point where he had moved into her house in Carlton Hill. They lived together until Zilliacus's death in 1967. The couple wanted to marry but Zilliacus's wife, Eugenia, refused to consider a divorce on the grounds of her Catholicism, whereupon Jan adopted the name Zilliacus and carried on from there.

Jan was born on 18 September 1912 in New York, the only child of Laurence

Trimble, a film director, and his wife Louise (née Trenton), who had been an op-era singer before her marriage. Jan spent most of her childhood in Hollywood, and attended Point Loma School in San Diego for a short spell, otherwise most of her education was by private tutor.

The Trimble family lived on a Californian ranch, with Tom Mix the famous screen cowboy and the Kelloggs family of cornflakes fame as their neighbours. Charlie Chaplin, Marion Davies and Pearl White were regular visitors to the ranch, and Rudolph Valentino had riding lessons there in preparation for his role in 'The Sheik'. Valentino took the young Jan to concerts at the Hollywood Bowl, and she was once a guest of newspaper magnate William Randolph Hearst at San Simeon, where she was shown his private zoo.

Her father pioneered the use of trained animals in films. His big chance came when the Trimble family's collie became famous on screen as 'Jean the Vitagraph Dog', and he then introduced the public to a new dog called Strongheart, which featured in several films as a rival attraction to Rin-Tin-Tin.[2]

Jan's parents split up when she was young, her mother moving off to teach singing in London, leaving Jan to be brought up by her father. He raised her as a tomboy. She sometimes did stunt work in his films and developed a close rap-port with animals, not least her father's pack of tame wolves.

As the 1920s drew to a close Larry Trimble's Hollywood career began to de-cline. The film company he worked for was taken over by Warner Brothers and the coming of talkies made Trimble's animal films appear rather old-fashioned to many moviegoers. The final blow came with the Wall Street Crash, which wiped out his financial assets. Larry Trimble then took Jan to live on an island he owned – the only piece of property he had retained – in the St Lawrence River.

One day Jan was skating on a frozen river when the ice gave way and she was rescued from the freezing waters by a young Canadian trapper called Alexander Harris. Three months later Jan married her rescuer and the young couple set up home together, supplementing their meagre income by running bootleg booze across the Canadian border into the USA. The marriage soon ran into difficulties and, after two years, Jan left with her one-year-old daughter, Dawn, to live with her mother, who had successfully established herself as a teacher of singing in London. While in London Jan gave birth to her second child, a son, Laurence.

In Britain Jan tried her hand as an entertainer, doing a song and dance act in cabaret. The pay was not very good and the work irregular so she became a door-to-door seller of vacuum cleaners and thoroughly enjoyed travelling from town to town across the country.

The world slump, which had brought such a change in her fortunes, in com-mon with those of millions of other people, had radicalised the political thinking of the young American. She had started to move in Hollywood's liberal and radi-cal circles, where she was introduced to Lillian Hellman and Dashiell Hammett among several other actors, directors and writers who were later to become victims of the McCarthyite purges of the 1940s and '50s. She attended the Berlin Olympics in August 1936, in the company of Paul Gallico the American sports journalist and author, where she had a first-hand look at Nazi Germany and did not like what she saw. When she returned to Britain, she picked up on the latest news from Spain, to learn that the Spanish generals' attempted coup had failed. The Republicans had successfully resisted a quick seizure of power by the military and Spain now faced a lengthy civil war. It was the opening events of the Spanish Civil War that prompted Jan to join the Communist Party because, as she later recalled, 'They were the only people prepared to do anything about it'.

However, she did not take easily to the strict discipline demanded by the Communist Party, and in her nine years as a member she was suspended from membership on three occasions for breaches of Party rules. If she thought the Party line was wrong she found it difficult not to say so. She could not support the signing of the Nazi-Soviet Pact and felt she had to speak out against it. Indeed she was unhappy with the Party's policy throughout the period September 1939 to June 1941, when the war against Germany, and later Italy, was designated an imperialist war. This was her political position when she first met Konni Zilliacus at the Café Royal in the autumn of 1939.

The entry of the Soviet Union into the war and the CPGB's switch into giving all-out support to the British war effort brought Jan back into line with Communist Party policy. She was on good personal terms with Harry Pollitt, who once told her that her difficulties in accepting Communist Party discipline were due to her bourgeois origins. There was also some socialising between the Zilliacus and Pollitt families at this time with Harry and his wife Marjorie occasionally coming to dinner at the Zilliacus' home in Carlton Hill. Claud Cockburn, who wrote for the *Daily Worker* under the *nom de plume* 'Frank Pitcairn', lived a few streets away and he and his wife, Patricia, were also dinner guests of the Zilliacus family from time to time. Zilliacus had known Claud before the war, when Cockburn was editing his famous cyclostyled newsletter of political gossip, *The Week,* and they met as old friends.

Britain, the USA and the Soviet Union were now allies and pro-Soviet sympathies in Britain probably reached their peak following the heroic defence of Stalingrad in the winter of 1942. It was some time in 1943 that Zilliacus was invited to become an undercover member of the Communist Party, while retaining his membership of the Labour Party.[3] Who made the offer is not known but such a matter would have had to be handled at the highest level and it could have been suggested by Pollitt on one of his visits to the Zilliacuses. In the event, Zilliacus declined the offer: firstly, because he felt that his proper place was in the Labour Party, and, secondly, because he considered it wrong and deceitful to operate in such a way.[4]

On the outbreak of war Jan's mother had decided to return to the USA, leaving her spacious house in St John's Wood in Jan's charge. Jan worked as a telephonist with the civil defence and when the blitz on London began she found a new role. Some of the staff at the Ministry of Information, who had been bombed out of their homes, were accommodated at Jan's house. Thus the house in Carlton Hill became a kind of boarding house, nicknamed the 'Mare's Nest' by those who stayed there, and Jan was kept busy looking after her war-time guests. In 1943 her second daughter, Linden, was born adding a baby to the Zilliacus household. When the general election campaign began in June 1945, Jan made appropriate domestic arrangements and followed Konni up to Gateshead to canvass on his behalf.

Chapter 13

The 1945 General Election

The timetable for the 1945 general election was that nomination day would be 25 June, polling day 5 July, and, to allow time for the servicemen's votes to reach the returning officer in each constituency, the ballot boxes would not be opened until 25 July, with the results being announced the following day.[1]

When Zilliacus reported to Gateshead in the second week of June it was to find preparations already underway. The month before, the Gateshead Labour Party had appointed a full-time election agent. This was Greg Purcell, who had been active in the Spanish Aid campaign of the 1930s and had served as a member of the Tyneside Joint Peace Council. He was a good organiser with responsibility for running the Labour Party's election machine in Gateshead.

The central committee rooms were located in the Labour Hall in Walker Terrace. Purcell had a small room for his office and the large meeting room, where Zilliacus had been selected as the Labour candidate six years before, was used as a general office and workroom. Several large trestle tables ran down the room with chairs placed along one side of each table. This was where the addressing of an envelope to each individual voter on the electoral register took place. There were 71,692 electors on the roll and each one was sent a copy of the Labour candidate's election address. It was a job performed mainly by people from the Labour Party's women's sections and the Co-operative Guild. Evening after evening people sat at the tables scratching away with steel-nibbed pens dipped in blue ink addressing envelopes. Once a street was completed the bundle of envelopes was tied up with an elastic band and stored in a cardboard box, and later each envelope was stuffed with a copy of Zilliacus's election address. The envelopes were then taken to the central post office from whence they were delivered to the addresses free of charge. It was a tedious yet important operation.

Zilliacus took great pains with the preparation of his election address and, because he was devoting such a lot of space to foreign policy, he considered it advisable to send a draft to Labour's head office at Transport House for their comments.

As he recalled:

> I wanted to make sure that there was nothing in the foreign affairs side of my election address contrary to our policy. I said I had based it on 'The International Post-War Settlement' and the policy page in 'Let Us Face the Future'. I got it back with

congratulations on an exceptionally fine address. I was asked to, and did, correct a small point about old age pensions. But there was no comment on the foreign policy section.[2]

This was as follows:

> Only a British Government friendly to Socialism can join effectively in making peace in Europe.
>
> Throughout Europe the overthrow of Fascism has meant the downfall of capitalism, because the political parties of the Right and the leaders of trade and industry, with a few exceptions, have been associated with the Fascist and Quisling dictatorships and Hitler's economic system.
>
> Throughout Europe, the resistance movements derive their main strength from the workers and their allies, and are largely under Socialist and Communist leadership. Their reconstruction programmes are based on sweeping advances towards Socialism.
>
> Europe can be reconstructed, pacified and united, and democracy can be revived, only on the basis of a new social order.
>
> To that policy the Soviet Union are already committed, and the French people have given their allegiance in the recent elections.
>
> On that basis a Labour Government can work together with the Soviet Union and with the popular and democratic forces in Europe that would be irresistibly encouraged by Labour's coming into power.
>
> That combination of states, bound together by such purposes and policies, would be so strong and so successful as to attract the friendship and cooperation of the American and Chinese peoples.
>
> On these lines Labour would put granite foundations under the flimsy scaffolding erected at the San Francisco Conference, and take the lead in building a world organisation capable of guaranteeing peace and promoting the common interests of nations.

He also promised in his address:

> If you put me into the House of Commons, I will fight for the whole of Labour's policy and defend the interests of Gateshead folk in the councils of the nation. But I appeal to you particularly to support me because I believe I have something real to contribute on the tremendous and overmastering issue of how to make peace secure. I have given all my adult life to that task, both as an international civil servant and as a student of world affairs. I want a chance to finish the job – or at best to go on trying.

Throughout the campaign Zilliacus averaged four public meetings a day. His day invariably began with a discussion with his election agent to review the campaign and sketch out the day's activities. Fergie Forster, the chairman of the Gateshead Labour Party, would sometimes attend these morning sessions. If there was time, Zilliacus might then fit in an appearance at some shopping centre to chat with members of the public before he made his first speech of the day at a lunchtime meeting in a factory canteen. After a break for something to eat he would be off to speak at an afternoon meeting of old age pensioners or women's groups, and in the evening he would address two more public meetings. Small meetings were usually held in schoolrooms, and larger meetings in the Gateshead Town Hall or the Co-operative Hall. Among those who came to speak on his behalf were Michael Foot, J.B. Priestley and Sir Charles Trevelyan. But perhaps the best remembered meetings of Zilliacus's campaign were those held in the open air at the Windmill Hills – the Gateshead equivalent of Hyde Park's Speakers' Corner – where huge crowds gathered to hear him attack Chamberlain's appeasement policy of the 1930s and to argue that to secure world peace Britain must work with both the Soviet Union and the USA under the auspices of the United Nations. Of particular interest to the Jewish community was his promise that, in accordance with Labour Party policy, there would be no limits on Jewish immigration into Palestine. On domestic policy he said that a Labour Government would give priority to housing and the maintenance of full employment.[3]

Meanwhile, Zilliacus's campaign team carried out the task of canvassing the voters to find out who were Labour supporters so that on polling day they could, if necessary, be prodded into voting, a process known locally as 'pulling out'. Jan Zilliacus, like most Americans, was a good mixer and she enjoyed going out 'on the knocker', canvassing people on their own doorsteps. Although widely travelled, Jan was shocked by the housing conditions she found in Gateshead's riverside area which she considered the worst slums she had seen anywhere in the world.[4]

Zilliacus's opponent was Thomas Magnay, a Liberal National who enjoyed the full support of the local Conservative Party machine. He was an accountant by profession and had been the Liberal candidate for Blaydon in the 1929 general election. In 1931 he was selected to fight Gateshead as the 'National' candidate when he had defeated his Labour opponent, Ernest Bevin, by 12,938 votes. After the election he was one of those Liberals who were prepared to accept the adoption of a tariff and had joined the Liberal National group under the leadership of Sir John Simon. Accordingly, as a Liberal National he had been adopted as the 'National' candidate in the 1935 general election, when he had retained the seat with a majority of 2,968 votes. Magnay had been a wholehearted supporter of Chamberlain's appeasement policy and had played a part in the setting up of the Team Valley Trading Estate on the outskirts of Gateshead. He was a devout Methodist and Sabbatarian: in 1941, he had led the opposition to the Government's attempt to allow theatrical performances to take place on Sundays. Magnay was on the defensive throughout most of the campaign, attempting to vindicate the National Government's record in the 1930s, and had little to offer in the way of policy except to urge the electorate to vote 'National' so that Winston Churchill could remain in charge of Britain's affairs.

Alison Readman, visiting Newcastle upon Tyne as part of Nuffield College's study of the 1945 general election, found little evidence of any massive shift in political allegiances there, although she reported 'The only rumour which had universal currency was that across the river in Gateshead Mr. Zilliacus was moving mountains for the Labour Party'.[5] However, in an analysis of North-Eastern constituencies carried out by the *Newcastle Journal*, a few days before polling day, the result at Gateshead was regarded as 'doubtful'.[6] Magnay's small majority could be overturned by a fairly modest swing to Labour, on the other hand as the 'National' candidate he might be returned to Parliament on Churchill's coat tails. No one could be sure.

Zilliacus had fought a vigorous campaign and he felt that it had gone well, but he was too old a dog to take anything for granted. After thanking all those who had worked so hard on his behalf he and Jan returned to London to see something of their family and enjoy a few days rest. They returned to Gateshead in good time to witness the counting of the votes.

Zilliacus was present on 25 July when the ballot boxes were emptied and the validity of the ballot papers first checked and then sorted into piles for each candidate. It was a peculiarity of this election that the votes were not counted until the following day, although it was evident from the stacks that Zilliacus had won. This was confirmed the next day when the official count took place and the Mayor of Gateshead announced the result:

Konni Zilliacus (Labour)	36,736
Thomas Magnay (Liberal National)	17,719
Labour majority	19,017

It was clear from the other results coming in that Labour had secured a landslide victory. The final results were: Labour 393, Conservatives and Allies 213, Liberals 12, Others 22, giving Labour an overall majority of 146 seats. At 7.25 in the evening Winston Churchill tendered his resignation to the King and, five minutes later, Clement Attlee was appointed Prime Minister.

Zilliacus was delighted with his own result, and the return of a Labour Government with a large majority was something he had wanted to see since he had joined the Labour Party in 1919. Nevertheless, he had his own reservations but managed to keep them to himself so as not to dampen the high spirits of his supporters, until one of his campaign team said: 'Zilly, you have worked so closely with our leaders and done so much for them in the past and you know so much about foreign affairs that surely they will give you a job in the Government'. To which Zilliacus replied, rather testily: 'No, I'm afraid you don't understand what is happening. They are going to carry on with the Tory foreign policy. I shall be fighting them and they will be calling me a Communist.'[7]

Thus with Zilliacus it was not a case of high hopes being disappointed after 1945. He already had misgivings before the Labour Government took office.

He had watched with disapproval the way the British and American governments had worked closely with Admiral Darlan's Vichyite forces in North Africa in 1943, how later in the same year the same governments had welcomed the cooperation of Marshal Badoglio's Government after the fall of Mussolini, and how de Gaulle had been installed in liberated France. But above all he was deeply concerned by the use of British troops in Greece in support of the Royalist Government. To Zilliacus this was armed intervention once again.[8] The Labour leaders in the Coalition Government were party to these actions and Ernest Bevin had stated his support for Churchill's policy in Greece. Zilliacus was also upset by a briefing of Labour Party candidates given by George Shepherd, the Party's national agent, just before the 1945 election campaign, when Shepherd had explained to them that there was virtually 'national unity' on foreign policy and Labour was going to concentrate the election campaign on home affairs. Zilliacus therefore resolved that 'In the circumstances there was nothing for it but to fight as hard as possible and hope against hope for the best. So far as I was concerned I made up my mind that the fight was going to include foreign affairs, and how'.[9]

After his victory, telegrams of congratulation began to flow in from all over the world and among them was one from Labour's Chief Whip in the House of Commons informing Zilliacus that he was expected to attend a meeting of the Parliamentary Labour Party at the Beaver Hall in London on 28 July at 11 o'clock. There was no time for extended celebrations in Gateshead. Zilliacus had to take his leave and board the next train for King's Cross.

Labour MPs in Prague, October 1947. Left to right: Ben Parkin, George Thomas, Fred Lee, Geoffrey Bing, Konni Zilliacus, Henry White, A.J. Chapman, interpreter, A.C. Allen

Chapter 14

Into Parliament

The meeting of the Parliamentary Labour Party in the Beaver Hall, held in the wake of the 1945 general election, is now part of Labour legend. Zilliacus remembered 'What a lot of us there were and what high enthusiasm'.[1] James Callaghan recalled that when the taxi driver, who drove him to the venue, learned that he was a newly-elected Labour MP attending his first meeting since his election, the cabby had refused to accept his fare;[2] Barbara Castle recalled, 'the hall was spattered with young men in uniform';[3] while Christopher Mayhew noted that the new MPs were 'all very keen to get their own voices heard and faces seen';[4] and Woodrow Wyatt observed 'Attlee was acclaimed as Prime Minister and Leader of the Party. In my innocence I knew nothing of the intrigues that Herbert Morrison had been busy with in the hope of becoming Prime Minister himself. I still thought all was sweetness and friendship at the top of the Labour Party'.[5]

As is now well known, the Beaver Hall meeting had been preceded by a struggle for power among the Labour leaders. On the previous afternoon Churchill had conceded defeat and informed Attlee – who was with Bevin, Morrison and Morgan Phillips in Transport House – that he would be recommending the King to send for him. Morrison argued that Attlee should not go to the Palace until there had been a meeting of the newly elected Parliamentary Labour Party, which would then have the opportunity of electing a leader. Morrison said that he would be a candidate for the leadership at such a meeting. Attlee was unperturbed, confident that the constitutional position was clear, and Bevin – who had already gained the support of Hugh Dalton on this question – urged Attlee to go to the Palace without delay, which he did.[6]

If there had been an election for the leadership at the Beaver Hall the likelihood is that Zilliacus would have voted for Morrison. In the *Gateshead Herald* of December 1943 he had written in praise of Morrison:

> But he is the only man big enough to be a national leader and able and willing to unite the forces of Labour and lead them to victory at the next election.

Zilliacus never forgot that Morrison had opposed the non-intervention in Spain policy back in 1936, when most of the Labour leadership had supported it, and he had always got on well with Morrison at a personal level, but above all he believed that Morrison had the right leadership qualities. Whether Attlee's success in leading the Party to victory in 1945 would have altered his views we do not know and, in any case, it did not matter because Attlee accepted the King's commission to form a government and had chosen the leading members of his Cabinet before the meeting of the Parliamentary Labour Party. Attlee, Bevin, Dalton, Morrison, Cripps, Jowitt and Greenwood went straight from the Palace, where they had received their seals of office from the King, to the Beaver Hall where the Chief Whip, William Whitely, introduced Bevin as the 'Foreign Secretary'. Bevin promptly moved a vote of confidence in Attlee that was received with loud cheers of assent. Attlee and Bevin then left the meeting to fly to Potsdam, leaving the Chief Whip to inform the new MPs of some procedural matters. Like many such occasions it was a mixture of high excitement and bathos.

Zilliacus was surprised and disappointed that Ernest Bevin and not Hugh Dalton had been appointed Foreign Secretary. His judgement of Bevin was:

> He was a great working class leader with a fine record. But he was tragically miscast as Labour's Foreign Secretary in 1945. For he did not have a clue to the problems facing him. He was too old and set in his ways to learn. Or rather, to unlearn and then learn afresh: that is, to do the kind of painful thinking that goes down to one's own prejudices and assumptions, tests them in the light of reason and facts, and then works out a policy that is genuinely 'realistic' because it is rooted in reality and not to an out-of-date conception of the world in which we are living, and harnessed to Labour's view of the national interest and not to that of the defenders of the old order.[7]

Zilliacus considered:

> Hugh Dalton would have been far better, first of all because he really did know a lot about foreign affairs; secondly, because he knew how to manage the Foreign Office officials, instead of being run by them; thirdly, because he was capable of learning from experience and correcting his mistakes; fourthly, because he would listen to the views of back bench colleagues instead of treating any criticism or comments as an insult and relying on blind trade union loyalties and the power of the block vote to impose on the Labour Party the Churchillian policies that the Foreign Office had induced him to adopt.[8]

The fact that Attlee changed his mind at the last moment and made Bevin Foreign Secretary instead of Dalton, reasoning that if both Bevin and Morrison were concerned with home affairs they were bound to clash, was, in Zilliacus's view, significant since it implied that it did not matter whether a Foreign Secretary knew anything about foreign affairs or not His officials were the experts who would guide him along the right path.[9]

Four days after the meeting in the Beaver Hall, MPs of all parties assembled for the first day of the new Parliament. This meeting took place in the House of Lords because the House of Commons had been severely damaged in a bombing raid. The Chamber was packed and when Winston Churchill came in to take his place the Tories stood up and sang 'For He's a Jolly Good Fellow'. Labour MPs responded by singing 'The Red Flag'. It was a rousing start to the new session.

It was shortly after this that Zilliacus bumped into his old friend Philip Noel-Baker in the lobby. Noel-Baker was feeling very pleased at being appointed Minister of State at the Foreign Office, and he chose to give Zilliacus some advice:

> Zilly, all the distrust for you of the leaders has disappeared. They are quite reconciled to you now, except Ernest Bevin. All you have to do now is to win his confidence.

Zilliacus admits to having been taken aback by this statement and replied:

> Listen, Phil, it is a question of whether Ernie earns my confidence. If he will act as we have promised we will do I'll back him in every way I can. But if he is going to go on behaving like a Tory in international affairs I am going to fight him.

As Zilliacus later observed, 'We did not have long to wait'.[10] On 20 August 1945, Ernest Bevin made his first speech as Foreign Secretary in the course of the debate in the House of Commons on the King's speech. Churchill opened the debate and spoke with restraint, although he did not conceal his distaste for what was happening in Eastern Europe and he expressed his concern that these developments did not augur well for the future. Bevin, in a wide-ranging speech, agreed that the governments that had been set up in Romania and Bulgaria were not representative of the views of the people and urged the Polish Government to honour its promise to hold free elections. He announced continued support for the Coalition Government's Greek policy and said he was opposed to intervention against Franco Spain. In other words, Bevin offered continuity in foreign policy, and Anthony Eden, when he spoke later in the debate, declared: 'What the Foreign Secretary has said represents a foreign policy on behalf of which he can speak for all parties in the country'.

Zilliacus did not speak on this occasion, he made his maiden speech three days later in the debate on the ratification of the United Nations Charter. In his speech he recounted his work for the League of Nations and expressed his support for its successor. He was pleased that both the USA and USSR were members and peace would be guaranteed provided the Big Five 'pulled together'. Zilliacus also argued that for peace to be secure in Europe there needed to be 'a sweeping advance towards socialism'.[11]

Clement Davies, the Liberal leader, congratulated Zilliacus on his maiden speech: 'We all realise that in entering the House he brings with him a vast store of knowledge and a great and almost unrivalled experience in foreign affairs.'[12]

Ernest Bevin's first weeks at the Foreign Office did nothing to convince Zilliacus that the former trade union leader would be a success in his new post.[13] The meeting of the Council of Ministers held in London in September-October 1945, convened mainly to discuss the terms of a peace settlement, was notable for the acrimonious exchanges between Bevin and the Soviet Foreign Minister, Molotov, and it ended in deadlock. After this bad start, relations between Britain and the Soviet Union remained frosty throughout the autumn. Zilliacus spoke in the Foreign Affairs Debate on 23 November 1945 saying 'We are agreeing too well with the USA', and he quoted the views of Field Marshall Smuts that an Anglo-American combination would turn Britain into a vassal state of the USA. Zilliacus was worried that Britain was trying to build up a balance of power against the Soviet Union. The Soviet Union certainly believed that we were and he wanted an assurance from the government that this was not the case.[14] His other interventions in these first months of the new Parliament were on events in Yugoslavia and Poland, when he spoke in defence of the actions of the new governments in those countries.

The American Secretary of State, the conciliatory James Byrnes, arranged a second Council of Ministers meeting in Moscow in early December and some progress was made on the drafting of peace treaties. However friction between Britain and the Soviet Union over policy in the Mediterranean and the Middle East continued into 1946, and on 5 March 1946 Winston Churchill made his famous Fulton speech warning of the fall of an 'iron curtain' across Europe 'from Stettin in the north to Trieste in the south'. The outlines of the Cold War were beginning to emerge.

In his early months in office, Bevin did not increase his popularity with Labour supporters by failing to carry out a purge of Foreign Office staff. For example, Sir Alexander Cadogan, the Permanent Under-Secretary at the Foreign Office since 1938, was due for retirement and Bevin asked him to stay on. Indeed, Bevin consistently retained and promoted career diplomats in Foreign Office posts, one of his few innovations being the addition of Labour Attachés to British Embassy staffs. Bevin was criticised at the Labour Party's Annual Conference in June 1946 for his failure to replace officials who were unsympathetic to socialist policies by others who held more progressive views, and he was adamant in his refusal to make politically-inspired appointments at the Foreign Office.

Bevin's first months at the Foreign Office, therefore, were very disappointing to Zilliacus, yet he did not make the mistake of heaping all the blame on to the Foreign Secretary's broad shoulders, for he believed that the Labour Party itself shared some of the responsibility.[15] Zilliacus held that Labour's domestic policies had been carefully worked out during their years spent in opposition. The maintenance of full employment, the nationalisation of the basic industries, and the creation of the National Health Service were successfully carried through by the Labour Government of 1945 to 1950. According to Zilliacus, however, the Labour Party had devoted much less attention to foreign affairs. The Party had done quite well in this field when in office in 1924 and from 1929 to 1931, but this had been in the halcyon days before the world slump. Labour had not brought itself up to date in foreign policy since then. The Labour leaders' attitude towards the Spanish Republic in 1936 and British military intervention in Greece in 1944 showed the lack of a socialist understanding of international affairs. This was aggravated, in Zilliacus's view, by the circumstance that the 1945 Labour leaders were ageing and tired men who had emerged from six gruelling years of office in a wartime coalition to find that the world had changed. A party cannot do fresh thinking when it is in office, for its leaders are too much taken up with routine work and the responsibilities of their position.

Furthermore, the Party's rank and file were content to leave foreign policy to their leaders who did not understand, and indeed to some extent feared, the social revolution sweeping the modern world. Zilliacus was always haunted by the actions of the German Social Democrats after 1918 who allied themselves with the Army in order to suppress a left-wing uprising in Germany. The result was the creation of the seriously-flawed Weimar Republic, which was successfully subverted by the Nazis. If the Social Democrats had instead put themselves at the head of left-wing forces in 1918 a Socialist Republic could have been created and, according to Zilliacus, the basis for fascism would not have existed in Germany. Zilliacus feared that Ernest Bevin was following in the footsteps of Scheidemann and Noske.

Zilliacus had prepared several memoranda on foreign policy for Attlee in the 1930s, when the two men had held broadly similar views on international affairs. In February 1946 Zilliacus was sufficiently concerned at the direction of Bevin's policy to prepare another memorandum for Attlee to consider. Zilliacus was neither surprised nor disappointed that he had not been given a post in the Labour Government. After all, he was new to Parliament and was not on particularly good terms with the Labour leadership: Bevin was hostile, Dalton was cool, Attlee was detached, and only Morrison showed any vestige of warmth towards him. He expected and received no favours from them. Nevertheless, he felt that his views on the international situation merited attention and he wanted to bring them to the notice of the Prime Minister.

His memorandum of 11 February 1946 to Attlee was 3,000 words in length and marked 'Private and Confidential'.[16] It was pragmatic rather than ideological in tone, and was accompanied by a note which read:

> Because we worked together for so many years before the war, particularly between 1931-5, that perhaps you may think my views worth considering. I am very much troubled indeed at our foreign policy and at the shape of things to come if we don't change it in time.

The main thrust of Zilliacus's memorandum was that Britain was overstretched: her commitments far exceeded her resources. Demobilisation had already been slowed down and Zilliacus foresaw the need to introduce peacetime conscription.

> The plain truth is that we must either share these commitments with others – which we could and should do in any case if they are genuine world peace commitments, that is what the United Nations is for – or else cut them by acts of unilateral abandonment.

He stressed the 'absolute' decline in Britain's position in the world. Both the USA and the USSR were now first-class world powers, he argued. Britain had recognised this fact in the case of the USA but had not yet done so in the case of the Soviet Union and it was impractical for us to attempt to build a balance of power against her. This was now beyond our strength.

Zilliacus urged the involvement of the United Nations in settling the trouble-spots of India, Indonesia, Iran, the Dardanelles, Suez, Tangier, the Dodecanese and Cyprus, and suggested that the Soviet Union should be encouraged to join in a settlement of the problems of the Middle East, which could no longer be treated as a purely British preserve. The development of atomic energy also needed to be regulated by international agreement.

Mr. Bevin had told the Security Council that the Communist Parties of the world were the enemies of the British Empire. Communism, however, wrote Zilliacus, was a reality in large areas of the world and this fact had to be recognised.

Zilliacus's memorandum concluded:

> In short, within a few months Labour foreign policy has reached a dead end and the government so far as foreign affairs are concerned are perilously near to political bankruptcy. They have been reduced to this condition because they threw overboard Labour's foreign policy and instead carried on with the foreign policy they inherited from the Tories ... Stop preparations for possible war against the USSR and join with fellow members of the Security Council to form an international police force and joint use of national forces.

Attlee's reply was brusque: 'Thank you for sending me your memorandum which seems to me to be based on an astonishing lack of understanding of the facts'.[17]

Yet although Attlee had curtly dismissed Zilliacus's memorandum the fact is that the Prime Minister was concerned at this time with the problem of an over-stretch of British power. In the last days of the wartime Coalition Government Eden, who was then Foreign Secretary, had expressed alarm at growing Soviet interest in the Mediterranean and the Middle East. Copies of his memorandum had gone to Churchill, Attlee as Deputy Prime Minister, and General Ismay of the Chiefs of Staff. Attlee sent a reply arguing that the British Government should not be misled by obsolete strategic arguments concerning this area. Air power had rendered naval power much less important. The financial cost also needed to be taken into account and we should not rule out the use of the United Nations to resolve possible rivalry in the area, and in a letter to Churchill on the same subject he pointed out that the USSR was now a world power and her interest in the area was understandable.

When Bevin and George Hall, the Colonial Secretary in the Labour Government, pressed for British trusteeship over Cyrenaica, with the Chiefs of Staff also wanting British control over a 'Greater Somalia' in order to dominate the Eastern Mediterranean, Attlee once again questioned the need for more bases at a time when naval power had become strategically less important. He also pointed out the financial costs of developing such bases and the likelihood of friction with the peoples of the area. These particular plans were abandoned, but Bevin still believed that British control of the Middle East was of paramount importance and there should be no scaling down of British commitment in the area. The arguments went on behind the scenes for nearly eighteen months, until 13 January 1947, when Attlee finally acquiesced to the demands of Bevin and A.V. Alexander, the Minister of Defence, supported by the Chiefs of Staff. None of this was made public at the time and 'Attlee's heresy', as it is now called, was not known until the relevant records were released in the 1970s.[18] Although Attlee would not have agreed with all of the points in Zilliacus's memorandum he was thinking along the same lines, yet he chose not to say so at the time. He certainly did not need to dismiss the memorandum quite so abruptly but that was always Attlee's style. The rejection of his memorandum however was the last straw for Zilliacus and he resolved to go on the attack.[19]

Vicky cartoon which appeared in the *News Chronicle*, 27 May 1947

Chapter 15

The Rebel

Zilliacus launched his offensive against Bevin's foreign policy during the Defence Debate in the House of Commons on 4 March 1946. From this date until his expulsion from the Labour Party in May 1949 he was in the thick of the struggle which took place inside the Party to change the direction of Bevin's foreign policy. He knew that few would listen to his warnings until some of the things he forecast started to happen. Even then he later came to believe that he had been over-optimistic in what he hoped to achieve. Looking back, he also came to recognise that he had had no clearly thought out tactics.[1] In the last years of his life he concluded: 'When it comes to winning friends and influencing people for what I believe to be true – getting them to face facts and see reason – I have not been, to put it mildly, a shining success, and my mistakes have been many and grievous.'[2] Like the high-minded founders of the Union of Democratic Control, who were his early radical influences, Zilliacus believed in the liberal virtues of education and discussion, and that out of the free play of ideas the broad mass of people would eventually perceive the 'right' policy to be pursued. Throughout his life Zilliacus also had a touching, almost Whiggish, respect for Britain's Parliamentary institutions and he never subjected them to any kind of Marxist analysis or indeed to severe criticism of any kind. Over the next three years he made speeches in the House of Commons, at Labour Party Conferences, and at numerous meetings across the country. He was also active with his pen and had letters and articles published in Labour's *Daily Herald*, the Co-operative Movement's *Reynolds News*, the Communist *Daily Worker*, and in Palme Dutt's *Labour Monthly* as well as *Tribune* and the *New Statesman and Nation*. He was articulate and knowledgeable and it was difficult for the Labour leaders to ignore his criticism.

In a letter to the *New Statesman and Nation* on 16 November 1946 George Bernard Shaw wrote:

The Prime Minister has not only shown that the Labour Party has no answer to Mr.Zilliacus, but it has quite definitely committed the Party to the old Foreign Office routine of Security first, Reparations second, sparring for the Balance of Power third, and Disarmament, after all the other States have disarmed, last. With, meanwhile, preparation for the next war.

This ancient program has fastened itself on the Labour Party simply because Nature abhors a vacuum. The Socialists have no foreign policy, having been completely preoccupied with domestic reorganisation.

Mr. Zilliacus is not a man to be ignored. I knew him in Geneva during his long connection with the League of Nations. He is the only internationally-minded member of any note in the House of Common. His queer name and extraordinarily composite nationality, backed by his supernational outlook and unique experience, to say nothing of his friendly and democratic private character, made him a marked figure in Geneva. He is a man who must be attended to and his question answered if another fiasco like that of Versailles and its sequel in 1939-45 is to be averted.

Zilliacus had been on friendly terms with Bernard Shaw since the 1920s, and in 1927 Shaw had been a guest at Zilliacus's home in Geneva. On that occasion Zilliacus's three-year-old son, Joe, had sat on Shaw's knee and fondled the playwright's ginger beard.[3] Shaw had read most of Zilliacus's books and thoroughly approved the line taken in them. Zilliacus was naturally gratified to receive support from such a quarter. Not that he was an isolated figure: many MPs and rank and file Labour Party members felt uneasy at the evolution of Ernest Bevin's foreign policy. Denis Healey, who at this time was head of the Labour Party's International Department at Transport House, summed it up:

> Much of the Party still took a Utopian view of world politics. Many at every level of the movement still had their pre-war illusions about Stalin's Russia as the workers' paradise. An even larger number distrusted the United States. Above all, there was general reluctance to accept that the defeat of Hitler and Mussolini had not in itself created the conditions for a lasting peace. With so much to do at home, the idea of continuing to direct resources to defence was universally unwelcome.[4]

Healey might have included the continuing strength of the 'Stalingrad syndrome': the enormous debt of gratitude that many people in Britain felt this country owed to the wartime efforts of the Soviet people. Until Hitler invaded the Soviet Union in June 1941 Britain stood alone against the might of Nazi Germany and her chances of victory looked extremely remote. The impressive fight back by the Red Army, after its initial defeats in the summer and autumn of 1941, culminating in the great victory over the German Sixth Army at Stalingrad in January 1943, was rightly regarded as a turning point in the conduct of the Second World War.[5] Russia's wartime sacrifices were still fresh in the minds of many people who found it difficult to believe that a 'gallant ally' had turned, almost overnight, into an avowed enemy of this country.

Zilliacus began his contribution to the Defence Debate on 4 March 1946 by quoting from a speech made by Clement Attlee in 1936 when the Labour leader had said, 'You cannot separate foreign policy from defence ... defence is the result of foreign policy. Very often defence proposals show what is the reality of foreign policy.'

Zilliacus went on:

> It is indeed so, and what is the reality? A slowdown in demobilisation and the prospect of conscription. One third of Britain's budget is on defence. I suggest that the price is too high ... I think that we can render better service to peace by scaling down our armaments to the point where we are solvent and can get on with our Socialist reconstruction, rather than by lowering the standard of living of our people and staggering into national bankruptcy under the burden of huge armaments.
>
> Since the general election there has been no sign of any realistic insight into what is happening in the world, no sober appraisal of our own position or the limitations of our power ... We have sunk into ancient ruts, running back to the nineteenth century, and punctuated by two world wars. We are trying to make the ghost of Palmerston walk again.[6]

'What is the way out?' asked Zilliacus, and his answer was to reduce Britain's overseas commitments, abandon 'the ill-starred policy we have inherited from the Coalition Government' and apply the Labour Party policy called *The International Post-war Settlement* adopted at the Annual Conference in 1944. This would mean 'sweeping concessions to the forces of social revolution in Europe' and make it necessary to come to terms with the forces of national emancipation in Asia. Britain also needed to reach an agreement with the Soviet Union through the United Nations and put a stop to all preparations for war. He concluded, 'I think that is the kind of lead the world is waiting for and that the people of this country expected when they returned the Labour Government to power.'

In a winding-up speech the First Lord of the Admiralty, A.V. Alexander, said that the Government 'stood clear' on the principles of the Atlantic Charter and the Four Freedoms with full support for the United Nations Organisation. He considered the criticism of the Foreign Minister to be 'unworthy'.[7]

Zilliacus returned to the attack at the next Labour Party Annual Conference held in the following June, when in a four minute speech he challenged Ernest Bevin to say whether the Labour Government accepted *The International Post-war Settlement* as setting forth in broad outline the Government's foreign policy. Bevin, in a wide-ranging speech to the Conference, lasting seventy minutes, did not answer the question, although the delegates did not seem to mind for he sat down to loud cheers and applause.[8] As *Tribune* observed, 'At the end of it all, Ernest Bevin retained his formidable place in the Labour Movement.'[9]

Zilliacus pressed the same point in the Foreign Affairs Debate in the House of Commons on 23 December 1946:

> I ask then that question, not only in my own name but in the name of my electors who returned me to this House. I fought my campaign as much on foreign affairs as on home affairs. I did not say that, if a Labour Government was returned, they would have their

home policy but that in foreign affairs they would have a black market under-the-counter coalition with the Tories.[10]

He concluded his speech by quoting from his election address and telling the Government that the way to win peace was to act as socialists in Europe 'as we have been given a mandate to do.'

Hector McNeil, Minister of State at the Foreign Office, winding up for the Government replied: 'I do not in any way subtract from the assertion that this is a Labour Government, that our policy at home and abroad is social democratic government.'[11]

Six days later twenty-one Labour backbenchers, headed by Richard Crossman, sent Attlee a confidential letter of protest against the Government's foreign policy. The missive asserted that British Social Democracy could provide a genuine middle way between 'the extreme alternatives of American free enterprise economics and Russian totalitarian socio-political life.' However Britain was playing power politics and 'gave the impression of being infected by the anti-Red virus which is cultivated in the United States.' The signatories condemned the division of the world into two hostile blocs and argued that only a Socialist Britain could overcome it. The letter concluded that 'the future of Britain and humanity is at stake in these matters, we cannot continue to remain silent and inactive.'[12]

Zilliacus was not involved in the drafting of this letter, which was largely the work of Crossman. He was seen as too much of a Sovietophile by the Crossman group and therefore his support was considered as likely to be an embarrassment rather than a source of strength, hence he was kept out of this particular attempt at influencing the Government's foreign policy.

The letter was followed by the tabling of a critical amendment to the Address on the King's Speech, supported by six formal signatories headed by Crossman, calling for the Government 'to review and recast the conduct of international affairs.' Zilliacus was one of fifty-eight MPs who eventually appended their names to the amendment.[13]

Ernest Bevin, who was in New York at the time, regarded the amendment as 'treachery' and Attlee was equally angry at this challenge to the Government's authority. When the amendment was debated on 18 November, Crossman made a sound speech in support and was answered by Attlee, who denounced the amendment as 'misconceived, mistimed and based on a misconception of the facts,'[14] but when Crossman tried to withdraw the amendment in order to avoid a division, he was thwarted by two Independent Labour Party Members who, when the Speaker asked the House if it agreed that the amendment should be withdrawn, shouted 'No'. The amendment was duly put to the vote, with the ILP members acting as tellers, and was defeated by 353 votes to nil. This meant that over a hundred Labour MPs had abstained and did not go into the lobby

in support of Bevin's foreign policy. Zilliacus was one of them, although he regarded Crossman's initiative as 'half-hearted and muddle-headed'.[15]

The year 1947 opened badly for the Labour Government with the 'big freeze'
of January and February leading to fuel cuts and short-time working in some industries. Britain's worsening economic position brought about a shift in foreign
policy: Bevin informed the State Department in Washington that Britain would
have to terminate her financial and military assistance to Greece and Turkey at
the end of March. This produced a major change in American policy when, in
mid-March, President Truman recognised the importance of supporting the
existing regimes in both countries and embodied this in the so-called 'Truman
Doctrine'. In order to ease his new policy through an economy-minded,
Republican controlled Congress, Truman gave it an ideological twist stating that
the USA must be 'willing to help free people to maintain their free institutions
and their national integrity against aggressive movements that seek to impose
upon them totalitarian regimes'. The Cold War was getting underway.[16]

In spite of the shedding of her commitments to Greece and Turkey Britain's
armed forces were still overstretched, and on the advice of the Chiefs of Staff the
Cabinet approved the introduction of a peacetime system of National Service
on the basis of an eighteen month term. Zilliacus opposed the National Service
Bill in the House of Commons. He said that he was not a pacifist and accepted
the principle of conscription, however he had to believe in what he was fighting
for and he did not consider that young men should be conscripted to serve in
Greece or Palestine.[17] Zilliacus was one of eighty-five MPs who voted against the
Bill. The outcome of this backbench rebellion was that the Government reduced
the proposed term of service from eighteen months to one year.[18]

In the first three months of 1947 a group of fifteen left-wing Labour MPs led
by Richard Crossman, Michael Foot and Ian Mikardo held a series of discussions on future policy. The outcome of these meetings was the publication in
April of the pamphlet *Keep Left*. The group's proposals covered both domestic
and foreign policy. In its foreign policy section the authors deplored the emergence of two armed blocs, one led by the USA and the other by the Soviet Union,
with Britain increasingly drawn into the American bloc. The Keep Lefters urged
Britain to show more independence in its conduct of foreign policy and lead a
'Third Force' in world politics. The group welcomed the recently signed Anglo-
French Treaty and favoured its expansion into a European Security Pact, which
would include a renunciation of atomic weapons. The pamphlet also argued for
an expansion of trade with European and Commonwealth countries thus lessen-
ing Britain's economic dependence on the USA.[19] Zilliacus was not a member
of the Keep Left group nor wished to be. Although he had favoured the creation
of an Anglo-French Union in 1944, he had envisaged that such a combination
would work closely with the USSR towards the creation of a socialist Europe. He
dismissed the idea of a Third Force as 'a phantom third alternative, the illusion

of a Western Union run by Social Democrats and independent of both the USA and USSR ... the policy of a little grey home in the West for pinks scared white by the reds'.[20]

The publication of *Keep Left* in the wake of the Left's tactical victory over the National Service Bill raised hopes and expectations that the Left would make further gains at the next Annual Labour Party Conference arranged for Whitsun 1947. Jennie Lee, writing in *Tribune* proclaimed that the Labour Movement was getting ready to 'lead its leaders'.[21]

Chapter 16

Margate and After

Ernest Bevin's position in the Labour Government was almost impregnable. Few people could match his long record of service to the Labour Movement. He was on close terms with the Prime Minister and his foreign policy was rarely challenged inside the Cabinet. Emanuel Shinwell and Aneurin Bevan occasionally offered some dissent behind the closed doors of the Cabinet room, but their main energies were engaged in running their own ministries. Harold Laski sometimes piped up against Bevin's policy on the NEC but that body was firmly under the control of the parliamentary leadership. At the Labour Party's Annual Conference Bevin could rely on the support of his own union, the Transport and General Workers' Union, which together with the block votes of the General and Municipal Workers' Union and the National Union of Mineworkers could beat down any opposition. The main opposition to Bevin's foreign policy at Conference came from the local Labour Parties and some left-wing unions.[1] Inside the House of Commons the votes of a hundred MPs could be mustered against aspects of Bevin's foreign policy, as was shown on the National Service Bill. However the Labour dissenters did not form a solid block of left-wing opinion.

First, there was a group of pro-Zionist MPs, led by Richard Crossman and Sydney Silverman, which opposed Bevin's Palestine policy. Zilliacus had Zionist sympathies and he supported this group. Secondly, there was a group of pacifists of whom Rhys Davies and Victor Yates were among the most prominent. Thirdly, there was the Keep Left group which favoured British backing for a Third Force in international affairs; and, finally, a group sometimes referred to as the crypto-Communists or the fellow travellers. Lester Hutchinson, John Platts-Mills, Leslie Solley and Konni Zilliacus, who were all to be expelled from the Labour Party for fellow-travelling offences, were usually regarded as the main core of this group. Some MPs straddled more than one group. For example, Richard Crossman and Ian Mikardo were pro-Zionist and Keep Lefters. S.O. Davies, who came close to being expelled from the Labour Party for his fellow-travelling activities, combined his Sovietophilia with a passionate support for Welsh Nationalism.[2] Labour's left-wing MPs resembled the colours of a kaleidoscope and when you gave them a shake the movement produced a different pattern.[3] Furthermore, many left-wing MPs were highly individualistic with strong views on particular issues and this was true of Zilliacus.

He was certainly sympathetic to the Soviet Union and its efforts aimed at building a socialist society, although he knew that the Soviet state was run by a Communist Party dictatorship under a ruthless leader. He believed the harshness of the Soviet regime had been brought about by Western intervention, followed by isolation in the 1920s, and the need to industrialise at breakneck speed in the 1930s. Nevertheless he always felt that given time and favourable circumstances the Soviet Union would evolve into a more democratic state allowing greater individual freedom to its citizens. He held that the totalitarian nature of its society was often exaggerated: the USSR covered a huge area inhabited by many different peoples and there was more diversity within its borders than was usually recognised by Western commentators. In foreign affairs he did not overlook the fact that the Soviet leaders were suspicious of the West and often awkward to deal with. In 1945, however, the USSR was in no position to fight a major war. Large areas of the country had been devastated and the Soviet people were exhausted by their wartime efforts. Zilliacus was convinced that the Soviet Union needed and wanted peace. He blamed Bevin for not persevering with the policy of post-war cooperation agreed by the Big Three at Yalta. The Labour Foreign Secretary's robust defence of British interests in his negotiations with Soviet representatives had helped to revive old fears in the Kremlin. Zilliacus also felt that the USA could have been given more encouragement by Britain to follow the path marked out by Roosevelt before his premature death in 1945. Instead Truman had been influenced by the hawks among his advisors and the result was that American suspicions of Soviet policy had given way first to ill will and then to outright hostility. On the eve of the Margate Conference Zilliacus saw the world dividing into two conflicting blocs, accompanied by the beginning of a new arms race. He was determined to do everything in his power to reverse Bevin's foreign policy and halt the drift to war.

Although Ernest Bevin was assured of getting his policy approved at the Labour Party's Annual Conference, he was keen to hit back at his critics. He had grown weary of the constant sniping from the Left, and Crossman's backbench revolt on the amendment to the King's Speech, in particular, still rankled with him. He thought that it would be a good idea to have a Labour Party pamphlet issued which would offer a defence of his foreign policy and counter the arguments put forward in *Keep Left*. Bevin was delighted to learn that young Denis Healey of the Party's International Department was preparing such a pamphlet.[4] Healey had obtained permission from the Party's general secretary, Morgan Phillips, and Hugh Dalton, then chairman of the NEC's International Sub-Committee, although the NEC itself had not been asked to give its approval as was usual practice.[5] Healey's pamphlet was called *Cards on the Table*. It was published a few days before the opening of the Party's Annual Conference and when delegates filed into the conference hall it was to find that a copy had been laid on each seat.

In the pamphlet Healey began by acknowledging that 'a minority of Labour's own supporters are seriously disturbed about the government's activities abroad … it is held to take sides with a Capitalist America against a Socialist Russia, or to entail a diversion of men and money from home production which this country cannot afford', and he went on, 'It is mainly to answer these general criticisms that this pamphlet is directed.'

Healey pointed out that Britain's foreign policy was not conducted in a vacuum, other countries had their own particular interests, and the effectiveness of British policy depended upon her power – economic, strategic, military and moral – and since the Second World War this was considerably less than it had been in the heyday of the British Empire. The United Nations Organisation had been intended to operate on the basis of agreement among the Big Three – Britain, the USA and the USSR. Such agreement had not been forthcoming, however, because of Soviet obduracy and Britain had been forced to look elsewhere for her security, namely, in the direction of closer links with the USA. The alternative option of Britain leading a European Bloc was dismissed as unrealistic because the countries of Western Europe had not yet recovered from the war. Scarce resources, therefore, needed to be devoted to maintaining British military power until such time as Soviet policy changed, and general disarmament and world peace was secured.

There was a rumpus in Labour's NEC when it was discovered that the pamphlet had been published without the NEC's authorisation, and Hugh Dalton was eventually forced to admit that he had given his approval. Some NEC members saw the issue as a procedural matter, others such as Harold Laski were equally concerned with the content of the pamphlet which criticised Soviet policy, justified closer links with the USA, questioned the effectiveness of the United Nations, and accepted the need for power politics and rearmament. For in *Cards on the Table* Healey had not only defended Bevin's foreign policy, he had also challenged the corpus of ideas provided by the Union of Democratic Control which had formed the basis of Labour's foreign policy since the 1920s.

The row spilled over on to the Conference floor during consideration of the work of the Party's International Department. Zilliacus intervened and argued that *Cards on the Table*:

'throws overboard the foreign policy on which this Party was returned to power … the basis of that policy is the United Nations … in this document the Charter is thrown overboard as the basis on which we are to deal with disagreements between the great powers. That is a complete rejection of the whole foundation of the Party's policy, and it is made on the grounds that it is impossible to settle differences with the Soviet Union through peaceful means; that we must line up with America in using the threat of war as an instrument of policy … It is a crypto-Fulton-Winston-and-water policy'.[6]

He asked the NEC to withdraw *Cards on the Table* and produce something 'in accordance with the foreign policy on which we were returned to power'.

Richard Crossman followed and he wanted to know who had authorised the publication of *Cards on the Table*, had it been approved by the Foreign Office and had it been written solely by Denis Healey?[7]

Hugh Dalton, replying on behalf of the NEC, warned delegates 'not to accept as completely accurate the version given by Mr Zilliacus' and 'before deciding whether or not you approve of this document I advise you to read it for yourselves'. He said it was a discussion document rather than a statement of policy and the NEC had yet to consider it.[8]

The Report was then approved by the Conference. Zilliacus returned to the rostrum in the International Policy debate to move a lengthy composite resolution on behalf of the Gateshead Labour Party, calling upon the Labour Government to base British policy on the fundamental principles of the United Nations Charter 'that the permanent Security Council members, and particularly Britain, the USA and the USSR, must cooperate as equal partners and must trust each other to keep the peace' and to give effect to this principle 'by instructing the Service Departments to frame their estimates and make their strategic dispositions on the assumption that Britain need not prepare for self-defence against either the USA or the USSR'. The resolution also pledged wholehearted support to a foreign policy based on the Labour Party's *International Post-war Settlement* and warned against excessive dependence on American capitalism, which would sooner or later involve Britain in another slump. Zilliacus said there was a choice between cutting military commitments and lowering Britain's standard of living.[9]

Before making his speech in reply to the Conference debate, Bevin had a chat with Attlee who told him that this was a time for 'letting them have it', and the Foreign Secretary agreed.[10] Bevin spoke for an hour and a half giving a review of his work at the Foreign Office. He opposed the motion proposed by Zilliacus and said that it had been drafted by 'an expert in deception'. Britain was not lining up with the USA in opposition to the USSR. 'We are doing nothing of the kind and I cannot accept what is implied in the resolution'. Turning to Crossman's amendment to the King's Speech nine months before, he discoursed on the need for loyalty. 'On the very day I was trying to get the Agreement with the Americans to prevent the bread ration going down – on that very day I was stabbed in the back', adding 'I grew up in the trade union, you see, and I have never been used to this kind of thing'.[11]

Bevin's demagogy plus the block vote carried the day. The resolutions that approved of his foreign policy were passed and the ones that were critical were defeated. Crossman neatly summed it up:

No one should be under any delusions about the extent of Bevin's victory. He carried the delegates with him in his demand that his policy should be condemned or accepted as a whole and in the implications which ran through his whole speech that criticism of it was an act of disloyalty. [12]

After eighteen months of fierce criticism the attacks on Bevin's policy became more muted after the Margate Conference. This was not so much due to Bevin's speech or Healey's pamphlet but because world events began to turn in Bevin's favour.

On 5 June 1947, speaking at Harvard, General George Marshall the American Secretary of State, proposed his plan for economic assistance to Europe, which led to a conference called by the British and French governments in Paris in July, to work out an organisation for European economic self-help and cooperation as the working counterpart of General Marshall's offer of American aid. The Soviet Government attended the conference, but after three days denounced the plan as involving an infringement of national sovereignty and forced its client states in Eastern Europe to refuse to participate, after Czechoslovakia had actually accepted, and Poland had indicated an interest in joining. The Marshall Plan was widely seen as a revival of New Deal idealism and it showed the USA in a favourable light, whereas the Soviet Union's refusal to participate and the pressure it put on other countries to do the same had the opposite effect.

Michael Foot in *Tribune* saw the Marshall Plan as:

> The offer of a fresh start: one which presented the chance to Britain, France, the Soviet Union and the United States of honourable association in the work of bringing sustenance to the hunger-stricken peoples of this tragic post-war epoch. This and nothing less is the meaning of the Marshall Plan. [13]

The *New Statesman and Nation* dithered over the Marshall Plan. The journal initially hailed Marshall's speech as statesmanlike. [14] A fortnight later, however, it was suspicious of possible political strings and it feared that if implemented it might deepen the division of Europe. [15] But when the USSR took the decision to withdraw, the *New Statesman and Nation* advised Britain and France to press ahead without the Russians. [16] By September the notoriously indecisive Kingsley Martin had reverted to his earlier support for a European Third Force. [17]

Zilliacus was at first favourably disposed towards the Marshall Plan, provided there were no political conditions attached. Soon after Marshall's speech Zilliacus wrote to his old friend from Geneva days, Zdenek Fierlinger, a left-wing Social Democrat who was Deputy Prime Minister of Czechoslovakia, and argued that the Czechs ought to test the sincerity of the American offer. Zilliacus's letter was read to the Czech Cabinet and it played its part in influencing the Czechs to accept the invitation to attend the Paris Conference. When the Russians decided to withdraw from the conference, Stalin forced the Czechs to follow suit. [18] Zilliacus believed that the European Economic Commission of the United

Nations should have been used to process the applications for aid instead of the Anglo-French sponsored steering committee. He believed that if this had been proposed it might have tipped the balance in favour of Soviet acceptance.[19] As it was, without the participation of the Soviet Union and the countries of Eastern Europe the Marshall Plan became, in Zilliacus's eyes, an arm of American foreign policy aimed at restoring capitalism in Western Europe.

Stalin took stock after his rejection of the Marshall Plan. The picture he saw was of the West European countries closing ranks behind the USA while in the Soviet sphere of influence in Eastern Europe different views were being expressed on important questions. Clearly, there was a need to tighten up discipline among the leading Communist parties of Europe. Accordingly, in August 1947 he summoned Andrei Zhadanov, the Politburo's ideologist, to his holiday villa on the Black Sea coast and instructed him to draw up plans for a new organisation to be known as the Communist Information Bureau or Cominform. Membership of the new organisation consisted of the Communist Party of the Soviet Union and the Communist parties of Bulgaria, Czechoslovakia, Hungary, Poland, Romania and Yugoslavia plus the French and Italian Communist parties; and all were invited to send two representatives to a secret inaugural meeting at Sklarsk Poremba in Western Poland on 21 September 1947.[20]

The keynote speech was given by Zhadanov who proclaimed a new phase in the development of world revolution. Since the Second World War, he went on, the world had become divided into two camps – 'one led by the USSR and other democratic countries' and the other led by the USA and Britain 'aimed at strengthening imperialism and strangling democracy ... The Marshall Plan is only the European part of a general plan of world expansion being carried out by the USA' Zhadanov attacked the 'treacherous policy of right-wing Socialists ... It is no accident that the foreign policy of British imperialism found in the person of Bevin its most consistent and zealous executor' and he urged the Communist parties to 'form the spearhead of resistance' to the 'plans of the aggressors'.[21] The Yugoslav delegates, Kardelj and Djilas, spoke in support and sharply attacked the French and Italian Communist parties for pursuing a parliamentary path to power.[22]

The creation of the Cominform signalled a new line for Communist parties throughout the world. In a two hour talk with Zilliacus, a month after the formation of the Cominform, Stalin had assured Zilliacus that the Cominform was different to the old Comintern. A single directing body for World Communism was no longer necessary because Communist parties throughout the world were now mature enough to make their own decisions. The newly created Cominform, according to Stalin, was merely a consultative body to exchange information and concert members' policies.[23] Whatever Stalin told Zilliacus, the Cominform was more than a consultative body: the Soviet Union determined its policies and the member Communist parties were expected to implement them. Furthermore, the policy directives sent out by the Cominform were followed by Communist parties throughout the world. The phase of People's Front coalition government was now over: the consolidation of Communist power was speeded up across Eastern Europe. Over the next three years the surviving Agrarian, Peasant and Smallholder parties were suppressed, then the remaining Social Democratic parties were absorbed by the dominant Communist parties, and, finally, the Communist parties of Eastern Europe were ruthlessly purged from top to bottom of all members considered 'unreliable'. In Western Europe the change of line was reflected in a wave of Communist led strikes in France and Italy, and in Britain Communist support for the Labour Government was replaced by outright opposition.[24]

The Communist Movement's change of line had important repercussions in Czechoslovakia. Since 1945, Czechoslovakia had been run by a left-wing coalition government with the Communist, Klement Gottwald, as Prime Minister and Jan Masaryk, son of the founder of the state, as non-party Foreign Minister, with Eduard Benes as President of the Republic. For the first two years the coalition had worked reasonably well. Popular measures of nationalisation had been carried out and reconstruction had made good progress and furthermore these changes had been achieved under a parliamentary system. After a visit to Prague in May 1947 Harold Laski had enthused 'If ever I saw a really democratic commonwealth I saw it in Czechoslovakia'. However the harvest of 1947 was a poor one and food shortages followed. The Communists, who had secured 38 per cent of the vote in the general election of 1946 and had emerged as by far the largest party, believed that they would not do so well in the forthcoming election of 1948 and this would reduce, or even end, their position in the Government. Their seizure of power, however, owed as much to opportunism as to careful planning. In February 1948 the non-Communist members of the cabinet resigned over the appointment of Communist sympathisers to senior posts in the police. They expected the Government to fall and that the President would then order fresh elections, in which they expected to do well. This did not happen because the Social Democrats supported the Communists in the crisis, allowing the Communists to carry on as the Government. The Communist-controlled police then arrested some members of the opposition, the radio stations and the newspapers were taken over, and armed workers' militias paraded in the streets of Prague in support of the Communist Government. A fortnight later the pyjamas-clad body of Jan Masaryk was found on the pavement several floors below an open window of his apartment at the Ministry of Foreign Affairs, and there was speculation on whether he had been thrown to his death or had committed suicide. The next election of May 1948 was held under a single-list system, confirming the Communists in power and enabling them to move to total control of the country.[25]

The coup in Czechoslovakia had a profound impact upon the Labour Left. Harold Laski was depressed to see the snuffing out of a functioning Social

Democracy in Eastern Europe.[26] Michael Foot wrote that the Russians were 'finally resolved to stamp out all opinions and political activities except those of their own partisans ... They have shown they are out for complete control wherever they can get it. Czechoslovakia is the latest example of this strategy'.[27] Richard Crossman, who travelled to Czechoslovakia with George Wigg to lay a wreath on the grave of Jan Masaryk, reported on his return that he had found 'a very quiet, cold terror' in the country. There was much talk at the time about 'another Munich', but Crossman was surely right when he compared Communist tactics with those of the Nazis in January 1933, when Hitler accepted the Chancellorship in order to destroy the Weimar Republic from within and then imposed his own dictatorship.[28]

Pre-coup Czechoslovakia was something close to the model that Zilliacus wanted to see adopted across Europe: a Popular Front-style government operating within a parliamentary system in an economy of which 80 per cent was under public ownership, yet he was prepared to defend the Communist takeover or at least justify it. In a letter to *Tribune* he wrote:

> The Czechoslovak workers acting pretty much unanimously through the trade unions and the Social Democratic as well as the Communist Party made a bloodless semi-revolution rather than allow the Right and centre to get away with their avowed object in bringing down the Government and forcing an anti-Communist coalition on the model of what has happened in France and Italy.
>
> Italy is now heading for a Dollfus or Franco type of pseudo-Christian Fascism and in France de Gaulle is an ever-present menace. American intervention in Europe is fostering fascism and incubating violent social revolution. It is the greatest single obstacle to a peaceful transition from capitalism to Socialism and thereafter the growth of democracy and political freedom.[29]

Very few people in the Labour Party agreed with Zilliacus on this point and he was becoming an increasingly isolated figure in his own party. Opposition to Bevin's foreign policy inside the Labour Party was melting away and many of those who had formerly agreed with much, if not all, of Zilliacus's analysis of events were now silent or had become supporters of Bevin's foreign policy. In the words of one historian 'Against its wishes and deepest instincts, the Labour Left was being driven into the arms of Ernest Bevin'.[30]

Chapter 17

The Titoist

A few weeks after the general election of 1945, Zilliacus was invited to join an eleven-strong party of British Parliamentarians, accompanied by selected journalists, to visit Yugoslavia and witness the country's first post-war elections.[1] The invitation was issued by Marshal Tito, and in November he sent his own plane to transport his British guests to Yugoslavia. The flight proved to be a hair-raising experience. The European airports where they would normally have stopped to refuel were fogbound and the plane flew straight to Belgrade, only to find the city's airport unable to give them permission to land. The plane eventually touched down at a partly-constructed and ill-lit airfield outside of Belgrade with, the pilot informed them after landing, no more than an eggcupful of petrol left in the tank.

The British group was warmly received wherever it went and on election day it watched Yugoslav voters flock to the polls to vote for the single list of candidates of the People's Front. Women were allowed to vote for the first time since the creation of Yugoslavia and they were determined to exercise their newly acquired right. The turnout was almost 100 per cent. It was not Westminster-style democracy but Zilliacus and most of the others in the British group were convinced that Tito's Communists and their allies, who had played the leading role in liberating the country, enjoyed the support of the bulk of the Yugoslav people. The country was devastated but the morale of the people was high, with a strong determination to maintain harmony between the different ethnic groups inside the federal republic and rebuild the shattered Yugoslav economy along socialist lines.

After the election results were announced there was folk dancing in the streets of Belgrade in which Zilliacus and Kingsley Martin, wearing garlands round their necks, did their best to participate. They were not the most nimble of men, but they joined in the fun and the crowds appreciated their attempts to dance the *Kolo*.

Zilliacus was deeply impressed by what he saw on this visit. Yugoslavia in 1945 reminded him of Russia just after the revolution and he afterwards took a special interest in Yugoslav affairs.[2] He became an active member of the British-Yugoslav Association, taught himself Serbo-Croat, and made a point of visiting the country at least once a year.

The British party met Tito and discussed Yugoslavia's urgent need for outside aid, especially food supplies, to see the country through the first post-war winter. It was Zilliacus's first meeting with the Partisan leader and it proved to be the beginning of a close friendship between the two men. Both were accomplished linguists and they had the choice of communicating in either German or Russian and, not surprisingly, they chose to speak Russian. They shared the experience of having lived in Russia during the early post-revolutionary years and both had visited Moscow in the 1930s. Zilliacus, however, was only one member of the visiting party and he could not monopolise the discussions with Tito. But he had made a favourable impression and knew that he would be welcome to return for further talks with the Yugoslav leader.

In 1946 and 1947 Zilliacus paid several visits to Czechoslovakia and Poland, and he found time to fit in trips to the Soviet Union, Bulgaria, Hungary, Romania and the Soviet Zone of Germany. During his visit to Czechoslovakia in September 1946 he had a four hour interview with President Benes, whom he had met many times at Geneva in the 1930s when Benes was Czech Foreign Minister.[3] Benes told him he believed that socialism could be achieved in Czechoslovakia by parliamentary means, with the Communist Party playing by the rules of the constitution. However, if there was a rift between East and West Czechoslovakia would opt for Russia and then things would change. Another of Zilliacus's former acquaintances, Zdeneck Fierlinger, had been Czechoslovakia's permanent delegate to the League of Nations and he was now Deputy Prime Minister. Zilliacus had long discussions with him and leading economists on the development of the Czechoslovak economy. Zilliacus also met for the first time Rudolf Slansky, general secretary of the Czechoslovak Communist Party from 1945 to 1951, and Vladimir Clementis, who succeeded Jan Masaryk as Foreign Minister in 1948.

Although Zilliacus had visited Poland several times in the 1920s and '30s, either when engaged on League of Nations business or on social visits with his wife, Eugenia, he had few old friends and acquaintances among the Polish leaders, who were little known men who had emerged from the backrooms of the Comintern or the Polish underground movement. Nevertheless, Zilliacus met the top people – Bierut, Gomulka, Berman, Minc and Cyrankiewicz, and had long discussions with them.[4] They explained the problems they faced in rebuilding a devastated country and incorporating the 'new territories' they had been awarded as part of the post-war settlement of frontiers. In return they were deeply interested in the programme of the newly elected Labour Government in Britain and Zilliacus was only too pleased to tell them how Labour had carried out the nationalisation of the Bank of England, the coal industry and civil aviation, and that the gas, electricity, railway and steel industries would follow.

During the parliamentary summer recess of 1947, Zilliacus arranged for a group of seven other Labour MPs to accompany him on a visit to Yugoslavia, the Soviet Union, Poland and Czechoslovakia. The party consisted of A.C. Allen of the Boot and Shoe Operatives Union, Geoffrey Bing the barrister, A.J. Champion of the National Union of Railwaymen, Fred Lee of the Amalgamated Engineering Union, Ben Parkin and George Thomas, both former schoolteachers, and Henry White, a Derbyshire miner. As was usual on such visits hospitality would be provided by the governments of the host countries with the visitors paying their own transport costs. Whether the other MPs knew it or not Zilliacus, who made all the travel arrangements for the party, subsidised their fares out of his own pocket.[5] The group left London for Belgrade on 25 September on the first stage of their tour. In Yugoslavia the MPs visited various industrial sites, talked with overseas students working on the famous Youth Railway, and concluded their visit with an interview with Tito.

The group found the Soviet Union in the early stages of recovery after the widespread devastation wrought by the Second World War. Zilliacus thought the people friendly but wary of becoming too intimate with their British visitors and he detected apprehension at the growing rift between the Soviet Union and her wartime allies.[6] The British MPs had hoped to meet Stalin on their visit but they had given up hope of meeting the Soviet leader when, on the eve of their proposed departure, they had a long interview with the Soviet Foreign Minister, Molotov, who told them:

> I understand you have expressed a desire to see the head of our government. Un-
> fortunately, Comrade Stalin is not in Moscow and you are leaving tomorrow. But
> if you could stay on twenty-four hours longer we could take you down by plane to
> see him at Sochi on the Black Sea and fly you from there direct to Warsaw.[7]

Naturally the British group accepted the offer and the next day flew from Moscow to the Crimea to meet Stalin. George Thomas, who was later to become Speaker of the House of Commons, recalled that Stalin was very affable: 'As he laughed and talked there was nothing to betray him as the ruthless murderer of his own people',[8] and Zilliacus later remarked to his wife: 'There is not a scrap of humanity in Stalin'.[9]

Stalin told them that he wanted friendship and cooperation between Britain and the USSR. It was not a question of choosing between East and West for he understood that Britain had close relations with the USA, but he advised Britain to balance these links by expanding its trade with the Soviet Union. Stalin said he saw no reason why socialism should not be achieved by peaceful means and he pointed out that in Poland Catholics and Communists were working together.[10] After their interview with Stalin one of his private planes flew the group to Warsaw.

The British MPs were impressed by the pace of reconstruction in Poland, especially in the rebuilding of Warsaw. They witnessed the brick by brick restoration of Old Town Square, completely destroyed by the SS in 1944, and saw the building of blocks of modern high-rise flats. The Poles, regardless of politics, were united in wanting to rebuild their devastated towns and cities. In Czechoslovakia the group found the same emphasis on reconstruction and economic development, led by a left-wing coalition government headed by a Communist Prime Minister. The MPs' programme included a meeting with the Deputy Foreign Minister, Vladimir Clementis, before they boarded a plane for London on 21 October.

Zilliacus was broadly sympathetic to the changes taking place in Eastern Europe from 1945 to 1947. As a left-wing socialist Zilliacus believed that socialism was both inevitable and desirable – the means to the creation of a better life for the broad mass of the people. Capitalism was defunct and there was always the danger that a moribund capitalist system would give way to fascism as a means of resisting the advance of socialism. Zilliacus believed in public ownership and economic planning, and he approved of the socialisation of the economies of the various East European states. Reconstruction and economic development, he believed, were proceeding hand in hand with the advance of socialism.

Zilliacus could also be described as a Popular Frontist. He wanted to see communists, socialists and other 'progressives' working together to advance the political objectives they held in common. He had supported Popular Front policies in the 1930s and was delighted when left-of-centre coalitions were formed in both Eastern and Western Europe in the immediate aftermath of the Second World War. Zilliacus had no sympathy for fascists and wartime collaborators who, he held, deserved the punishments meted out to them after the war. He was not naïve enough to believe that the People's Democracies, as they termed themselves, were perfectly functioning democracies. There were restrictions on civil liberties which would have been considered unacceptable in the more mature democracies of Western Europe. However, apart from Czechoslovakia, all of the East European states had been ruled by right-wing authoritarian regimes of one kind or another before the Second World War, and before that they had formed part of foreign-imposed empires. The imperfect democracies of the 1945-47 period, therefore, were a big improvement on what had gone before.[11] Furthermore, in Zilliacus's view, the breaking up of the big landed estates and the nationalisation of large-scale business enterprises held the promise of an improved standard of living for the vast majority of people. Yet at the very time Zilliacus and his party of Labour MPs boarded their plane at London airport, the inaugural meeting of the Cominform was being held at a remote spa in western Poland. This meeting of Communist leaders would end this particular phase of Popular Frontism and usher in a new period of harsh and uncompromising Communist rule in Eastern Europe.

At the Cominform meeting the two delegates from the Yugoslav Communist Party had shown the greatest zeal in supporting Stalin's new line, yet it was the Yugoslav Party that was the first to fall foul of the new policy. Tito had always shown more independence in his dealings with Stalin than any other Communist

leader. He had led the Partisans in their victorious struggle against German occupation and had not come to power in the wake of the Red Army. He had
firmly resisted Soviet penetration of his police and security forces, and had been
tough in his trade negotiations with the USSR. Tito had also shown a large measure of independence in his foreign policy, pressing his claim to Trieste, assisting
the Communist rebellion in Greece, and discussing with the Bulgarian leader,
Dimitrov, the possibilities of a Balkan Federation. These actions had brought
reprimands from Stalin but Tito in return had protested his loyalty to the Soviet
Union and Stalin had appeared satisfied with Tito's replies.

This rift between the USSR and Yugoslavia first became apparent in March
1948, when Stalin withdrew all Soviet military and technical advisers from
Yugoslavia.[12] There followed a number of letters between the two men in which
Stalin dredged up alleged slights suffered by Soviet personnel and criticised the
Yugoslav Communist Party for its absence of internal democracy and of favour-
ing the peasants at the expense of industrial workers. Tito did his best to avert a
split and answered Stalin's criticisms point by point. However the Soviet leader
was intent on Tito's overthrow and his replacement by someone more subservi-
ent to the USSR.

A meeting of the Cominform was arranged for the last week in June 1948 to be
held in Bucharest, and Tito was summoned to attend. The Yugoslav Communist
Party's central committee, however, rejected the invitation and Tito did not go.

In his absence the Cominform passed a resolution accusing the Yugoslav leadership of pursuing 'an incorrect line on the main questions of home and foreign policy, a line that represents a departure from Marxism-Leninism'. Tito's
government was called a ' Turkish terrorist regime … suffering from boundless
ambition, arrogance and conceit', which led it to meet comradely criticism
'with belligerence and hostility'. By such conduct the central committee of the
Yugoslav Communist Party had placed itself and the Party 'outside the fraternity
of Communist Parties, outside the ranks of the Cominform'. Tito's Yugoslavia
had taken a nationalist line which was bound to end in 'Yugoslavia's degenera-
tion into an ordinary bourgeois republic', to the loss of its independence and to
its transformation into a colony of the imperialist countries. The main charges
in home affairs were an excessively conciliatory policy towards the peasantry
and the merging of the Communist Party in the People's Front. There was an
overall charge of hostility to the Soviet Union.

The expulsion of Yugoslavia from the Cominform on 28 June 1948 came as
a surprise to many observers of the international scene. There had been some
evidence of tension between Yugoslavia and the Soviet Union but few people
knew the full facts or had quite realised the seriousness of the situation. Zilliacus
had good sources of information and he knew that a crisis in Soviet-Yugoslav
relations was impending and he wanted to know more. He had therefore written
to Tito asking to see him during the summer recess and the Yugoslav leader had

agreed to a meeting at his summer villa in Bled.[13]

Zilliacus was a busy man and he did not see as much of his family as he would have liked. It was therefore his practice to arrange a family holiday in the summer months.[14] At the end of the war Jan Zilliacus's mother had returned to London to reclaim her house in Carlton Hill and the Zilliacus family had moved to a house a short distance away in Abbey Road. Konni and Jan had also rented a spacious cottage, called 'The Clamp', located on a bank of the River Orwell in Suffolk. This was a popular retreat for the family but in the long summer recess Zilliacus liked to take his family abroad. Zilliacus therefore planned to take his wife, stepdaughter Dawn, and daughter Linden, to Yugoslavia for a holiday and at the same time fit in his meeting with Tito. He was also suffering badly from gout and decided to travel to Yugoslavia through Czechoslovakia, where he would visit the spa at Piestany, in the hope that its sulphuric mud baths would give him some relief.

From the minute they crossed the border into Czechoslovakia the Zilliacus family found themselves treated with suspicion. The Cominform campaign against Tito was getting underway and Zilliacus, known to be Tito's friend, was travelling through Czechoslovakia to visit the arch-traitor himself. The Czechoslovak security services, therefore, were on the alert and kept the Zilliacus family under close scrutiny.

Zilliacus took ill in Piestany and was admitted to hospital but he persuaded his wife and family to go on ahead without him and after a tedious rail journey across Czechoslovakia and Hungary they were relieved when they finally crossed the border into friendly Yugoslavia. Zilliacus spent an unpleasant five weeks in hospital and as soon as he felt fit enough to travel he left Czechoslovakia and met up with his family at the Excelsior Hotel in Dubrovnik. He told Jan that he had been treated with great hostility when a patient in the Piestany hospital and had even feared for his life. After a few days of rest at Dubrovnik Zilliacus was sufficiently recovered to make the journey to Tito's lakeside holiday residence at Bled in Slovenia, where the Marshal gave him a warm welcome.

Zilliacus was the first 'Westerner' to meet Tito after Yugoslavia's expulsion from the Cominform. Tito told him that all the talk about ideological differences between the Soviet Union and Yugoslavia was nonsense. The only point on which they differed was in their policy towards the peasants. Tito wanted to avoid the errors of breakneck collectivisation. Yugoslav peasants had owned their land for centuries. They had to be persuaded to enter co-operatives and this would take time. The real issue, said Tito, was the relations between socialist states. These should be on the basis of friendship and cooperation and not on coercion and exploitation.

'I'm glad it has fallen to us to settle this issue once and for all', Tito told Zilliacus. 'Any other Communist Party would have broken before Stalin. But we shan't. We're going to stand up to him'.[15]

Zilliacus had no doubt that Tito was correct in making a stand against Stalin, who he believed was always inclined to be unnecessarily harsh and brutal in his methods. Zilliacus's Finnish background also made him sympathetic to the right of small nations to develop in their own way. He was very much aware that every country had its own national identity, shaped by history and geography, and that such factors needed to be taken into account when introducing socialist measures. In later years he always argued that references to the Soviet bloc often concealed the enormous differences between the Communist states of Eastern Europe. Zilliacus did not want to see these differences ironed out, creating a dull uniformity among countries each one of which had its own distinctive culture. He therefore hoped that the rift between Yugoslavia and the Soviet Union would be settled without further conflict and Yugoslavia allowed to develop socialism in her own way. For the next twelve months Zilliacus watched events closely but made no public statements on the dispute.

Tito also hoped for reconciliation with the Soviet Union and in the first months following the rift he did nothing to provoke Stalin's wrath. Stalin was not used to being thwarted, however, and he took it very badly. All trade between Yugoslavia and other Communist countries was cut off, and diplomatic relations were suspended. A purge of Communist leaders suspected of being sympathetic to Tito was carried out in all the Communist states of Eastern Europe and a series of show trials took place: of Xoxe in Albania, Rajk in Hungary and Kostov in Bulgaria. This was accompanied by a virulent propaganda campaign against Tito. Finally, Stalin began to mass troops along the Yugoslav border.

When Zilliacus visited Yugoslavia in September 1949 he found widespread apprehension at reports of Soviet troop movements along the country's borders with Bulgaria, Hungary and Romania.[16] Tito informed Zilliacus that if the country was invaded it would defend itself and Yugoslav units would take to the mountains if necessary as they had done during the war. However Tito did not believe it would come to that.

Zilliacus recalled that at a meeting with a group of Yugoslav leaders one of them had said to him:

'Look here. When are some of you socialists in the West going to speak out about this business? You know we are standing for a principle that concerns you as much as it does us.'

Zilliacus replied:

I explained that the reason why the Left in the West had been keeping quiet so far was partly because we had clung to the hope of the whole thing ending in a compromise and did not want to add fuel to the fires of the cold war. The Left wanted an accommodation with the Soviet Union through negotiation and compromise, and did not want to give a handle to those who thought in terms of preparing for or threatening war as an instrument of their policy towards the Soviet Union. And we wanted our country to be independent of the United States, as much as the

Yugoslavs wanted to be independent of the Soviet Union. But beyond a certain point a political question ceased to be merely political and became a moral issue, where it was one's duty to speak out and tell the truth, regardless of consequences, I believed that point had been reached now in the Soviet-Yugoslav conflict, and when I returned home I would say exactly what I thought.[17]

Zilliacus kept his word, and on his return to Britain he reported that he had found strong support for Tito among the Yugoslav people and he gave a generally favourable account of conditions inside the country.

Tribune pointed out that the Soviet press was reporting that Yugoslavia had degenerated into a fascist state at the very time Zilliacus was praising its socialist achievements:

Zilliacus's statement is therefore one of real courage. It seems that the Soviet attack on Tito has stuck in his gullet, and that fact does him credit. One comment of Marshal Tito, reported by Zilliacus, is of special interest. He is reported as saying 'that if Socialism does not mean humanism, if it does not mean human dignity, more respect for freedom, truth and justice, it would not be worth working for'.

After the praise for Zilliacus came the barb:

We regret that these humanist principles did not provoke Zilliacus to protest against the savage persecutions which have been pursued in the countries of Eastern Europe against thousands of people including Socialists – countries which hitherto Zilliacus has hailed as people's democracies.[18]

It is true that Zilliacus said nothing in public concerning those Communists and non-Communists who were arrested, imprisoned, and sometimes tortured and executed in Eastern Europe as part of the process of Stalinisation carried out after September 1947. There were three main reasons for his silence. Firstly, Zilliacus believed that the creation of the Cominform was Stalin's response to the Truman Doctrine and the Marshall Plan; and 'as Anglo-American policy got tougher and tougher and more and more bellicose, the Communist regimes became harsher and more suspicious, drew together, clung to the Soviet Union and mounted guard against the enemy within and without. The Soviet leaders became more and more insistent, on security grounds, on the welding together of the Soviet Bloc and the purging of any weak-kneed or doubtful elements'.[19] He held that a relaxation in the rigours of the Cold War would allow a return to a more relaxed political situation in the Communist states of Eastern Europe, therefore he was reluctant to say anything that might make the situation worse. Secondly, he was aware that an anti-Communist campaign was underway in the West, particularly in the USA, and he wanted no part of it. Finally, although he knew that the East European show trials were based on fabricated evidence he considered public criticism of Communist regimes was often counter-productive and it was more useful to make a protest or to petition in private conversations with Communist leaders. Zilliacus certainly used his high level contacts to speak up on behalf of some of those languishing in Communist prisons, and although there is no evidence that he was successful in getting anyone released from confinement in Cominform countries on balance his pressure and enquiries probably did the prisoners more good than harm.[20]

He was more successful in his dealings with Marshal Tito, who was, in any case, a friend but also more humane than most of the 'little Stalins' who ruled Eastern Europe at this time. One case in particular was that of Jovan Obican.[21] Obican was a Yugoslav journalist who had fallen foul of the country's censorship laws and been imprisoned. Zilliacus took up his case with Tito who ordered Obican's release. On regaining his freedom Orbican decided that journalism was too risky an occupation and he opened a pottery in Dubrovnik. In order to make a living he turned out items of pottery for the tourist trade but, when time allowed, he produced more ambitious pieces and became one of Yugoslavia's leading ceramists. He then turned to painting with considerable success, and in the 1950s there were exhibitions of his work held in London and New York. He was deeply grateful to Zilliacus for taking up his case and securing his release from prison.

The rift between Stalin and Tito affected the activities of the British-Yugoslav Association (BYA). The Association was formed in 1944 'to further friendship, mutual understanding and co-operation between the peoples of Great Britain and Yugoslavia'.[22] When Zilliacus was elected to Parliament in 1945 he became one of the BYA's Sponsors. The Association was a broadly-based organisation and other Sponsors included Fitzroy McClean, a Conservative MP; Lady Megan Lloyd George, a Liberal MP; and trade union leader Arthur Deakin. The BYA's first President was Professor R.W. Seton-Watson, who was succeeded by Sir Henry Bunbury. Zilliacus was an active member of the BYA and joint-author of the pamphlet *Yugoslavia Faces the Future.*[23] Many of the BYA's rank-and-file members were Communists or Communist sympathisers, but the Association was by no means a Communist-controlled 'front organisation' and when the Cominform-Yugoslav dispute broke out in the summer of 1948 the executive committee of the BYA decided to remain neutral between the disputants and this policy was unanimously approved at the Association's annual general meeting held in January 1949.

When Zilliacus returned from Yugoslavia in September 1949 he was determined to swing the BYA behind Tito, and he organised a slate of fifteen pro-Tito candidates for the same number of places on the Association's executive committee, and put forward a resolution of support for Tito's Yugoslavia on the agenda of the BYA's next annual general meeting. The pro-Stalin faction in the BYA responded to the challenge and nominated fifteen pro-Cominform members for the places on the executive committee, and put an anti-Tito resolution on the agenda. The voting was by postal ballot and at the BYA's annual general meeting held on 17 November it was announced that all fifteen of the pro-Cominform candidates had been elected, with the left-wing barristers D.N. Pritt and John Platts-Mills topping the poll. The pro-Tito resolution was defeated by 72 to 58 votes and the anti-Tito passed by 72 to 57 votes. To crown their victory the pro-Cominform faction elected D.N. Pritt as the new President of the Association. Thereupon the pro-Tito members led by Zilliacus resigned from the BYA *en masse*, and formed a new organisation called the British-Yugoslav Friendship Society, with Sir Henry Bunbury as President.

In the Cominform journal, published later in the month, the pro-Cominform members of the BYA were said to have prevented Zilliacus from using the organisation as 'a vehicle to slander the Soviet Union, the Communist Parties and the peace movement'.[24] A month later the same journal accused Zilliacus of embarking 'on a campaign in favour of the Tito gang' and of showing 'a suspicious love for the Belgrade fascists'.[25] Zilliacus was to be vilified by the Cominform press in similar fashion for the next four years. It was some consolation to him that his activities were favourably reported in the Yugoslav media where he was accorded, to his embarrassment, something approaching hero status. The author Bernard Newman, visiting Yugoslavia in 1950 in order to collect material for one of his travel books, observed that in Yugoslavia Zilliacus was 'rated far above the importance which British politicians would allot to him'.[26]

Chapter 18

The Road to NATO

In January 1948 Ernest Bevin put four foreign policy papers before the Cabinet for its information and approval. One background paper outlined the hostile policies pursued by the Soviet Union since 1945. Bevin did not consider that the Soviets were planning a war against the West, although he maintained they hoped to achieve their aims by other means. According to Bevin, Stalin believed the West would not make a successful post-war recovery and Western Communist parties would be well placed to capitalise on any economic difficulties. Bevin thought that attempts at coups in Czechoslovakia and Italy were a possibility. In a second paper Bevin emphasised the need for Social Democracy to put forward its case with greater vigour and confidence. A third paper argued the case for close integration of the three Western zones of Germany, including the introduction of a single currency and a greater measure of self-government. In a final paper Bevin proposed to work for closer unity among the West European democracies. Bevin received the Cabinet's support for his policy. In the longer term he hoped to draw in the USA, but he knew the time was not yet ripe for such a move. Nevertheless, he sent copies of his papers to George Marshall at the State Department and received a favourable response.[1]

On 22 January 1948, in a Foreign Affairs debate in the House of Commons, Bevin unveiled the policy he had outlined to the Cabinet three weeks before. In the debate that followed his policy was supported by several Conservatives, including Winston Churchill and Anthony Eden, as well as loyalists from the Labour benches. The main opposition came from Zilliacus, the two Communist MPs Willie Gallacher and Phil Piratin, the fellow-travellers John Platts-Mills and William Warbey, and the Keep Lefter Richard Crossman. Gallacher's and Piratin's speeches followed the Communist line without deviation, Platts-Mills and Warbey were critical of Bevin's policy and sympathetic to the Soviet position, while Crossman, while criticising some aspects of Bevin's line, was in the process of abandoning his support for a Third Force in favour of a more pro-American stance. Zilliacus's speech was his distinctive blend of UDC thought combined with a sympathy for the foreign policy being pursued by the Soviet Union:

> The course of the debate has shown how far we have come along the road we have been treading for two years – the road towards a new balance of power, a new arms race, and preparations for a new world war, between an Anglo-American alliance

on the one hand, dominated by Washington, and a combination of states which have passed through a social revolution on the other hand … I fear very much that the proposals that are being discussed tonight about the organisation of Western Europe on the basis of the Marshall Plan must be viewed as part and parcel of this wider policy, of this return to power politics

Zilliacus spoke of his recent visit to Sweden, where he had found Swedish socialists prepared to participate in some form of Western Union, provided there were no military commitments involved. He urged the British Government to take the lead in setting up an Assembly of Parliamentarians, drawn from all the states of Western Europe, including the Scandinavian countries, to discuss current problems.

He concluded:

> We must settle all our differences even with the USSR by peaceful means, and must never use force in our dealings with that country. On that choice hangs the issue of peace or another world war.[2]

Zilliacus was followed by Jack Lawson, a miners' MP who sat for the neighbouring constituency of Chester-le-Street. Lawson warned the Commons that Zilliacus 'does not speak for the majority of his party nor does he speak for the working classes of this country', and he went on to praise Ernest Bevin for his work at the Foreign Office.[3]

Bevin moved swiftly and was soon in discussions with France and the Benelux countries on the drawing up of a mutual defence pact. News of the Communist coup in Czechoslovakia helped to speed up the negotiations and the Treaty of Brussels was signed on 17 March 1948.

In April a row blew up over the sending of what came to be called the Nenni Telegram. A general election was to take place in Italy on 18 April and its outcome would be an important factor in the Cold War. In the campaign the Christian Democratic Party and its allies were ranged against the Italian Communist Party and its allies. The Italian Socialist Party had split, with its left wing under Pietro Nenni supporting the Communists and its right wing under Giuseppe Saragat backing the Christian Democrats. On the afternoon of 13 April, Attlee, Morrison, Dalton, Shinwell and Morgan Phillips met in the Prime Minister's room at the House of Commons to discuss statements by Platts-Mills and Zilliacus 'that appeared to be subversive of Party policy'.[4] By pure coincidence, the two Labour Members in question were engaged at that moment in canvassing signatures for a message to be sent to the Nenni Socialists. The message itself read: 'Greetings to our Italian Socialist Comrades and warm hopes for your triumph in the election'. Where the original idea for sending such a message came from is obscure.[5] Both Zilliacus and William Warbey were certainly among the first to consider such a move and Geoffrey Bing is credited with drafting the message.[6] Zilliacus and Warbey began to collect signatures and when they had to go abroad the task was taken over by Maurice Orbach. After gathering a dozen names he asked Platts-Mills to help and the barrister then took over the project. In this game of pass the parcel it was the unfortunate Platts-Mills who was left holding the parcel when the music stopped.

John Platts-Mills was born in New Zealand in 1906. After a brilliant scholastic record in his own country he came to Britain on a Rhodes scholarship, and after studying at Oxford he stayed on to qualify as a barrister. On the outbreak of war he joined the RAF. His work at the Bar had brought him into contact with Sir Stafford Cripps who, in 1941, recommended him to Churchill to head a semi-official unit organising propaganda in support of the Russian war effort. He did this very successfully for a couple of years and then worked for a spell as a miner in Yorkshire. He had joined the Labour Party in 1936 and won the parliamentary nomination for the Finsbury constituency during the war years. He went on to win the seat in 1945. One historian has described him as the 'least disguised' of the crypto-Communists in the Parliamentary Labour Party,[7] and there is no doubt that he was one of the most prominent of the fellow travelling group of Labour MPs in the 1945-50 Parliament. Oscar Wilde once advised that one should choose one's enemies with great care. Platts-Mills was careless in this respect for he had made enemies of both Ernest Bevin and Herbert Morrison, and although he had been a member of the Labour Party for over ten years he did not have deep roots in the Labour Movement. He was unlucky in that he had been handed final responsibility for sending off the telegram to Nenni.

By late afternoon of Friday 16 April, Platts-Mills had secured thirty-seven names when Geoffrey Bing burst into his room in the Commons. Bing told him he had heard that the Whips would press for the expulsion of all signatories and he strongly advised his fellow barrister not to send the message. Platts-Mills held back from sending the telegram, spent the evening doing some work in his room, had a bite of supper, and at nine o'clock drove to the all-night post office in the City, where he despatched the telegram in the name of all the signatories. He then rang round the news agencies and newspaper offices, reporting what he had done.[8]

The Nenni Telegram made the next day's newspapers and the story rumbled on for several days. There were even questions raised in the House of Commons as to whether there had been a breach of parliamentary privilege. The Speaker ruled there had not: the incident was a party and not a parliamentary matter, and Herbert Morrison promised that it would be dealt with by the appropriate Labour Party authorities.[9] Accordingly, Morgan Phillips wrote to all the signatories asking them to confirm that they had signed the telegram and asking for any observations they had to make. In the event, fifteen of them managed to dissociate themselves from the telegram and, after protracted correspondence with Morgan Phillips, the remainder promised not to take part in organised opposition to Party policy and to work within the framework of the Party's rules and constitution.[10] The Labour leaders recommended that Platts-Mills be expelled from the Party for the leading part he had played in organising the sending of the telegram and for his previous record of opposition to the Government's policies. His expulsion was confirmed at the next Labour Party Annual Conference. Zilliacus and several other signatories could think themselves lucky that they had not been caught in the same net. However the Labour leadership had given notice that there were limits to how far Labour MPs could go in criticising the Government's policies and in associating with Communists. The expulsion of Platts-Mills was a warning to all Labour MPs that in future they must toe the line or face the consequences.

The incident of the Nenni telegram was soon eclipsed in the news by a much more serious development: a deepening crisis over the future of Berlin. A month after his foreign policy speech in the House of Commons Bevin hosted a conference to discuss the future of West Germany. Invitations were sent to the three Western occupying powers – Britain, France and the USA – plus the Benelux countries. The outcome of these discussions was the issuing of a communiqué expressing the view that, while Four Power agreement on Germany was still possible, there were pressing political and economic problems needing to be settled affecting the future of Germany and Europe. The implications were obvious: a West German republic was about to be set up and incorporated into the Marshall Plan.

The Soviets protested and made it clear that the creation of a West German state would affect the position of Berlin. Nevertheless, the Western governments pressed on with their plans. There was to be economic integration of the three Western occupation zones, a constitution for a West German federal republic was to be drawn up, and a new German currency was to be introduced into the Western zones on 18 June. The Soviet response was to cut off all road and rail communications between West Germany and the three Western occupation zones in Berlin, leaving West Berlin isolated in the middle of the Soviet zone. The Soviet blockade of Berlin started on 24 June 1948 and ended on 12 May 1949. The Western sectors were not starved or frozen out, as many expected, because supplies were brought in by a massive Western airlift. The Berlin crisis ended without armed conflict, but on several occasions during the eleven months the blockade lasted the outbreak of war looked imminent.[11]

Zilliacus voiced his views on the Berlin crisis in a speech he made in the Commons' Foreign Policy debate on 9 December 1948, when he argued that the deadlock over Berlin could only be solved as part of a wider settlement. He favoured the unification of Germany, with public ownership of its heavy industry and Four Power control of the Ruhr. He wanted to see a moratorium on reparations until such time as Germany had made a successful economic recovery. Therefore he wanted to see the occupation zones abolished and a central authority established so that all-German elections could be held. Then all Allied troops could be withdrawn, to be replaced by an international force.[12]

Whatever the merits of Zilliacus's proposals, the Berlin crisis had made them less likely of acceptance than they would have been before the imposition of the blockade, for the blockade had hardened American attitudes towards the Soviet Union. During the summer of 1948 there were discussions between the Americans and the Brussels Pact countries. In December, the governments of Canada, Denmark, Iceland, Italy, Norway and Portugal were invited to join the new alliance. Dean Acheson, one of its main architects, became Secretary of State in January 1949 and he brought the treaty negotiations to a successful conclusion. On 4 April 1949 the North Atlantic Treaty was signed in Washington. Ernest Bevin, who signed the treaty on Britain's behalf, told the journalist Francis Williams that the signing was 'one of the greatest moments of all my life'.[13]

Zilliacus saw things in a different light. To him the creation of NATO marked a return to power politics and an acceleration of the arms race. It was a reversion to the system of armed alliances. For three years he had worked to prevent this happening and had failed. As he later came to recognise the odds had been stacked against him, but he had done his best, and was determined not to give up hope that a Third World War, probably fought with atomic weapons, could be averted. He would continue his work for peace.

On 12 May 1949 the House of Commons held a debate to approve the signing of the North Atlantic Treaty. Ernest Bevin opened the debate and was followed by Winston Churchill, who gave his support. William Warbey delivered a long speech, critical of the treaty. Zilliacus rose to speak at 7.10 p.m. and spoke for twenty-five minutes.

He said he was concerned that Franco Spain and a re-Nazified West Germany would become members of NATO. The Soviet Union was not solely to blame for the present situation, although it bore some responsibility. However he was convinced that the Soviet Union wanted peace.

He went on:

The more we arm the more we increase fear and suspicion. The more we increase armaments, the less strong we feel ourselves and the more we feel the other fellow's strength. In order to sustain the burden and sacrifice of the arms race, one has to foment and sustain a psychological condition in the people, who are bearing the strain, that unfits them for peacemaking ... So much for the Atlantic Pact: it scraps the Charter and returns to the balance of power. It commits us to a new arms race ... I beg the Government to find some way before it is too late to come back to the Charter of the United Nations ... to be conciliatory and moderate in their attitude, not to be rushed or stampeded into recrimination, not to put their faith in armaments, but in a wise and conciliatory policy.[14]

Philip Noel-Baker, Secretary of State for Commonwealth Relations, wound up for the Government and the treaty was approved by 333 votes to 6. The tellers for the Noes were Emrys Hughes and Ronald Chamberlain, and the six members who voted against were: Tom Braddock, Willie Gallacher, Phil Piratin, John Platts-Mills, D. N. Pritt and K. Zilliacus.

Harold Macmillan, an observer on the Conservative benches, thought D. N. Pritt and Zilliacus 'the most effective in argument against the treaty' although he considered Zilliacus the 'more sprightly and engaging of the two'.[15]

Zilliacus followed up his opposition to the North Atlantic Treaty by bringing out a pamphlet, published at his own expense, *Dragon's Teeth – the background, contents and consequences of the North Atlantic Pact.* Collet's was responsible for the pamphlet's distribution and it did not enjoy a wide circulation.

Chapter 19

Alarums And Excursions

The expulsion of Platts-Mills from the Labour Party should have served as a warning to Zilliacus that he stop, or at least moderate, his attacks on the Labour Government, tone down his support for Soviet foreign policy, and distance himself from Communist-dominated organisations. However, he did the opposite. Far from keeping his head down, in the twelve months from May 1948 to May 1949 he was rarely out of the news in a series of headline-catching incidents. Zilliacus did not court expulsion by deliberately provoking the Labour leadership: he felt that the circumstances of the time made it imperative that he speak out against what he conceived as the drift to war. There was also a certain innocence about Zilliacus, like the cartoon character, the short-sighted Mr Magoo, he was often oblivious to the commotion he left in his wake.

On 1 May 1948, speaking at a May Day Rally in Blaydon, Zilliacus used the occasion to put forward his views on foreign policy, and when referring to the strength of Communism on the continent he said:

> It is not our business to tell the workers of Europe how to run their own affairs in their own countries and even if it were there is nothing we can do about it. The story of the big bad wolf and the three little pigs is still a fairy tale when told in reverse: even the most blow-hard little pigs in Transport House can not huff and puff the big bad wolf of revolutionary working class leadership out of Europe [1]

It was a speech that was reported in the national press[2] and its content was carefully noted by Morgan Phillips at the Labour Party headquarters in London.[3]

Later in the month Zilliacus was in action at the Labour Party's Annual Conference at Scarborough, where he emerged as the leading critic of Bevin's foreign policy. On 20 May, Will Lawther of the National Union of Mineworkers moved a resolution expressing firm support for Labour's foreign policy. Zilliacus moved an amendment which called for a return to Labour's traditional foreign policy, condemned Churchill's Fulton speech, reaffirmed support for the United Nations, called for a British withdrawal from Greece, and urged partnership with the Soviet Union in the Middle East. If passed the amendment would have completely negated the resolution, and it is some measure of the growing support for Bevin's policy inside the Labour Party that it was defeated by four million votes to 224,000.[4]

Once the conference was over, the chairs had hardly had time to be rearranged for the next Max Jaffa concert at the Spa in Scarborough before Zilliacus was planning a visit to Poland. On 21 May he wrote to James Griffiths, the newly-elected Chairman of the Labour Party, informing him that he had accepted an invitation to speak to the Foreign Affairs Group of the Polish Parliament and as his stay in Poland would overlap with the International Socialist Conference being held there he hoped to attend this meeting as a visitor. 'I believe that wholly informal and personal contacts of that kind may serve a useful purpose in keeping our Party, to some extent, in touch with and informed of developments in the Socialist Parties of these countries, now that all official contacts have ceased ... I should like to send you a report when I get back'.

James Griffiths replied that he did not consider there would be any objection to Zilliacus speaking to the Foreign Affairs Group of the Polish Parliament, however he thought the NEC would have 'misgivings' if he attended the International Socialist Conference. 'My view is that it will be better if you do not attend'. Zilliacus replied that he was surprised at Griffiths' advice that he should not attend as an observer therefore 'in order to remove any anxiety on your part, I wish to assure you that I will not attend as an observer ... if I attend any of its meetings it will be as a mere visitor.' The difference between attending as an observer and as a visitor was not pursued by James Griffiths, who was no doubt satisfied that his advice had been clear enough.[5]

Zilliacus's lecture to the Polish Foreign Affairs Group was a critique of British foreign policy, and it was reported in the *Daily Herald*,[6] as was his presence at a press conference of the International Socialist Conference which he explained he had attended 'as a guest, to meet old friends'.[7] The Polish press reported that Zilliacus had sat on the platform of the International Socialist Conference and had 'said a few words about the fight of the British working class for peace'.[8] These reports were duly noted by Morgan Phillips back in London.

Zilliacus was quiet for the next two months when he was incapacitated by a severe bout of rheumatic gout, and he then set out for Yugoslavia via Czechoslovakia and Hungary, as described elsewhere.

On his return from visiting Tito he was active throughout the year, writing articles and addressing meetings across the country. After the publication of a long letter by Zilliacus in the *New Statesman and Nation* on 30 October which contained a blistering attack on Bevin's foreign policy and referred to the Labour leaders as playing 'the shabby and shameful part of MacDonaldites', Hugh Dalton wrote to Morgan Phillips 'I feel we cannot, much longer, avoid dealing with Zilliacus as we did with Platts-Mills. What do you think? Have we got a dossier on him?'[9] Phillips, of course, did have a bulky file on the activities of Zilliacus and several other Labour MPs which he called his 'Lost Sheep' file, and he continued to add to it.

On 29 January 1949, Zilliacus appeared at the Palais de Justice in Paris to give evidence in the case of Kravchenko versus Sim Thomas-Morgan – *Les Lettres*

Françaises. Victor Kravchenko had been a Soviet trade official working in the USA when he had defected to the Americans in April 1944. In the following year he had published an autobiography, deeply critical of the Soviet Union, under the title *I Chose Freedom.* In November 1947 a review of Kravchenko's auto-biography by Claude Morgan appeared in the Communist weekly *Les Lettres Françaises.* The reviewer accused the writer of anti-Soviet bias and claimed to have information from a certain Sim Thomas that the book had been ghosted by someone working for American Intelligence. American Communists had made similar charges against the book but Kravchenko had ignored these and openly declared, both before and during the Paris trial, that he had decided to launch a libel action in France because here was a Communist Party that mattered. Kravchenko never denied that he intended the case to be a political operation. The French Communist Party responded to the challenge by lining up a number of Communists and fellow travellers to give evidence, and some witnesses were flown in from the USSR.

Zilliacus volunteered to appear as a witness on behalf of the defence and his offer was accepted. He explained his reason for appearing:

> I consider that this book forms part of the infamous propaganda which is being spread everywhere throughout the Western world in order to make people believe in the necessity of waging a third world war.[10]

Zilliacus appeared as someone who had visited the USSR on several occasions, including two meetings with Stalin, and who had studied Soviet affairs for many years. In his evidence he challenged Kravchenko on three main points: Zilliacus defended the collectivisation of agriculture as being necessary on economic grounds, he argued that the purges of the 1930s had rooted out a potential fifth column in the Soviet Union, and he maintained that the Nazi-Soviet Pact had been used by Stalin to strengthen Soviet defences.[11]

Much of the trial was concerned with the existence or otherwise of forced labour camps in the Soviet Union. Perhaps the most impressive witnesses for Kravchenko were people who had experienced life in the gulag. Zilliacus was not involved in this particular controversy. He was not asked any questions on the topic by either the plaintiff or the defendants. He knew that forced labour camps did exist in the USSR, never attempted to justify their existence, and looked forward to the time when they were wound up.[12]

When questioned about civil liberties in the USSR he replied:

> It is obvious that the conception of civil liberties in Russia is not at all the same as ours. If there are still people among those present who show any surprise on hearing this, or ignore this fact, I am certainly not one of them. Frankly I believe that it will need at least another thirty years before countries where there has been a social revolution, including Soviet Russia, can accept a conception of individual liberty and rights of political mi-

norities, such as exists in our countries. This can only take place if a policy of friendship towards such countries is pursued ... If one talks of war, of intervention, it is evident that such regimes will react and mobilise. And as a result the misdeeds of the police state will increase.[13]

The Kravchenko Trial was given massive publicity across the world. It was well covered in the press and millions of cinema-goers watched newsreels of Zilliacus giving evidence at the trial. Judgement was delivered on 4 April 1949 in favour of Kravchenko, who was awarded 50,000 francs in damages.

Zilliacus was a Francophile. He spoke French like a native and loved the country, its people and its culture. He dismissed the French Socialist Party as a bunch of 'MacDonaldites'– he had never forgiven Leon Blum for withholding French support from the Spanish Republic in the 1930s – and he believed that the powerful French Communist Party, with its magnificent Resistance record, was the authentic voice of the French working class. Furthermore, he saw the French Communist Party as the spearhead of a growing peace campaign in France which was drawing considerable support from outside its own ranks.[14] This development had a great appeal to Zilliacus who was always attracted to Popular Front movements. In April Zilliacus was back in Paris attending the World Congress of the Partisans of Peace held in the Salle Playel. The French, Italian and Soviet delegations were the strongest of the groups from fifty-nine countries represented there. It was for this Congress that Picasso painted his famous Dove of Peace. The Congress was presided over by Professor Frederic Joliot-Curie, and Zilliacus was elected to the organisation's International Committee.[15]

Zilliacus explained his reasons for attending the Congress:

> At the Paris Congress it was reasonable to hope that the Partisans of Peace would develop into a broadly based peace movement, a forum for those in both world camps who wanted peace and understood that we could get peace only through negotiation and mutual concessions resulting in a live-and-let-live agreement between the Capitalist democracies and the People's democracies.[16]

The Congress concluded with a mass rally at the Buffalo Stadium at which Zilliacus was one of the principal speakers. In his speech he said he regretted that the Labour Party had chosen not to be represented at the Congress, he described Churchill as the 'spiritual father of the Atlantic Pact', and proclaimed that 'the workers of Britain will not fight or be dragged into fighting against the Soviet Union'.[17]

Paul Robeson also attended the Congress, where he spoke and sang. Robeson and Zilliacus had met in London in the 1930s and got on well together, as well as sharing a similar political outlook. Robeson was planning his programme of free 'workers' concerts' in Britain and Zilliacus invited him to visit Gateshead. Robeson therefore agreed to launch his tour at Gateshead and then move on to give concerts in Liverpool, Manchester, Sheffield and Clydebank.[18]

Paul Robeson arrived at Newcastle Central Station at midday on Friday 6 May 1949, where he was met by Zilliacus, who escorted him to the Bensham Cinema in Gateshead. The concert was free and many people were turned away. Robeson's repertoire included such old favourites as 'Water Boy', 'Old Man River', 'Swing Low Sweet Chariot', and the Canoe Song from the film *Sanders of the River.* Robeson and Zilliacus then had tea at the home of Kit Esther, Chairman of the Gateshead Labour Party and Trades Council. After this, Robeson attended an informal service at St John's Church, Sheriff's Hill, where he gave a recital of Negro spirituals. He ended the day by giving an evening concert to an audience of two thousand people at the Gateshead Town Hall.[19]

The 'Lost Sheep' of the 1945-50 Parliament

John Platts-Mills

Konni Zilliacus

Leslie Solley

Lester Hutchinson

Chapter 20

The Lost Sheep

In October 1948 the Boundary Commissioners divided the existing constituency of Gateshead into two constituencies: Gateshead East and Gateshead West, and on 3 December of the same year, in preparation for the next election, Zilliacus was unanimously selected by the newly formed Gateshead East Constituency Labour Party as its candidate. Gateshead East was the first to hold its selection meeting and hence Zilliacus accepted its nomination. The feeling in the local party was that Zilliacus would have won the nomination of the Gateshead West constituency if he had so desired.[1] In the event, John Hall, a colliery engine driver, was chosen as the Labour candidate for Gateshead West at the subsequent selection meeting. Both of the newly created constituencies were safe Labour seats and Zilliacus and Hall could look forward to being returned as MPs at the forthcoming election.

After the selection of a candidate at constituency level the procedure was for the candidate's name to be put before the NEC's Election Sub-Committee which would make a recommendation to the NEC. Normally, approval would follow as a matter of course. This did not happen when Zilliacus's name was forwarded to Transport House. The Election Sub-Committee decided to defer making a decision and sent Zilliacus a letter asking him to appear before the Committee on 17 January 1949. Attached to the letter was a 'charge sheet', which began by stating:

> Over the last three years, Mr Zilliacus's speeches and writings have for the most part taken the form of violent attacks on the Labour Government's foreign policy. He is recognised in Cominform literature as the leading British exponent of left wing Socialists whose substantial agreement with Cominform policies ultimately lead them into complete agreement with the Communists.[2]

It went on to quote from various speeches Zilliacus had made since 1946, to provide copies of the relevant correspondence on the Nenni Telegram incident and Zilliacus's correspondence with James Griffiths concerning his attendance at the Warsaw International Socialist Conference, to list Zilliacus's speaking engagements to organisations proscribed by the Labour Party, and, finally, details of his recent visits to Czechoslovakia and Yugoslavia.

Before the scheduled meeting with the Election Sub-Committee, Zilliacus responded to the charge sheet in writing.[3] He dismissed the charge that alleged he followed Cominform policies on the grounds that he was unfamiliar with Cominform literature. However he admitted that the main charge that he had opposed the Government's foreign policy was 'a true bill'. Zilliacus stated that Bevin had abandoned socialist principles and so he had to oppose it. Moreover:

> I hold it is my prime duty as a Member of Parliament to stick to the foreign policy statements and pledges on which I fought the general election and to do all I can to secure compliance with those pledges.

He explained his attitude towards Communism. He pointed out that over the years he had never been uncritical of Communist policies, however he believed that the split between Communists and Social Democrats in the 1920s and 1930s had been disastrous, and in Britain he had always argued that the Communist Party should dissolve itself, and its members join the Labour Party. The situation in France and Italy, he argued, was 'fundamentally different and we must accept the facts of the situation and pin our faith to the traditions of European liberalism and democracy, and the political maturity of the peoples of Europe, as contrasted with Russia, gradually transforming Communism from within'. For this to happen, he went on, Europe needed a period of peace, increased trade between East and West, and 'some measure of working class solidarity'.

He argued that he had never knowingly spoken to any organisation on the Labour Party's proscribed list, some of those quoted had not been proscribed when he had addressed them. He said that the press had misrepresented aspects of his visit to the Warsaw conference, and he had attended one social function there because it would have been discourteous to have refused the invitation. Why mention his visits to Czechoslovakia and Yugoslavia, he wanted to know, and not refer to his visits to Sweden, Denmark and the USA? In any case, he had visited Czechoslovakia for medical treatment and had travelled to Yugoslavia in order to interview Tito.

He concluded:

> I know I must appear an awkward and self-righteous sort of beggar. But I don't do it for fun. As I see it, this is the fight for peace that I have been waging for most of my life and that has long become inseparable from Socialism and world government. I don't want to fight our side – apart from sentiment, after thirty years in the Labour Party, which is more than a party, I don't believe there is any other political instrument that can do the job. I want to fight the Tories. But in foreign affairs as things are, it is almost impossible to go for the Tories without having a slam at our leaders … But I hope that in the light of this memorandum and after the meeting the Committee may feel reassured and able to report accordingly to the NEC.

The proceedings began on 17 January 1949. Zilliacus was asked if he had anything more to say. He said that he had three points he would like to make. First, he reminded the Committee of his thirty years of service with the Labour

Party and emphasised his loyalty to the Party. Second, he asked the Committee whether it seriously thought he was taking orders from the Communists. Third, he stated that the reasons he opposed the Government's foreign policy was because he 'sincerely and wholeheartedly' believed that Labour had abandoned its election pledges.

There followed what Zilliacus described as 'a confused discussion' in which the Committee conceded his constitutional right as a Member of Parliament to put forward his views; however, because the Party's Annual Conference had overwhelmingly endorsed Bevin's policy he should tone down his attacks on government policy.

Finally, Mr Attlee intervened, and after some exchanges with Zilliacus he said: 'You are just like the old ILP. You claim the right to run your own policy inside the Party'.

To which Zilliacus replied: 'I am standing by my election pledges'.

Attlee left early to attend another meeting and after he had gone the Committee voted unanimously by 9-0 to recommend that Zilliacus's candidature be endorsed.[4]

Zilliacus was warned that the real fight would take place in the NEC, where his enemies were Clement Attlee, Herbert Morrison and Sam Watson.

According to Zilliacus:

Mr Attlee was bent on getting me out because Mr Bevin didn't want me in the Party and had mobilised the trade union bloc. He was supported by Mr Morrison, who believes in boss rule, and wants to appease the middle class and reassure the Tories by cowing and purging the Left in the Labour Party ... To this was added Mr Sam Watson's personal hostility.[5]

Sam Watson was Secretary of the Durham Miners and the elected nominee of the National Union of Mineworkers on the Labour Party's NEC. He was small in stature, with twinkling eyes and a ready smile. At the age of fifty-one his red hair was thinning and brushed straight back. He was not a great platform orator but he had the power to hold the attention of an audience by the force of his personality, for above all Sam Watson had gravitas. At his home in the city of Durham he had a library of over 2,000 books: he was well read and widely travelled. He was famous for his 'Bible classes': these were adult educational classes he ran on Sunday mornings at Red Hills, the miners' headquarters in Durham. Watson would often lecture on economics or politics, and sometimes he would invite 'big names' to address his classes of young trade unionists. In the 1930s Sam Watson had been on the Left of the Labour Movement, a supporter of Popular Front politics and an active member of the Left Book Club. The Nazi-Soviet Pact of 1939, followed by the Soviet Union's attack on Finland, made him critical of the USSR, and in the 1940s he became increasingly anti-Communist in his views. He was a staunch supporter of Bevin's foreign policy.[6]

Sam Watson made a bad enemy and Zilliacus had rubbed him up the wrong way. The cause of the rift between the two men began when Zilliacus took up the grievances of a group of miners who lived in his constituency, and wrote to the National Coal Board on their behalf. Watson challenged Zilliacus's right to do this without the consent of the NUM. Zilliacus, in his correspondence with Watson acknowledged that he should have consulted the NUM before he acted, but he resented Watson telling him that he was 'not allowed' to deal with the concerns of his constituents without first obtaining the permission of an outside body. Zilliacus threatened that if Watson made such a claim publicly he would report him to the Speaker of the House of Commons for breach of privilege. Hugh Dalton, who represented a Durham mining constituency, was not noted for his tact but he always treated Watson with the utmost respect, as did most people in the area. Zilliacus, however, in his own words had 'refused to kiss the rod'. The spat between the two men was smoothed over, but Zilliacus always believed that Watson continued to harbour a grudge against him and 'He has never, indeed, abandoned what seems to me the extraordinarily dangerous claim that Labour MPs are the mere tools and agents of the Party and must conform to the decisions of Party Conferences and of the National Executive'.[7]

Zilliacus's patron of his early years, Josiah Wedgwood, would have approved of this statement, but, then, Wedgwood was a Liberal MP who had joined the Labour Party in 1919, where he had found Labour Party discipline 'more irksome than the easier control of the Liberals'.[8] Wedgwood, in an echo of Edmund Burke, believed that an MP should 'offer electors his judgement, his conscience and his knowledge, not simply a party label'.[9] To Ernest Bevin, who believed in the trade union practice of accepting majority decisions, and Herbert Morrison, whose experience in local government had taught him the merits of caucus rule, these liberal sentiments had little place in the Labour Party of the 1940s, especially as the Cold War was ushering in a period of political intolerance.

It was a feature of Zilliacus's clash with the Labour leadership that he enjoyed the support of his local party. From the time he started his attacks on the Government's foreign policy in 1946, Zilliacus regularly received votes of confidence from the Gateshead Labour Party. Did this mean that the Gateshead members were in wholehearted agreement with his criticism of Bevin's foreign policy? Some undoubtedly did agree with his analysis to a greater or lesser extent, but some had other reasons to support him. Alderman Mary Gunn said, after chairing a Party meeting, 'We should be proud of the fact that we have an MP who states his position honestly and clearly',[10] and at another meeting Zilliacus was loudly cheered and praised for not being a 'Yes man'.[11] Some of those who may not have agreed with his general line on foreign policy nevertheless felt he had the right to state his views, and he gave lively reports to his local party on the political situation which were very popular with members. Furthermore, Zilliacus proved to be a good constituency MP. Although he was very much an international affairs specialist, Zilliacus found that he enjoyed his constituency work. 'There is something satisfying and real about helping those in trouble – that is the direct, human, personal side of an MPs job'.[12] He was the first Gateshead MP to hold surgeries and his facility for drafting letters was put at the service of his constituents. Finally, he had a likeable personality: he was pleasant and approachable.

The first cracks in the strong local support for Zilliacus came in January 1948 when the Ravensworth lodge of the NUM, which was affiliated to the Gateshead Labour Party, passed a resolution:

> The members desire Mr Zilliacus to note that they loyally support the policy of the Labour Government and are dissatisfied with the constant attacks he is making against the Government's policy.

The Ravensworth lodge put the same motion on the agenda of the February meeting of the Gateshead Labour and Trades' Council where it was defeated by 45 votes to 5. Later in the same month Sam Watson arranged for Hector McNeill, Minister of State at the Foreign Office, to speak at Gateshead in defence of the Government's foreign policy.[13]

In the following month Watson wrote to Morgan Phillips claiming that Party organisation in Gateshead was being allowed to run down, and he observed:

> It is true that Mr Zilliacus receives the support of the majority of members who attend the Gateshead Labour and Trades' Council, but they are small in number and in my opinion by no means reflect the feeling of the majority in Gateshead.[14]

Hence, Sam Watson's attempts to chip away at Zilliacus's local support were not a great success. The Gateshead Labour Party continued to give him its backing and, as we have seen, the Gateshead East Labour Party unanimously selected him as its candidate to fight the 1950 general election. However Zilliacus's support in the Parliamentary Labour Party and in the wider Labour Movement had diminished to the extent that the Labour leadership now felt strong enough to deal with him as it had dealt with Platts-Mills the year before. This was the position when the NEC met in Transport House on 23 February 1949 to consider whether to endorse Zilliacus's candidature as recommended by the Election Sub-Committee.

The NEC, on a resolution moved by Clement Attlee and seconded by Sam Watson, decided not to endorse Zilliacus's candidature. The NEC's decision was discussed at the next meeting of the Gateshead Labour and Trades' Council, where it was held to be 'unacceptable' and it was agreed unanimously that the choice of a Labour candidate was 'purely a domestic question' for the Gateshead Labour Party to determine, and it decided to circularise all constituency Labour Parties, arguing that 'the action of the National Executive is dictatorial and un-

British, and unworthy of the great Labour Movement', and warning that 'the
Gateshead East Division could just as easily have been your division'.[15] The issue
of the circular was obviously an attempt to influence local parties in the run-up
to the next Labour Party Conference which was the 'final court of appeal' on
such matters.

Zilliacus had little faith that the NEC would relent or the Annual Conference
reverse the NEC's decision, and he decided he would not compromise. 'I was
pretty sure my attendance at the World Peace Conference would be thankfully
seized on as a pretext for turning me out of the Party, but I went there because it
was part of the fight for peace'.[16]

On 16 May, Zilliacus was again invited to appear before the Labour Party's
Election Sub-Committee, when the only matter to be discussed was his attendance at the World Peace Conference. Herbert Morrison was in the chair and
in summing up he said that it was not only Zilliacus's attendance at the World
Peace Conference which worried the NEC but his overall approach to Labour's
policies. It was true, Morrison went on, that the NEC had already decided not to
endorse Zilliacus's candidature, but what concerned them now was whether the
NEC ought not to exclude him from the Party. Mr Attlee added a few remarks
about it being obvious that Zilliacus's whole outlook was now out of sympathy
with that of the Party. The Sub-Committee relayed its findings to the NEC and
two days later Zilliacus was expelled from the Labour Party, subject to the approval of the Party's Annual Conference.[17]

The Annual Conference opened at the Blackpool Winter Gardens on 6 June
1949. The day before the NEC had held its pre-Conference meeting and Harold
Laski, who had indicated to his fellow NEC members that he wanted to speak
on Zilliacus's behalf, was told that as a member of the NEC he must accept the
principle of collective responsibility. Laski, therefore, was not allowed to speak
in the debate,[18] and it was also decided by the Conference that Zilliacus would
not be allowed to speak in his own defence.[19] Zilliacus sat with Leslie Solley in
the gallery, looking down on the Conference delegates below. Solley was the
Labour MP for Thurrock and a barrister who practised at the Common Law Bar.
Like Zilliacus he had been critical of the Labour Government's foreign policy,
especially the use of British troops in Greece, and the NEC had decided to expel
him along with Zilliacus. Although Solley's expulsion was on the Conference
agenda, he was not such a colourful personality as Zilliacus and hence his case
was inclined to be overlooked by the press.

Those who spoke in support of Zilliacus tended to emphasise the right of
free speech to those inside the Party. Geoffrey Bing MP stated that no matter
what Zilliacus's position was he would uphold his right as an MP to speak his
mind. T. G. Healey, the delegate from Streatham CLP, saw the issue of Zilliacus's
expulsion as 'the right to speak, to differ, and to have their opinions democrati-
cally discussed without fear of expulsion and fear of threats'. N. Whine, from St

Marylebone CLP, said that Zilliacus was a member of his constituency party and its members knew him very well and 'they are convinced that Mr Zilliacus is a man of the greatest integrity, one of the most honest members in the Labour Party, who has never at any time hidden his views on foreign policy, and who has always been accepted inside the Labour Party as a free critic of the Government'. Harold Davies MP believed that 'there is seeping into our Party the fear of criticism'; Sydney Silverman MP argued 'if the Party expels Zilliacus for exercising the right of dissent, we shall be doing damage to the cause of social democracy;' and Benn Levy stated that the only grounds for expulsion would be if Zilliacus was either a Communist or a Tory, and he was neither, 'his expulsion is part of the NEC's heresy hunt'.

Support for the NEC came mainly from the trade union wing. Arthur Deakin of the Transport and General Workers' Union and Ernest Popplewell, an MP sponsored by the National Union of Railwaymen, saw the main issue as one of accepting majority decisions, while Will Nally MP, of the Co-operative Party, accused Zilliacus of 'always siding with the Soviet Union'. J.W. Besford of the NUM believed 'the action of expelling Mr Zilliacus is long overdue'. Paul Cowen, who was a member of the Gateshead's Ravensworth lodge of the NUM, struck a wrong note when he said: 'All of us hold in our hands *Labour Believes in Britain*. I wonder if we also believe in Britain? Can't we get an Englishman into the House of Commons?' This statement was met with boos and catcalls from all sides of the hall.

Sam Watson wound up the debate on behalf of the NEC:

> There is no other way of running a democratic organisation like the British Labour Party than by deciding our policy after full discussion in Annual Conference ... Mr Zilliacus and Mr Solley were expelled by the Executive because they had persistently and consistently opposed the policy of the Party in relation to foreign affairs as decided by Annual Conference.

The decision to expel Zilliacus and Solley was approved by 4,711,000 votes to 714,000.

Two months after the expulsion of Zilliacus and Solley, Lester Hutchinson, the Labour MP for the Rusholme division of Manchester, was expelled from the Party, joining the small flock of 'lost sheep' in the 1945-50 Parliament. Hutchinson had been educated at the Universities of Neuchatel and Edinburgh. He had worked as a journalist in Germany and India during the inter-war years, and while in India had been imprisoned for helping to organise a trade union for Indian workers. He had spent the first two years of the war working as a temporary civil servant and had then volunteered for the Royal Navy, where he had served on an anti-submarine trawler. Like the other expelled Labour MPs he had been an outspoken critic of Bevin's foreign policy, and this included touring the USA speaking in support of Henry Wallace, the Progressive Party's presidential candidate in 1948. His Rusholme constituency was destined to disappear in boundary changes in the 1950 general election, but in 1949 he had been selected for the newly created constituency of Middleton and Prestwich. The NEC, however, had refused to endorse his candidature and then proceeded to expel him from the Labour Party.[20] It is likely he would have been included in the cull along with Zilliacus and Solley if he had not been on a speaking tour of the USA at the time of their expulsion.

The four expelled MPs teamed up with D. N. Pritt, who had been expelled from the Labour Party back in 1940 over his support for the Soviet invasion of Finland. Pritt had held his seat in the 1945 general election, standing as a Labour Independent. The five MPs called themselves the Labour Independent group in the House of Commons but they were never a closely-knit team. They often ate together in the House of Commons dining room, and sometimes met for dinner at Zilliacus's house in Abbey Road where, although they exchanged the latest political gossip, there was little discussion of policy or tactics.[21] Nevertheless they continued to harry the Government in the Commons, criticising Bevin's foreign policy, calling for friendship with the Soviet Union, cuts in defence expenditure, and an increase in East-West trade. But their efforts were like those of gadflies stinging the rump of a horse, irritating ministers without doing the Labour Government any serious harm.[22]

Zilliacus broke with the group in the autumn of 1949, and the breach occurred over Yugoslavia. Pritt, Platts-Mills, Solley and Hutchinson supported the Soviet criticism of Tito, whereas Zilliacus found the Cominform's anti-Tito campaign, then reaching its peak, totally unacceptable and, as described earlier, he spoke out against it and fought Pritt, Platts-Mills and their Stalinist allies for control of the British-Yugoslav Association. As the general election approached the Independent Labour group published a manifesto on which the four members intended to fight the election. Zilliacus drew up his own for the coming contest in Gateshead.

Chapter 21

Crusade for Peace

Zilliacus hoped the Gateshead East Labour Party would not adopt an official Labour candidate and thereby give him a free run against his Conservative opponent. After his expulsion he wrote a letter to the local party which he asked to be read out at the next party meeting:

> I, for my part, will do nothing to split the Party and would regard it as a calamity if it did split. That is why I do not ask any of you to come and help me. That is why, too, I hope some of you will not try to put up a candidate against me.[1]

There was certainly strong support for this move in the Gateshead East Labour Party, for when the NEC instructed them to set in motion the procedure for the selection of a Labour candidate, they stalled for a couple of months until the National Agent insisted that the matter be dealt with as soon as possible. Whereupon Kit Esther, the Chairman of the local party, resigned his chairmanship and announced he would campaign for Zilliacus at the next general election. Esther was fifty-five years of age and a full-time official of the Confederation of Health Service Employees. He had been a member of the Gateshead Borough Council since 1938 and was prominent in its affairs. His lead was followed by two other councillors, a member of the local party's executive committee, and several rank-and-file Labour Party members. All those who announced they would support Zilliacus were automatically expelled from the Labour Party.

Up to this point the Gateshead East Labour Party had been broadly supportive of Zilliacus. This now began to change. The anti-Zilliacus faction in the local party grew stronger, and even those members who remained sympathetic felt the pull of loyalty to the party they had served for many years. Attitudes began to harden against Zilliacus and those who followed him into the political wilderness. When Esther's daughter used the address of her council flat to appeal for funds to help finance Zilliacus's campaign, the Gateshead Council said that she had infringed housing regulations and ordered her eviction. She took the Council to court and the court blocked the eviction order. Kit Esther was removed from membership of all his committees on the Gateshead Council, and Zilliacus was informed that he would no longer have free use of the Town Hall.[2]

Ten per cent of Gateshead's electors were Roman Catholic, the descendants of Irish immigrants who had come to the town in the nineteenth century in search of work, and most were Labour voters. Although Zilliacus was an agnostic he did his best to serve all his constituents regardless of creed, and he tried to keep on good terms with the local clergy of all denominations. However he was aware that the charge of 'Communist' being levelled against him was undermining his position with some of his constituents and he determined to counter it. At the World Peace Conference in Paris he had met the Abbé Boulier, the Professor of International Relations at the Catholic Institute of Paris. The Abbé, dressed in his black cassock, had cut an impressive figure and Zilliacus had invited him to speak at Gateshead. The priest had accepted the offer and the meeting was duly held at the Gateshead Town Hall on the evening of Friday 17 June 1949.[3]

The Abbé was billed to speak on the topic 'Peace and Christianity'. He gave his lecture in French, with Zilliacus, who chaired the meeting, acting as interpreter. In his talk he began by saying that he was not a Communist or a fellow-traveller, although he had some points in common with the Communists and was a fellow traveller in the cause of peace. He went on to say that he believed it was the duty of the West to make peace with Soviet Russia and he denounced what he described as 'the sort of holy war which is being waged against Communism, especially in the religious press'. He described the Atlantic Pact as 'a potential menace to peace' because 'we have been handed over, bound hand and foot, to the Americans. It is an arrangement for going to war at the drop of a hat without giving UNO a chance to consider the matter.'

At question time, Father Higgins, the local parish priest who attended the meeting, supported by a couple of dozen of his parishioners asked: 'Is it not a fact that you are under an interdiction by the Bishop of Paris for your Communist tendencies?'

The Abbé replied that this was not true, although on several occasions individual bishops had asked him not to speak in their dioceses and he had respected their wishes.

Father Higgins then asked whether Boulier had been expelled by his own bishop and forbidden to say mass in his own parish. The Abbé admitted this was the case because he had 'refused to subscribe to his superiors' "Vichy-Petain" sympathies'.

When Father Higgins rose to ask a third question there were cries of protest from other members of the audience who said they were being denied the chance to ask questions.

Zilliacus appealed to Father Higgins: 'May I suggest that you discuss this at length privately with Father Boulier?' But the Gateshead priest was not to be put off:

'Father Boulier is advertised as being a Professor of International Relations at the Catholic Institute of Paris. Today I have been in touch with the Institute who tell me that Father Boulier is under suspension.'

Father Boulier confirmed he had been suspended from his academic post after his attendance at the World Peace Conference in Paris, but he remained a priest of the Roman Catholic Church, and he handed his celebret to Zilliacus who rue-fully observed: 'This defeats me because it is in Latin but I understand that this document accredits Father Boulier as a priest.'

'I am a priest', affirmed Boulier.

There were shouts from the audience of 'He is not a priest' and 'He is not a Catholic', with counter cries of 'Let him speak'.

Zilliacus struggled to restore order and there was a welcome burst of laughter when some wag in the audience asked: ' Does Mr Zilliacus's appearance on a plat-form with a Catholic priest mean that he has been converted to Christianity?'

After the meeting the Abbé said to reporters, 'This is my first meeting in England and it has been strenuous', adding with a smile, 'and stormy'.

Zilliacus launched his 'Crusade for Peace', as he called his campaign, to an enthusiastic audience of over 650 people in the Gateshead Town Hall on 8 September 1949, with Kit Esther in the chair. Zilliacus said that he was fighting for the right of constituency parties to select their candidates for Parliament on the conditions laid down in the Party's constitution without having their choice dictated to them by the NEC's abuse of its right to refuse endorsement.

> 'It is the duty of a Member to keep faith with those who sent him to Parliament by speaking his mind on great issues according to his conscience and judgement in the light of his election pledges, even if that means disagreeing with his Party leaders'.

Zilliacus said he would continue to fight for a socialist foreign policy:

> 'It is mainly because I realise that the drift to war is wholly unnecessary and know how peace could be made by a foreign policy similar to that for which the Labour Party received a mandate in 1945 that I am waging this campaign and shall at the general election stand as a Labour Independent candidate in Gateshead East ... A campaign that will not only have national but international repercussions, that will be not only a campaign but a crusade'.[4]

As part of his preparations for the coming general election, Zilliacus wrote to George Bernard Shaw asking his permission to quote from the letter Shaw had written to the *New Statesman and Nation* in November 1946, and asking for Shaw's endorsement.[5] Shaw wrote back:

> The very worst mistake the Labour Party made in forming its Cabinet was not to make you Foreign Secretary and Ernest Bevin Home Secretary. Nobody else in the Party had the international outlook that there is such a place as Europe. Your book on the League of Nations made you the leading authority on foreign affairs from the supernational point of view. Never was there a more obvious choice.[6]

Shaw went on to criticise the Labour Government's foreign policy accusing it of 'declaring that everything must give way to the supreme necessity of a Jingo war on Russia', and concluding:

> It is for Gateshead to come to the rescue by returning you to the House of Commons with an unequivocal and overwhelming majority. The issue is clear between Jingo Trade Unionism (Bevinism) and a Democratic Socialism on Fabian lines of which you are by far the most instructive champion. Gateshead can change for the worse only, and can win the leadership of democratic public opinion in the country by supporting you. A vote for you is a vote against another war.

In November, Zilliacus visited Shaw at Ayot Saint Lawrence, where the two men talked over old times and discussed the current political situation.[7]

Zilliacus had a letter published in the *New Statesman and Nation* appealing for funds, and as well as contributions from supporters in Britain he received money from people in Canada, Mexico, Switzerland and the USA. The total amount, however, was not large and the main cost of Zilliacus's campaign was met from his own pocket.

In another move Zilliacus placed an advert in the *New Statesman and Nation* as follows:

> General Election. Capable whole-time campaign organiser wanted to help hold Gateshead for Socialism and peace. Reply K. Zilliacus, House of Commons, giving qualifications, references and terms. [8]

And after sifting through the applications and carrying out some interviews he appointed Russell Kerr. The twenty-eight year old Kerr was born in Australia and had first come to Britain in 1942 as an officer in the Royal Australian Air Force. For the reminder of the war he served as a navigator flying Lancaster bombers, and became a member of Bomber Command's Pathfinder Force. In the 1945 general election he had assisted Ian Mikado's election campaign in Reading, before returning to Australia. He came back to Britain in 1948, where he read about Zilliacus in the newspapers and sympathised with his stand. When he saw the advertisement in the *New Statesman and Nation* he decided to apply for the job. Kerr was full of drive and energy, and as an Australian was a good 'mixer', this together with his fine war record meant he had little difficulty in fitting into Zilliacus's election team at Gateshead.[9]

In October 1949, Zilliacus's book *I Choose Peace* was published as a Penguin Special, conveniently timed to feed into his 'Crusade for Peace'. The book was a substantial paperback of 509 pages, and was described by one reviewer as 'the fattest Penguin ever to waddle on the bookshelves'.[10] The book had been commissioned thirteen months earlier, when it had originally been titled *The Price of Peace – Inquest on the Labour Government's Foreign Policy and the Case for a Socialist Policy*[11] but in an obvious echo of Kravchenko's *I Choose Freedom*, it had been given the sharper title of *I Choose Peace*.

In his new book Zilliacus brought together the views on foreign policy he had expounded as 'Vigilantes' plus his more up-to-date criticism of post-war British and American foreign policy. Ernest Bevin was shown as continuing Winston Churchill's war-time suspicion of Soviet aims, with Britain bridging the gap until the USA was prepared to take over the main burden of 'containing' the Soviet Union or, as Zilliacus saw it, attempting to check the forces of social revolution then sweeping the world.

In *I Choose Peace* one historian has credited Zilliacus with writing one of the first 'revisionist' histories of the Cold War, in which the Cold War begins with Allied intervention in Russia in 1918, and continues with the isolation of the Soviet Union in the 1920s, followed by the appeasement of the fascist powers in the 1930s. The 'Grand Alliance' of 1941-45 provided a brief interlude of cooperation in the joint struggle against Hitler, with a return to Cold War policies by the West in the closing stages of the Second World War.[12]

On matters of immediate policy, Zilliacus advocated British withdrawal from NATO, followed by the opening of direct negotiations with the Soviet Union in order to reach a settlement of their differences. He argued for closer links between Western Socialist and Communist parties, and he believed that many Communists in Eastern Europe were potential Titoists who wanted to build Socialism in their own way. However, the Cold War needed to be relaxed if they were to acquire greater influence in their own countries.

Most reviewers found the book interesting, although too inclined to give the Soviet Union the benefit of every doubt while base motives were attributed to almost every action undertaken by British and American governments. One reviewer summed up for many when he said Zilliacus's book 'compels attention if not agreement'.[13]

In October 1949, the Gateshead East Labour Party adopted Arthur S. Moody as the new Labour candidate. Moody, a former joiner, was sponsored by the Amalgamated Society of Woodworkers. He was a member of Labour's NEC and the sitting Member for the Fairfield Division of Liverpool, although the constituency was to disappear in 1950 as a result of boundary changes. The fifty-nine year old, snowy-haired Moody lacked charisma, nevertheless he was shrewd and experienced. After his selection he said his main concern was with the bread and butter issues affecting the people of Gateshead, adding 'I am not interested in the problems of the Volga boatmen or how long it takes a slow boat to reach China'.[14]

When Prime Minister Attlee announced on 11 January 1950 that Parliament would be dissolved on 3 February, with polling to take place on 23 February, Zilliacus was ready for the contest. Nominations for Gateshead East were completed on 11 February and, in addition to Arthur Moody as the Labour candidate, Zilliacus faced Douglas Clift, a solicitor standing as a Conservative and

National Liberal. Moody forecast he would win the seat with a small majority and Clift hoped the Labour vote would divide between Zilliacus and Moody in such a way that he could come through the middle and win. Zilliacus knew he faced the well-organised machines of the two parties and that the odds were not in his favour, nevertheless he was determined to go down fighting.

In his election address Zilliacus had the endorsement of J.B. Priestley as well as Bernard Shaw. He argued that peace was in jeopardy and Britain, the USA and the Soviet Union must resolve their differences through the United Nations, and he pointed out that he had stuck to his election pledges of 1945. Arthur Moody used the slogan 'Britain for the British' in his election address, and six members of the Labour Party protested that this was a Fascist slogan used by Oswald Mosley in the 1930s. Moody retorted that it had been used even earlier by the socialist pioneer, Robert Blatchford, to mean that Britain should belong to the British people and he refused to withdraw it. It was reported that Sam Watson, who had been looking forward to delivering a 'counterblast to Zilliacus's views on foreign policy', had caught influenza and would be unable to speak in support of Moody.[15] Moody usually described Zilliacus as a blackleg, and there was a whispering campaign on the doorstep against Zilliacus, alleging that he had Communist sympathies. Zilliacus, however, did not enjoy the assistance of the Communist Party during the election – his championing of Tito made sure of that – and local Communist Party members were engaged in supporting the three Communist candidates contesting seats in North-East England. Zilliacus's campaign team included many people who did not normally engage in electioneering but were attracted by his 'Crusade for Peace'.[16] Most were left-wing socialists who were not members of the Labour Party, and a party of duffel-coated students from Sheffield University were also active in support of Zilliacus.

The 1950 general election was dominated by domestic issues and foreign affairs played little part in the national campaigns of the major parties.[17] The Conservatives broadly supported Bevin's foreign policy and there was therefore little scope for disagreement between the Labour and Conservative leaders on international affairs. However, in an election broadcast, Churchill said he favoured the holding of 'top-level talks' in an attempt to ease international tension. A delighted Zilliacus said he welcomed Churchill's statement, adding 'I have been saying this for the past two years. Is Churchill now fellow-travelling with me?'[18]

The intrusion of foreign affairs into the national election campaign was short-lived, and the major parties were soon back to debating issues such as full employment, nationalisation, housing, taxation and rationing. Zilliacus's emphasis on foreign policy in his own election campaign, therefore, went against the national trend.

In what was regarded by many as the rather dull national campaigns conducted by the major parties, Zilliacus's 'Crusade for Peace' raised more than its fair share of press attention. The special election correspondent of the *Northern Echo* thought that Zilliacus's campaign:

> will show whether there is still room in the British party political system for the individualist, the rebel and the crank; moreover whether lost causes and romantic adventurers still attract public sympathy, and, finally, whether it is still possible to appeal to the electorate on moral principles rather than the bread and butter politics.[19]

And Aylmer Vallance, Assistant Editor of the *New Statesman and Nation,* observed:

> He will have against him at Gateshead the mobilised opposition of the Catholic Church and the vitriolic enmity (ci-devant Leftist) of the President [sic] of the Durham Miners. If he is beaten, it will be a defeat for something that is worthwhile in internationally minded British Socialism.[20]

Polling took place on Thursday 23 February in mild weather for the time of year, and the result, declared after midnight, was:

Arthur S. Moody (Labour)	15,249
Douglas Clift (Conservative and National Liberal)	13,530
Konni Zilliacus (Labour Independent)	5,001
Labour majority	1,719

When all the results were announced over the next two days it emerged that the Labour Party had won 315 seats and the Conservatives and their Allies 298. The Liberals had been reduced to nine seats, and the Communist Party had lost its two Members. The Irish Nationalists had elected two Members in Northern Ireland constituencies. The Labour Government would be able to continue in office with an overall majority of six seats. 'An outstanding feature of the election was the way in which the electorate ruthlessly crushed minority parties and groups in an effort to concentrate on one or other of the two main parties'.[21]

There was no room for Independent MPs in the newly elected House of Commons and Zilliacus's colleagues in the Independent Labour group of expelled Labour MPs all lost their seats. Platts-Mills, Pritt and Solley were able to devote themselves to their law practices, which they did with some success, and Lester Hutchinson took a teaching post at a private school. At the age of fifty-five with no job and little money Zilliacus's prospects looked bleak.

Tito welcomes Zilliacus to Belgrade, September 1949

Zilliacus family holiday, Briani, April 1950. Left to right: Dawn Harris, Laurie Harris, Konni, Linden, Jan and Joe Zilliacus, with Tito's dog, Tigar

Chapter 22

Tito and Slansky

In March 1950, Zilliacus and his family were invited by Tito to spend a holiday with him on the island of Brioni. In the days of the Habsburg Empire this small island off the Adriatic coast had been privately owned by an Austrian aristocrat, who had built himself a summer residence there. After the First World War Brioni had become a popular Italian tourist resort, and the island had been occupied by the Germans during the Second World War. Brioni had been ceded to Yugoslavia in 1945 and Tito used it as a presidential retreat. The island had first-class facilities for swimming, horse riding and tennis, and the Zilliacus family was grateful for Tito's invitation.

The years 1948-50 had been years of considerable strain for Zilliacus. In some ways they were the most miserable years of his life, and he welcomed the chance of a break.[1] Between 1948 and 1950, as the Cold War had gathered momentum, Zilliacus had been squeezed by personal and political pressures. He had been expelled from the Labour Party after membership of thirty years during which he had rendered the Party many valuable services. Many of his former friends had turned their backs on him: some no doubt believed that he was a crypto-Communist or at least a fellow-traveller, those who knew he was not nevertheless felt he had shown poor judgement in his political career, and others held he had been disloyal to the Labour government by his constant sniping at Bevin's foreign policy.

Zilliacus also had many left-wing friends outside of the Labour Party, some of them members of the Communist Party, others sympathetic to its policies, and Zilliacus's support for Tito had opened up a rift with many of them. For example, Zilliacus and his wife, Jan, had been good friends and neighbours of Claud and Patricia Cockburn for many years, but after the Cominform-Tito break there had been a distinct cooling off on the part of the Cockburns and this had hurt Konni and Jan Zilliacus very much.

In November 1950 the rift between Zilliacus and his Communist friends widened even further when he published an open letter to the delegates of the Sheffield Peace Conference announcing his resignation from the executive of the British Peace Committee and the International Committee of the Partisans of Peace.[2] In his open letter of resignation he explained that he was the only member of the British Peace Committee who was 'not an all-in fellow traveller or a member, whether secret or open, of the British Communist Party' and he wrote that the Partisans of Peace had become 'a mere voluntary annexe of the Cominform, run by Communist parties whose only idea is to wage their side of the cold war through an alleged peace movement'. Furthermore, he had been upset, he explained, by the way in which the Partisans for Peace had accepted without question the Cominform's case against Yugoslavia and then expelled the Yugoslav Peace Committee from the organisation.

The news from the USA was also depressing. In 1947 The House Committee on Un-American Activities had started a purge of Hollywood and many of Jan Zilliacus's friends were caught up in the net over the following years.[3] Lillian Hellman was subpoenaed to appear before the Committee and escaped relatively lightly with her integrity intact, but her partner, Dashiell Hammett, served a six-month jail sentence for refusing to cooperate, and several other friends had their lives blighted by the Committee's purge of the film industry. Zilliacus had visited the USA in November 1947, when he had addressed a number of meetings and had taken part in a radio programme broadcast from New York. However when he applied to visit the country in 1949 he was denied an entry visa. Jan Zilliacus was asked to return her American passport to the US Embassy in London, which she did in all innocence, and it was over twenty years before it was reissued to her.

Zilliacus was aware that he was being kept under surveillance by the British security service: his phone was being tapped, he suspected his mail was being examined, and sometimes he was shadowed in the street. These measures did not upset him too much, for he felt he had nothing to hide and he regarded much of the business of spying as rather childish. At the same time it was not pleasant to be regarded as some kind of security risk.

Ten days after his defeat at Gateshead Zilliacus and his family set out for Yugoslavia on a much-needed holiday.[4] After their unfortunate experiences on their previous visit when they had travelled by rail through the hostile territories of Czechoslovakia and Hungary, the Zilliacus family decided to travel to Yugoslavia by plane. At Frankfurt airport, however, their take-off was delayed by a security alert, and although the German police never discovered who was responsible for scattering pieces of metal on the runway Zilliacus was convinced the action was directed at him.

The incident was not allowed to spoil the family's three-week stay on Brioni, which was enjoyed by everyone in the party. Tito usually worked in his office from early morning until lunchtime, but after this he enjoyed relaxing in the sun, reading the newspapers, chatting to his guests or playing chess, and in the evening the party usually played billiards or watched a film in Tito's private cinema.

Tito's famous German guard dog, Tigar, was, of course at the holiday home with his master. On the first morning of her stay as Tito's guest Jan Zilliacus wandered into the ante-room to Tito's office, where the Marshal sat working at his desk. At first Tigar was suspicious of Jan but she advanced towards him displaying friendliness and confidence, and the dog responded, leading her into Tito's office. When Tito saw her standing in the doorway stroking his guard dog he laughed.

'You are the only one, except myself, he has ever allowed to do that', he remarked.

Jan explained that she was the daughter of a Hollywood film director who had specialised in making animal films in the 1920s. His most popular films had featured an alsatian dog called Greatheart, and he had kept a pack of tame wolves for use in his movies. As a girl Jan had played with these animals and learned to handle them, hence she had soon won the confidence of Tigar.

A party of American senators came on a fact-finding visit to meet Tito while the Zilliacus family holidayed at Brioni, and the portly Marshal dressed in a smart white uniform decorated with gold braid and wearing a high-fronted peaked cap prepared to meet them, when he was stopped by Jan Zilliacus:

'May I give you some advice?' she proffered. 'Yes, of course,' said Tito. 'Don't wear that uniform to meet the Americans,' replied Jan. 'Why not?' 'They'll say you look like Hermann Goering,' said Jan. 'Do you think so?' 'Yes,' she replied. 'It would look much better if you wore a suit.'

Tito considered the matter for a moment, then returned to his room to change his clothes. His meeting with the senators passed off well. Yugoslavia was already the recipient of American aid and it was important to Tito that it should be continued. A successful meeting helped to ensure this.

Zilliacus was a bit shaken at his wife's bluntness but she had given Tito sound advice and the Marshal knew it. Tito had a known weakness for fancy uniforms, but he was always prepared to listen to what others had to say and this served him well. He liked Zilliacus and his feisty wife and at the end of the holiday he invited the Zilliacus family to return the following year.

Zilliacus returned from Yugoslavia with an invitation from Tito for H.N. Brailsford to visit the country later in the year.[5] Brailsford, the veteran radical and socialist journalist, had served in the Philhellenic Legion of the Greek Army in 1897, in one of its campaigns against the Turks, and after hostilities he had paid several visits to the Balkans, taking a special interest in the affairs of Macedonia. Tito wanted Brailsford to view the progress of the 'New Yugoslavia' and Zilliacus brought him the invitation and made the necessary travel arrangements.

Once back in London the problem of the shortage of money had to be faced. When Zilliacus's mother died in 1938 she had left a substantial estate to her two sons, Konni and Laurin. Konni Zilliacus , in turn, when separating from his wife Eugenia in the same year, had given her half of his personal assets and she had taken up residence in Guildford. Zilliacus had enjoyed a reasonably good salary as a League of Nations official, although with the open house he maintained in

Geneva he probably did not live within his income. He had been on a modest civil service salary during the war, and from 1945 to 1950 he had his parliamentary salary of £1,000 per annum.[6] This was not a particularly generous payment for the circumstances of the time and economies had to be observed by Zilliacus, such as travelling from Tyneside to London on an overnight sleeper after visiting his constituency, in order to avoid the cost of staying at a Newcastle hotel. Zilliacus's frequent trips abroad were largely at his own expense and the cost of secretarial and research services, in connection with his Parliamentary work, came out of his own pocket. He was a prolific writer but many of his articles were not written for money and he received no payment for their publication in left-wing journals, and several of his pamphlets were published at his own expense. He also had to finance most of his election campaign in February 1950. Therefore, after the loss of his Parliamentary income there had to be a reining-in on expenditure. The house in Abbey Road was put up for sale, and the family moved to more modest accommodation in Maida Vale. His daughter, Linden, continued to attend local state schools. Zilliacus always had a soft spot for his old school Bedales, where he had spent several happy years, and he might have considered sending Linden there if he had been able to afford the fees.

Zilliacus began work on a biography of Tito, financed by an advance payment from the publisher, Michael Joseph. The book was written with Tito's full cooperation and Zilliacus, who now spoke fluent Serbo-Croat, did his own research and conducted his own interviews. Jan took a temporary job in a sausage-making factory until she found more congenial employment on the staff of a London mental hospital. Zilliacus referred to the period 1950-55 as his 'years in the wilderness' and it was not an easy time for him or the members of his family.

In the summer of 1951 the Zilliacus family spent another holiday at Brioni as Tito's guests. This time they travelled on the Simplon Express from Paris to Belgrade. A rough draft of Zilliacus's book on Tito was packed into one of the family's suitcases and loaded aboard the train at the Gare du Lyon. However, when the suitcase was opened by Zilliacus in his hotel room in Belgrade, he found that the manuscript of his new book had been shredded. Who carried out the shredding can only be the subject of speculation, although one of the arms of the Soviet security service must be the prime suspect. It was certainly not an act of random destruction because it had been done very thoroughly and nothing else in the suitcase had been damaged or stolen. Hence Zilliacus had to begin the tedious task of re-writing the book from notes. The book was published in September 1952 as *Tito of Yugoslavia* and Zilliacus always maintained that the loss of the manuscript made it a poorer book than it otherwise would have been. With the rough draft to work on he had intended to go through it with Tito at Brioni, check out some references, and afterwards spend more time than he subsequently was able to do polishing it up for publication. In the event, the reviews were favourable: the exception being one by Randolph Churchill who thought that Zilliacus had been far too generous in his praise of Tito 'there is not a single criticism of Tito or the Yugoslav Communists. From start to finish, Mr Zilliacus is more Titoist than Tito and very much more partisan than the Partisans'.[7] A. J. P. Taylor in his review detected the same tendency to treat Tito as a hero but nevertheless considered it 'an excellent book as a picture of an individual'.[8]

Zilliacus's admiration for Tito was soon to be portrayed in a more sinister light. On 20 November 1952 the trial of Rudolf Slansky and thirteen co-defendants opened in Prague.[9] Slansky was a former Vice-Premier and General Secretary of the Communist Party of Czechoslovakia. All the accused were veteran Communists who had served in leading positions in post-war Czechoslovak governments. Eleven were Jews and were described as such by the prosecution.

The Chief prosecutor accused the defendants of being Trotskyite, Titoite, Zionist and bourgeois nationalist traitors 'in the service of the US imperialists', guilty of spying, undermining the State, damaging the economy, and weakening the unity of Czechoslovakia in order to restore capitalism and take the Republic into the imperialist camp.

So began the last of the major show trials to be held in a Communist state, and it closely followed the pattern of the Moscow show trials of the 1930s and the Rajk and Kostov trials of the 1940s. The defendants had first been interrogated, then mentally and physically tortured for over a year, and after being broken in mind and body they were then forced to memorise their lines from a carefully prepared script, followed by a series of rehearsals in preparation for the trial.

Zilliacus emerged as one of the key figures in this scenario. His fact-finding visits to Eastern Europe in 1945-48 were put forward as intelligence-gathering missions on behalf of the British secret service and the memoranda he had prepared to assist the new members of the Ministry of Foreign Affairs to carry out their duties at the United Nations appeared as instructions given to his agents in the Czechoslovak Government. The defendants, Slansky, Clementis, London, Frejka, Loebl, Margolius all testified to being Zilliacus's agents. The Labour MPs, Richard Crossman and George Wigg; the former *Daily Worker* correspondent Claud Cockburn; and, incongruously, the playwright Noel Coward, were also woven into the plot.

The accused were shown as being lifelong traitors to the Communist Movement and spies in the pay of the diabolically clever Western security services. The charges of Zionism were a thinly disguised cover for a bout of old-fashioned East European anti-Semitism directed against the Jewish defendants in the dock. Some of the accused recounted bizarre incidents. Slansky confessed he had shouted 'Long live Trotsky' in public in 1927;[10] André Simone that he had lunch with Noel Coward, 'who held an important position in the British intelligence service', in the private room of a Paris restaurant in 1939 where Coward had recruited him to serve as a British intelligence agent;[11] and Eugene Loebl described how, as Deputy Minister for Foreign Trade, he had sabotaged the Czech

economy by the export to Israel of machinery for the making of pencils.[12]
  As Zilliacus recalled:

> It was queer to read in the reports of the trial detailed confessions by people I have
> known in London and Prague to things that neither they nor I had ever done.
> What I found significant was that all of this was mixed with some of the things that
> had actually happened, but in strangely distorted forms. [13]

On 27 November 1952 the Presiding Judge pronounced the court's verdict: all
thirteen were found guilty of high treason, espionage and sabotage and eleven
were sentenced to death. Pleas for clemency were rejected and the condemned
men were hanged on 3 December 1952.
  Zilliacus was severely shaken by the conviction and execution of these innocent men, some of whom he had regarded as his friends. He condemned the
trial as a frame-up whose 'ultimate object was to brand all attempts at national
independence and democratising Communist regime as being Titoist treason,
and that this was done on directives from Stalin', and added:

> but this had in no way weakened the case for peaceful co-existence: on the contra-
> ry, these evil things were largely the products of the cold war; the forces for democ-
> racy and freedom within the Socialist camp could gather strength and ultimately
> prevail only in the context of peace, trade and friendly relations. [14]

Chapter 23

Gorton

In February 1952 Zilliacus was re-admitted to the Labour Party. The political climate in Britain had changed since his expulsion two years before. Although McCarthyism raged in the USA and an increasingly paranoiac Stalin planned more purges in the Soviet Bloc, the anti-Communist fervour of the period between the Berlin blockade and the early months of the Korean War began to wane in Britain. Curiously, the return of Winston Churchill to Downing Street in October 1951 helped to calm things down, for Churchill was anxious to demonstrate his moderation in both foreign and domestic policy.[1] Bevanism was also gathering strength inside the Labour Party, challenging the Party's right-wing leadership.[2] The charge that Zilliacus was a crypto-Communist or fellow traveller began to appear difficult to sustain in the light of the abuse he had received from Communist sources over his support for Tito. Furthermore, Tito's regime had become respectable in the eyes of the Labour leadership and a Labour Party delegation to Yugoslavia that included Zilliacus's old adversaries Morgan Phillips and Sam Watson gave a generally favourable report on its return. Indeed, Zilliacus had helped to facilitate this visit to Yugoslavia. So when Zilliacus appealed to be re-admitted to the Labour Party he was knocking at an open door and was delighted to be allowed inside again.

Zilliacus often remarked to his family 'You have no friends in politics',[3] and perhaps he can be forgiven for thinking this. Yet after his re-admission to the Labour Party he found a good friend in Stephen Swingler. Swingler was the Labour MP for Newcastle-under-Lyme and a leading Bevanite. He admired Zilliacus's deep knowledge of foreign affairs and his socialist perspective. Swingler often popped into Zilliacus's home in Maida Vale for a chat. He wanted to see Zilliacus back in the House of Commons and was prepared to do what he could to secure his return. Unfortunately, with a Conservative electoral recovery underway, safe Labour seats were at a premium and when Zilliacus did get his chance of returning to the Commons it was not due to the backing of some organisation or the influence of a particular MP but because an individual in a constituency party had chosen to nominate him. When George Willey, the Labour MP for Cleveland, died in July 1952, Zilliacus received a nomination and was shortlisted for the seat, and at the selection conference he was runner-up to Arthur Palmer, a candidate sponsored by the Co-operative Party. Palmer went on to win the seat at the subsequent by-election.

When Zilliacus got his next chance to return to Parliament it came unexpect-edly. On 15 April 1955 the new Prime Minister, Sir Anthony Eden, announced that Parliament would be dissolved on 6 May, with the election following on 26 May. Whereupon William Oldfield, the Labour MP for Manchester Gorton, declared he would not be standing at the forthcoming election. He had held Gorton with a majority of 7,948 at the 1951 general election therefore it could be regarded as a safe Labour seat.

Gorton was an industrial suburb of Manchester, although the Gorton con-stituency extended beyond the city boundaries, taking in the districts of Denton and Audenshaw. Several famous engineering firms were located in Gorton, in-cluding the former Gorton Tank, since nationalisation part of British Railways, where Harry Pollitt had served his apprenticeship as a plater, and the locomo-tive engineers Beyer Peacock, where Pollitt was employed after he had served his time. Other famous firms in the area were Hans Renold the chainmakers and Armstrong Whitworth. The Amalgamated Engineering Union was very influential in the area and a local trade union official called Hugh Scanlon was beginning to make his mark.[4]

The Gorton Labour Party had been a mainstream constituency party during the period of the Attlee Government but it had acquired a Bevanite tinge in the 1950s.[5] There were dozens of nominations for the seat and among them some-one living in Audenshaw had nominated Zilliacus. The Gorton Labour Party's Executive drew up a shortlist of five consisting of C.W. Loughlin, an organ-iser of the Union of Shop, Distributive and Allied Workers from Birmingham; Alf Morris, a school teacher from Wythenshaw; Sir Frank Soskice, a barrister who served as Solicitor-General and Attorney-General in the 1945-51 Labour Governments; his constituency of Sheffield Neepsend was being abolished in a reorganisation of boundaries and he was seeking another seat; Henry Wimbury, the Secretary of the Gorton Labour Party who had been nominated by his union the Electrical Trades Union; and Konni Zilliacus.

The selection conference was held at the Labour Party rooms in Hyde Road on Sunday evening, 30 April 1955, with seventy-four people in attendance. In his speech Zilliacus admitted he did not know the area and lacked an industrial background, however he promised that if selected he would work hard to reme-dy these defects. His main interest lay in securing world peace and he said he was very concerned at the development of nuclear weapons. He pointed out that he was not sponsored by a trade union but he promised to donate £400 a year to lo-cal party funds to match the amount normally paid by a trade union in support of one of its sponsored MPs. The selection was carried out by an exhaustive bal-lot, with the candidate gaining the lowest number of votes being eliminated after each count, until Zilliacus defeated Soskice by three votes on the final ballot.

Afterwards there were allegations that Zilliacus had 'bought the seat' by offer-ing to subscribe £400 a year to Party funds. It should be pointed out that Zilliacus was by no means well off and this sum represented a substantial proportion of his parliamentary salary. Soskice, on the other hand, was a wealthy barrister and he offered to contribute £100 a year to party funds, a much less generous offer, especially when he could have afforded to pay more, and perhaps this did influence some delegates to vote against him.[6]

Delegates can also have long memories and some of them remembered how Transport House had put great pressure on local members to select William Wedgwood Benn at a by-election for the Gorton seat back in 1937, and how four years later Benn had been created Viscount Stansgate. Sir Frank Soskice was undoubtedly perceived as the candidate favoured by Transport House and some of the older delegates remembered the Benn incident and were determined this time round to assert their independence.

There are always cross currents at work in any selection conference and these are open to conjecture. The fact that mattered was that Zilliacus had been successful at the selection conference and the next question was: would the NEC endorse his candidature? In view of Zilliacus's record this was by no means a foregone conclusion.

It was the practice at this time for the NEC to suspend its normal activities during the period of an election campaign. However some provision had to be made for the endorsement of candidates. Hence the NEC set up a special panel consisting of three NEC members to act on its behalf in respect of endorsements. This trio met, together with Sara Barker the National Agent, to consider the endorsement of late-selected candidates, such as Zilliacus.

Sara Barker immediately proposed that the panel should reject Konni Zilliacus, who had been selected for Gorton, and Ernie Roberts who had been selected for Stockport South. Ian Mikardo, who was one of the panel, asked why.[7] Whereupon Sara began leafing through two files which she had on the table in front of her, and read some passages from them, consisting of criticism Zilliacus and Roberts had made of the views and activities of certain Labour leaders.

Mikardo then reached across the table and said to Sara: 'Give me those files, I want to have a look at them'. 'Oh, no', she replied, 'you can't do that, they're private'.

Mikardo exploded. 'Don't be daft, those files are not your personal property, they're the property of the Party', and he snatched them from her hands.

He recalled:

They were an eye-opener. No MI5, no Special Branch, no George Smiley could have compiled more comprehensive dossiers. Not just press cuttings, photographs and document-references but also notes by watchers and eavesdroppers, and all sorts of tittle-tattle. I'm convinced that there was some input into them from government sources and from at least a couple of Labour Attachés at the United States Embassy who were close to some of our trade union leaders, notably Sam Watson.

Mikardo than turned to his two colleagues and said: 'I move that the candidatures of Zilliacus and Roberts be endorsed. I must tell you that if I am voted
down I shall walk out of here and announce publicly that I am resigning from
the Executive as a protest against my friends, and doubtless myself as well, being
spied on as though we were criminals, and that will make a great story to start
our election campaign'. Mikardo's motion was carried unanimously.

In his budget of April 1955 R.A. Butler, the Chancellor of the Exchequer, had
paved the way for the election by announcing a number of tax reductions, and
the new Prime Minister, Sir Anthony Eden, was still basking in the afterglow of
his diplomatic success as Foreign Secretary at the Geneva Conference, where he
had played a major role in bringing the war in Indo-China, at least temporarily,
to a halt. The electoral tide was flowing in favour of the Conservatives.[8]

Zilliacus, in any case, faced a difficult campaign, for he had had no time to get
to know his constituency or for the people of Gorton to get to know him. He did
not compromise: at his first public meeting held on 10 May in the Levenshulme
Town Hall he announced to an audience of thirty people that the theme of his
campaign would be peace, because he believed it overrode all other issues. He
was convinced that peaceful coexistence with Russia and China could be achieved
and he promised to do all he could to bring this about. He added he was no great
admirer of Anthony Eden. He had observed him close-up at Geneva in the 1930s
and had not been impressed.[9] The cover of Zilliacus's election address showed a
nuclear explosion as he warned of the dangers of nuclear war.

Zilliacus's Conservative opponent was Bruce Campbell, a barrister, who
hammered away at the improvement in the economy under the campaign slogan 'Conservative freedom works', and at Anthony Eden's wide experience in
foreign affairs. On polling day Zilliacus mustered 21,102 votes to Campbell's
20,833, giving Zilliacus a slim majority of 269 votes. The Conservative vote
had remained remarkably stable but Zilliacus polled 7,661 fewer votes than the
Labour candidate had in 1951. The result was hardly a sweeping endorsement
of Zilliacus's candidature, nevertheless it was good enough to return him to the
House of Commons.

Soon after his return to Parliament representing a Manchester constituency,
Zilliacus was invited to be one of the main speakers at a meeting held in the
Lesser Free Trade Hall organised by the Let Paul Robeson Sing Committee. Since
the 1930s Robeson had used his position as a world-famous figure to speak out
on a range of political issues, notably expressing his support for the demands of
black people seeking fairer treatment in the USA. Robeson was also an avowed
admirer of the Soviet Union and at the World Peace Congress in Paris on 2
April 1949 he had stated that black Americans would not support a war against
the Soviet Union. On his return to the USA Robeson was denounced as a trai-
tor, many of his concerts were banned, and in the summer of 1950 his passport
was withdrawn by the State Department on the grounds that 'Robeson's travel

abroad would be contrary to the best interests of the United States'.[10]

McCarthyism silenced any effective protest in the USA but a worldwide campaign, 'Let Paul Robeson Sing', was organised outside its borders. On 11 March 1956 the Committee held a mass meeting in Manchester with Will Griffiths MP, trade union leader Rowland Casasola, and Cedric Belfrage former editor of the *National Guardian*, lining up on the platform alongside Zilliacus. In his speech Zilliacus recounted his long friendship with Paul Robeson and praised the black singer's courage in speaking out in difficult times.

Robeson had recorded an address to the people of Manchester, followed by a recital of the 'Ode to Joy' from Beethoven's 9th Symphony with special lyrics written by Robeson.[11] It was a memorable occasion and the campaign continued across the world until, in June 1958, the US Supreme Court ruled that passports could not be withheld because of a citizen's 'beliefs or associations'. With his passport restored Paul Robeson did not linger in the USA and in the following month he departed for London, where he received a warm welcome from his many friends.

Zilliacus (right) with election helpers at Gorton, September 1959

Labour Party Conference, Scarborough, October 1960. Right to left:
Will Griffiths, Michael Foot, Konni Zilliacus with others

Chapter 24

Westminster and Beyond

When the new Parliament assembled in June 1955 Zilliacus was welcomed back by his left-wing friends Stephen Swingler and Harold Davies, and by Philip Noel-Baker, who no longer shared Zilliacus's views on foreign policy but was nevertheless pleased to see him return to the Commons. Among absent friends was Geoffrey Bing, who had lost his seat in the election and was soon to embark on a new career in Nkrumah's Ghana. Michael Foot, whose relationship with Zilliacus had its ups and downs over the years, was another victim of the Conservative electoral victory and was missing from the new Parliament. Outside the Commons an old friendship was revived. Claud Cockburn had left the Communist Party in 1948 and taken up residence in the Irish Republic. He earned his living by freelance journalism, and this sometimes brought him to London where he and Zilliacus met and repaired the friendship put under strain by the Stalin-Tito dispute seven years before.[1]

Much had changed in the five years that Zilliacus had been absent from the Commons. Sir Anthony Eden was now Prime Minister at the head of a Conservative Government with an overall majority of fifty-eight, and Labour in opposition was deeply divided over policy and personalities, reflected in the 'Bevanite split'. Another big change occurred later in the year when Clement Attlee resigned the Labour leadership and was replaced by Hugh Gaitskell, who defeated Aneurin Bevan and Herbert Morrison in the contest for the post. Zilliacus had voted for Bevan, a man he admired, although he was not on close personal terms with him. Bevan was never noted for his team work, yet he regarded Zilliacus as too individualistic in his approach to politics and too pro-Soviet in his views. Zilliacus was never a Bevanite; he was not invited to Bevanite meetings, and he never attended the convivial lunches for Bevanites held at Richard Crossman's house in Vincent Square. Nor was he invited to dine with the Bevanite group at the Gay Hussar in Soho. He was not even a member of the Bevanite 'second eleven', the outer fringe of Bevanite organisation, although he sometimes appeared as a panellist on *Tribune* brains trusts. In Ian Mikardo's words Zilliacus was 'sometimes among us but never totally with us'.[2] Zilliacus's friendship with Stephen Swingler and Harold Davies served as his bridge to the Bevanites, with whom he usually made common cause.

In one particular aspect of his thinking Zilliacus had moved closer to the Keep Left Group's position of the 1940s. Prior to 1948 Zilliacus had poured scorn on

the idea of a third force in world politics led by Britain and France, preferring
to see Britain and France working in partnership with the USSR as part of a
socialist Europe. By the mid-1950s this policy was obviously unrealistic, for by
this time Britain and France had moved to the right and were firmly embedded
in the Western Alliance. However, Zilliacus believed that Yugoslavia's defection
from the Soviet Bloc and Tito's subsequent role in helping to create the non-
aligned movement had opened up new possibilities: a third force was emerging
which offered an alternative to membership of one of the two power blocs facing up to each other in the Cold War. Over the next few years many people on
the left in Britain came to share Zilliacus's view that the non-aligned movement
could play a constructive role in world politics, for example by voicing its opposition to nuclear tests.[3]

Zilliacus also took a renewed interest in Sweden because of its domestic socialism and foreign policy based on neutrality. He was very proud of his Swedish
ancestry and often accepted invitations to address meetings in the country. As
Zilliacus saw it, Sweden had once been a so-called Great Power and had successfully adjusted her foreign policy to match her diminished position in the
world. He considered that a similar change would be in Britain's best interests,
although he knew there was little likelihood that any British Government would
adopt such a course: Britain's 'Great Power' complex was still too strong.[4]

Back in Parliament Zilliacus's main interest, as before, was in foreign affairs. He
continued to attack NATO, as he had done since its formation, and now wanted
to see both NATO and the Warsaw Pact dissolved. He pressed for the People's
Republic of China to be admitted to the UN, and was opposed to Franco's Spain
becoming a member of NATO. He believed that Britain spent too much on armaments and this gravely weakened her economy, and he favoured an increase
in East-West trade. He wanted to see the Suez crisis resolved through the UN,
and was strongly opposed to the Anglo-French invasion of Egypt in 1956. But
above all he was concerned at the development of nuclear weapons. To him this
was the supreme issue of the time.

Zilliacus believed that Britain's possession of nuclear weapons was largely
irrelevant in defence terms and amounted to little more than an expensive ges-
ture. He argued that Britain's abandonment of the H-bomb would give a lead
to the other nuclear powers and help to prevent the spread of nuclear weapons.
He wanted to see the Labour Party commit itself to the outright repudiation of
nuclear weapons and was as disappointed as anyone when at the Labour Party
Annual Conference of 1957, Aneurin Bevan, the acknowledged leader of left-
wing opinion in the Labour Party, spoke against the unilateralist case. Unilateral
resolutions, Bevan declared, 'will very greatly embarrass a Labour Government'
and put it into 'diplomatic purdah'. The unilateralists were guilty of 'an emotional spasm' and would send a British Foreign Secretary 'naked into the conference chamber'. The British H-bomb should not be abandoned but negotiated

away in order to achieve wider gains.[5] Bevan's supporters were shocked by what they heard and Bevan had the rare experience of being booed at an annual conference. This speech marked the end of Bevanism as a political force.

After the debate there was much talk of betrayal among delegates, and the criticism continued in the correspondence columns of *Tribune*. Zilliacus was more charitable than most: he believed that Bevan had been subject to enormous pressures behind the scenes, by Sam Watson and others, to compromise in the interests of party unity, and he also speculated on the state of Bevan's health.

When the Campaign for Nuclear Disarmament was launched in February 1958, calling on Britain 'to renounce unconditionally the use or production of nuclear weapons', Zilliacus supported it with enthusiasm and spoke at CND meetings across the country.[6] The campaign proved hugely successful in attracting many non-political supporters as well as the politically-conscious into its ranks. The first CND march took place in 1958, with an estimated ten thousand people making the journey from London to Aldermaston, and in the following year the march was even more successful when it reversed direction, starting at Aldermaston and ending with a mass rally at Trafalgar Square. Zilliacus was unable to do the march himself because of his bad foot and poor state of health, but he did address the crowd on several occasions from the plinth at the foot of Nelson's Column. For Zilliacus it was like old times working alongside friends such as Kingsley Martin and J. B. Priestley once again.[7] He also engaged in friendly correspondence with Frank Cousins, the general secretary of the Transport and General Workers' Union, on the subject of nuclear disarmament.[8] Cousins supported CND in an individual capacity and in the summer of 1959 he persuaded his union to adopt a unilateralist position, which gave him the mandate he needed to attempt to convert the Labour Party to the same policy.[9] Zilliacus was delighted with the way things were moving.

In February 1958 Zilliacus was one of a group of Labour MPs who re-launched an organisation called Victory for Socialism (VFS). The body had been formed in 1944 'to ensure that Labour's day-to-day policies are related to Socialist aims', and for several years it had played an educational role inside the Labour Party. By the 1950s it had become moribund until a group of left-wing MPs decided to revive it as a replacement for the defunct Bevanite group. Stephen Swingler became Chairman and Jo Richardson its Secretary. Zilliacus served on its Executive Council alongside fellow-MPs Frank Allaun, Harold Davies, Ian Mikardo, Walter Monslow and Sydney Silverman. The VFS had originally intended to organise branches throughout the country but when challenged by Hugh Gaitskell, who warned that Labour's NEC would not tolerate the creation of 'a party within a party',[10] the VFS leaders replied that this had never been their intention.[11]

Zilliacus quickly established himself as the VFS's foreign affairs guru and the revamped organisation's first pamphlet, *Policy for Summit Talks*, although it was published as representing the views of VFS members, was drafted by Zilliacus.

It argued in favour of Britain ceasing to be a nuclear power and using its influence to replace NATO and the Warsaw Pact by an all-European security treaty.
All foreign forces would be withdrawn from both East and West Germany as a
pre-condition for reunification. Finally, it urged that Communist China should
be admitted to the UN and encouraged to assist in a settlement of Far Eastern
problems.

The Labour leadership viewed the activities of VFS with some suspicion but
the organisation managed to avoid being proscribed and over the next four
years, when the Labour Party was racked by the issue of nuclear disarmament,
the VFS played its part in arguing the case for a unilateral approach to the question. Zilliacus was in the forefront of this campaign and he brought out his own
pamphlet, *Mutiny against Madness*, to supplement the VFS's *Policy for Summit
Talks*.

After Khrushchev had paid his penitential visit to Tito in October 1955, ending the six year dispute between the Soviet Union and Yugoslavia, Zilliacus
began to receive invitations to East European embassy functions once again;
and when the Soviet leaders Bulganin and Khrushchev visited Britain in April
1956 Zilliacus, who was usually brought to the fore on such occasions because
he spoke Russian, had chatted to Bulganin in the Royal Gallery of Parliament.
The Soviet Prime Minister had told him 'I want you to know that we are very
sorry about the things we have been saying about you for the last few years'.[12]
There followed an invitation from the Soviet Institute of World Economy and
International Relations in Moscow for Zilliacus to deliver a lecture on the
topic 'The Labour Party and the parliamentary path to Socialism'. A date was
fixed for October and Zilliacus accepted other invitations to visit Yugoslavia,
Czechoslovakia and Poland, and worked out a timetable to visit the countries
consecutively. However he insisted that the Czechoslovak Government must
first withdraw the false allegations made against him at the Slansky trial before
he would consider entering their country and only when this was done did he
accept an invitation to visit Czechoslovakia.

Zilliacus saw himself as

> someone whose record was familiar over the previous ten years, in some cases even
> from Geneva days, and was regarded not as a Communist or fellow traveller but
> as an inconveniently awkward and outspoken, but on the whole consistent Labour
> friend, whose views had been broadly confirmed by events.[13]

He arrived in Moscow on 10 October and stayed for ten days. Moscow, he recorded, felt like the capital of a world power. Living standards had improved and
people were more relaxed than when he had last visited the city in 1947. Tourism
was being encouraged and the academic staff at the Institute of World Economy
informed him that there was now less political interference in their work.

On his eighth day in the capital Zilliacus was granted a two hour interview with Nikita Khrushchev, now First Secretary of the Soviet Communist Party and Prime Minister. Zilliacus liked Khrushchev: he found him 'highly intelligent, earthy, with plenty of confidence and drive',[14] and he was in sympathy with what the Soviet leader was trying to achieve in the USSR. At the 20th Congress of the Communist Party of the Soviet Union, held earlier in the year, Khrushchev in his 'secret speech' to delegates had exposed some of Stalin's crimes and started the process of releasing prisoners from the gulags. Khrushchev told Zilliacus that his country wanted coexistence with the West, and the end of the Cold War with a halt to the arms race so that resources could be put to more constructive uses. Khrushchev recognised the dangers of nuclear war whose consequences, he clearly saw, would be disastrous for everyone. The USSR, however, would remain militarily strong in its own defence, but would not seek to impose Communism on other countries by force of arms. Communism would triumph because it was inherently superior to capitalism. Khrushchev said he had wanted Yugoslavia to re-join the 'socialist camp' but Tito had opted for membership of the non-aligned group of states.

Zilliacus left Moscow for Belgrade on 21 October. He found the Yugoslav capital swarming with visitors from all parts of the world, eager to study the economic reforms Tito had introduced in Yugoslavia.[15]

Moving on to Czechoslovakia, Zilliacus found that country still under the tight control of the Communist Party, although he thought the economic position of the workers had improved since his last visit. The Czech leader, Antonin Novotny, told Zilliacus that he was concerned about the situation in Hungary, which he believed was due to too hasty liberalisation by the Communist Party in that country. Czechoslovakia, he said, would not make the same mistake.[16]

In Poland Zilliacus witnessed the early days of Gomulka's return to power. Gomulka had promised Khrushchev that he would keep Poland in the Soviet Bloc and not restore capitalism, and in return had received from the Soviet leadership a large measure of independence on how he tackled Poland's internal problems.[17]

Zilliacus believed, on the basis of what he had seen on this tour, that Communism was in transition from Stalinism to something more liberal in nature. The rigid central control formerly exercised by Stalin was no longer feasible and the various East European Communist parties would, in future, enjoy more freedom to do things their own way, provided they remained within the framework of the Soviet Bloc. If they attempted to break free from the Soviet Bloc they could expect to experience the harsh treatment meted out to Hungary by Soviet forces in 1956. Poland had escaped this fate by a very narrow margin. The new Soviet tolerance had its limits.

Konni, Jan and Linden Zilliacus went on holiday to the Soviet Union in the summer of 1958, and while visiting the Crimea Konni took ill. He had suffered from gout for several years, but when he was taken to one of the top hospitals in Moscow, where he was given a thorough medical examination, he was diagnosed as suffering from chronic lymphatic leukaemia. Fortunately, his condition was stable and he was told that his ailment could be kept in check by taking regular doses of Vitamin C. Zilliacus followed this course of treatment for the next nine years and thus was able to carry on as an MP. The previous year – on 11 October 1957 – he had been speaking to a group of students at a meeting near Windscale in Cumbria, when there had been a serious radiation leak from one of the reactors at the nearby atomic plant: Zilliacus was convinced that this was the source of his leukaemia.[18]

In the following year the Zilliacus family enjoyed the sun and beaches of Romania's Black Sea coast, already popular with holidaymakers from Eastern Europe and keen to attract Western tourists. Zilliacus was not in good health and he pushed himself hard throughout the year. Therefore, with a general election expected in the autumn it was important that he should have a good summer holiday. In Romania he got away from politics and enjoyed a period of sunbathing and swimming, with visits to local places of interest.[19]

It was a joke in Gorton that although Zilliacus could find his way across Russia and Eastern Europe without any trouble, he had difficulty in making his way from the local railway station to the Labour Party rooms in Hyde Road.[20] It was true that Zilliacus could be absent-minded about mundane matters and the street layout of Gorton sometimes baffled him. However the joke was unfair to Zilliacus if it implied that he neglected his constituency: this was not the case. He always attended his monthly surgery in Gorton, he gave regular reports to the general management committee of the Gorton Labour Party, and he rarely turned down an invitation to speak to any group or society in Gorton, however small it might be. He was also diligent in answering letters from his constituents. Very few of these letters were concerned with foreign affairs. Most of his local correspondence was from people experiencing problems with the receipt of their pensions or social security benefits.[21] He was, of course, aware that he held Gorton with a very small majority and only a modest swing was needed to defeat him, it was therefore important to his political survival that he should build up some local goodwill. Nevertheless, dealing with his constituents' problems was never a chore to Zilliacus. He regarded it as an important part of his work as an MP and he gained great satisfaction from helping people with their personal problems.

Harold Macmillan had succeeded Sir Anthony Eden as Prime Minister in January 1957 and, against the odds, proceeded to raise Tory morale in the aftermath of the Suez debacle. He went on to restore the Conservative Party's fortunes by some skilful moves on the international stage, assisted by an economic boom at home. In early September he gave five weeks notice that a general election would be held on 8 October 1959.[22]

The Conservatives began the campaign with a comfortable lead in the opinion polls, but Labour fought back strongly and midway through the campaign had cut the Conservative lead by half. The Conservatives counterattacked by focusing on Labour's spending programme and asked: 'how would this be financed?' In reply, Hugh Gaitskell promised that there would be no increase in income tax under a Labour Government. Many people found this implausible and Labour was thrown on the defensive for the remainder of the campaign. The result of the election was a Conservative majority of 100.

In Gorton, Zilliacus's Conservative opponent was Donald Moore, the headmaster of a technical high school. Moore pointed out the general improvement in living standards and the reduction in taxation achieved under Conservative rule. Zilliacus countered with Labour's promise to increase pensions, and he expounded on his party's proposals for checking the spread of nuclear weapons and for securing disengagement in Central Europe.

The result in Gorton was:

Konni Zilliacus (Labour)	23,337
Donald Moore (Conservative)	22,480
Labour majority	857

Zilliacus had trebled his majority against the electoral background of a small national swing to the Conservatives and was reasonably satisfied with his result. When he scanned the list of successful candidates he was sorry to see that Ian Mikardo had lost his seat at Reading. However, John Mendelson, who had been elected Labour MP for the Penistone Division in the West Riding of Yorkshire at a by-election in June 1959, had been safely returned in the general election. Mendelson had come to Britain as a refugee from the Nazis in the 1930s, and had served in the British Army during the Second World War. After graduating from the London School of Economics he had become an adult education tutor at Sheffield University. He and Zilliacus shared a cosmopolitan background and held similar views on foreign policy. Not surprisingly, therefore, they found themselves working closely together in the new Parliament and Mendelson became a frequent visitor to Zilliacus's home in Maida Vale, where the younger members of the Zilliacus household were impressed by his encyclopaedic knowledge and nicknamed him 'the Brain'. Mendelson quickly mastered the procedures and routines of the Commons and soon became an influential figure in the Parliamentary Labour Party.[23]

East-West Round Table Conference, Rome, September 1961.
Left to right: Zilliacus, Reg Prentice and George Thomson

Zilliacus with Robin Cook and Malcolm Rifkind at the
Edinburgh University Union, 1966

Chapter 25

Gaitskell and Khrushchev

The return of the Conservatives to power for a third term of office prompted some rethinking at the top of the Labour Party. On the Sunday morning after the general election Hugh Gaitskell invited a group of his political friends to a meeting at his home in Hampstead. Among those present were Herbert Bowden, Tony Crosland, Hugh Dalton, Douglas Jay, Roy Jenkins and Patrick Gordon Walker. The aim of the meeting was to consider what should be done to avoid another Labour defeat at the polls and there was broad agreement that Labour's failure had been due to the unpopularity of nationalisation, the trade unions, and Labour-controlled councils plus the Party's old-fashioned, proletarian image. Anthony Wedgwood Benn popped in for a chat with Hugh Gaitskell in the afternoon, and in the evening Gaitskell dined with Tony Crosland and Woodrow Wyatt, where there was further discussion of the issues. These were informal gatherings, discussions among friends, however details of the meetings reached the press and these reports spread alarm among Labour's left-wing members and the traditionalists of the Party's centre-right. There were fears that a dilution of Labour's socialist principles was being planned by a small, London-based clique.[1]

The warning signs were clear yet Gaitskell chose to press ahead, against the advice of some of his friends, with proposals to change Labour's constitution by revising Clause Four: the section dealing with the taking into 'common ownership of the means of production, distribution and exchange'. At the next Labour Party Annual Conference held at Blackpool in November 1959, Gaitskell argued that Clause Four:

> lays us open to continual misrepresentation ... It implies that we propose to nationalise everything, but do we? Everything? Every little pub and garage? Of course not. We have long ago come to accept a mixed economy ... had we better not say so instead of going out of our way to court misrepresentation.[2]

Michael Foot, in a barnstorming speech, attacked the proposal to change the constitution and received a great ovation from the delegates,[3] and he was supported by a speech from Frank Cousins of the TGWU. Charlie Pannell and Denis Healey were among those who spoke in support of Gaitskell. Aneurin Bevan wound up the debate with a speech, conciliatory in tone, in which he criticised the priorities of the affluent society and argued that there was still a need for public ownership. Hugh Gaitskell recognised this fact, he went on, and Labour must do its best to convince the electorate of the merits of the case.[4]

It became clear to Gaitskell over the following months that he would not be able to secure NEC backing for a straightforward repeal of Clause Four, and at the NEC meeting on 16 March 1960 it was agreed to retain Clause Four but supplement it with a statement of aims put forward by Gaitskell, which was accepted by the NEC after some amendment. The revised text would be presented to the next Annual Conference for its approval.[5]

Gaitskell had failed in his attempt to remove Clause Four from Labour's constitution and he had to be satisfied with the addition of a statement of aims. Was it worth four months of bitter infighting to achieve this? Most definitely not; Gaitskell had shown himself tactically inept and had aroused suspicions that he wanted to change the nature of the Labour Party, but above all he had undermined the support he enjoyed in the trade unions.

In the spring and summer of 1960 there was a surge in public sympathy for CND's campaign to 'Ban the Bomb' and this was reflected in the decisions taken at trade union conferences. The TGWU was already committed to unilateralism and the Shopworkers' and Engineers' unions went unilateralist at their Easter conferences, followed by the Boilermakers, the Building Workers and the Electricians. It began to look extremely likely that the next Labour Party Annual Conference would see the Party adopt unilateralism as the basis of its defence policy, and if this happened could Gaitskell retain the leadership of the Labour Party or, indeed, would he want to?

The VFS group, with Ian Mikardo in the lead, worked hard to achieve the outcome of converting the Labour Party to unilateralism and ousting Gaitskell in the process; and Michael Foot used the columns of *Tribune* to further the same end. Zilliacus supported these aims and in July 1960 CND published his pamphlet *Anatomy of a Sacred Cow*, which not only put the case for unilateralism but also contained some sharp criticism of Hugh Gaitskell.

In Zilliacus's words:

> As a leader Hugh Gaitskell has a sincerity, courage and outspokenness which I admire, and a belief that it is the business of a leader to lead, which I share. But as the leader of a Socialist Party he has a serious defect: at his press conference at Transport House after he was appointed leader Mr. Gaitskell was asked whether he agreed with Earl Attlee's dictum that the proper position for the leader of the Labour Party is left of centre. He said yes, he did. But with the best will in the world, he has never been able to get anywhere near to that position. His sincere and strongly held economic and political convictions put him so far to the Right as to make him indistinguishable from a Liberal in home affairs and from a Tory in foreign policy. That is his personal tragedy and the Party's misfortune.[6]

Hugh Gaitskell had been forced to compromise on Clause Four but he was determined not to compromise on defence policy at the forthcoming Annual Conference, and he scorned attempts by George Brown and Richard Crossman to broker a compromise with Frank Cousins on the issue of nuclear disarmament. Instead he moved to shore up his position by seeking a vote of confidence from the Parliamentary Labour Party. At a PLP meeting on 30 June he received 179 votes of support and Zilliacus was one of seven MPs who voted against Gaitskell's leadership. Six days later Aneurin Bevan died of cancer. Bevan, the former left-wing rebel, had acted as a conciliator at the 1959 Annual Conference and he would not be available to act as a peacemaker at the 1960 Conference to be held in October. Furthermore, although Bevan had cooperated, somewhat reluctantly, with Gaitskell over the previous three years, in the interests of party unity, he had remained the most significant figure on the left and a credible alternative leader to Gaitskell. As the Party paid tribute to the dead Welshman the question was being asked: who, if anyone, would take his place?

As a break from the cut and thrust of British politics Zilliacus spent a month in the Soviet Union during the summer parliamentary recess. While in Moscow he interviewed Khruschev, who arranged for him to attend the trial of the American U-2 pilot Gary Powers, whose spy-plane had been shot down over Soviet territory. The trial took place in the Hall of Pillars, where the show trials had been held in the 1930s, although Zilliacus considered the Powers' trial 'was unexceptionable in terms of procedure and fairness, and the verdict was reasonable'. He followed this with a week at Yalta, swimming in the Black Sea and sunbathing on the beach. He then flew to Kiev to see his friend Alexander Korneichuk receive the Lenin Prize for his services to Soviet drama, and ended his holiday with a week in Moscow where he attended the premiere of Korneichuk's latest play. Refreshed by his holiday he returned to the fray in mid-September.[7]

As the Annual Conference convened in the Spa Grand Hall at Scarborough on 3 October 1960, there was a general feeling that Hugh Gaitskell and the defence policy he supported would be defeated. The key debate on foreign policy and defence opened on 5 October with the presentation by Sam Watson of the joint TUC-NEC document *Policy for Peace*.[8]

Sam Watson told the conference:

> It is not a question of being for or against the H-bomb; that is an over-simplification of this important problem. It is not for or against peace: we are all for peace. The question is how to get it.

Watson explained that the NEC's policy document supported the United Nations and 'all-round comprehensive and controlled disarmament' but it also stood for collective security and NATO provided this. 'Why should the Western Alliance give up nuclear weapons while Russia retained hers?' asked Watson. The policy statement, he went on, 'rejects pacifism, it rejects neutralism, it embraces

the basic principles which have guided our movement throughout its history ...
Britain cannot abdicate its role and responsibilities in international affairs'.

Sam Watson was followed by the mover of an Associated Society of Locomotive
Engineers and Firemen (ASLEF) resolution, warning of growing Nazi influence
in the Bonn Government and the dangers of allowing West Germany to have
nuclear weapons.

Then a straightforward unilateralist resolution was moved by L. Misledene of
the Amalgamated Engineering Union, and was seconded by Ian Mikardo.

Frank Cousins then moved a resolution on behalf of the TGWU which rejected 'any defence policy based on the use of strategic or tactical nuclear weapons' called for 'the cessation of the manufacture or testing of nuclear weapons'
and opposed 'patrols of aircraft carrying nuclear weapons ... operating from
British bases' and pressed for urgent discussions on how to secure world disarmament. The resolution was seconded by John Horner of the Fire Brigades'
Union. A pro-NATO resolution was then moved by the Amalgamated Society
of Woodworkers.

In the general debate that followed, the MPs Philip Noel-Baker, George
Brown, Denis Healey and James Griffiths mounted the rostrum and spoke
in support of the NEC's position while Harold Davies, Michael Foot, Emrys
Hughes and Anne Kerr made speeches against. Zilliacus wanted to speak in this
important debate but he was one of many delegates to the Conference who failed
to catch the Chairman's eye.

Hugh Gaitskell rose to wind up the debate at 3 p.m. and he launched into an
attack on unilateralism and neutralism, for he believed the two to be closely
linked. He stated that an adverse vote could not turn him and many others into
'the pacifists, unilateralists and fellow travellers that other people are' and in
a passionate peroration he promised 'to fight and fight again' to reverse any
Conference decision in favour of unilateralism.

The resolution on Germany was remitted to the NEC, and when voting on
the others had been completed it was announced that the pro-NATO resolution
had been defeated, the two unilateralist resolutions had been carried by small
majorities, and the NEC's policy statement had also been defeated by a small
majority.

Zilliacus was delighted at this outcome. Labour Party policy on foreign affairs and defence had moved significantly closer to his own views and in a
post-Conference speech he mounted a fierce attack on Gaitskell. He accused
the Labour leader of 'arrogance and fanaticism' and claimed that 'the amateurs
of genocide are wrecking the Party and making a burnt offering to Pentagon
brinkmanship of the British people'.[9] The trade union group of Labour MPs
believed that Zilliacus had gone too far and had infringed the 1952 rule against
personal attacks. Accordingly they raised the matter at the December meeting of
the Parliamentary Labour Party, where their complaint was upheld. The Deputy

Leader and Chief Whip were deputed to reprimand Zilliacus but he refused to meet them, feeling that his comments had been fully justified. The matter was not pressed further, leaving some Labour MPs, such as Jean Mann, feeling that Zilliacus had got off too lightly.[10]

However, Zilliacus was soon in trouble with Labour's NEC, for publishing an article on the Labour Party in the international Communist review *Problems of Peace and Socialism*. The German Social Democratic Party had been in touch with Labour Party officials at Transport House, complaining that a British delegation consisting of four Labour Party members had visited the German Democratic Republic in December 1960 as guests of the Communist Government. The group was made up of three MPs – Richard Kelley, Sir Leslie Plummer, and Konni Zilliacus – plus Ian Mikardo as the former MP for Reading. The group stayed at the Johanneshof Hotel in East Berlin and had been shown the city's housing developments together with some industrial sites. The Labour Party visitors had viewed the new construction with approval and Zilliacus had expressed himself in favour of a demilitarised, neutral, democratic, united Germany. The SPD, in the same letter of complaint to the Labour Party, had made reference to Zilliacus's article in the Communist journal.

Zilliacus was never a great admirer of the German SPD and he replied that the NEC and Transport House officials should not 'act as an agent and branch office of the SPD leadership'.[11] He accused the SPD of moving to the right in an attempt to be 'better cold warriors and devotees of modern capitalism than Adenauer'.

As for the East German regime:

> I don't think any of us has illusions about the absence of democracy and full national independence in the GDR. On the other hand, its social and economic success is very considerable, and it is politically pretty solid and a reality which has come to stay and with which we must reckon. And although the SPD leadership naturally feels embarrassed about it, the fact seems to me indisputable that the international policies of the GDR, although not as close to Labour's policies as those of the SPD used to be, are a good deal nearer to ours than the present ersatz Adenauer line of the SPD. Above all the GDR is safe for peace, which is more than one can say for the German Federal Republic.

He went on to remind the NEC of a resolution passed at the Labour Party's Annual Conference in 1957 urging the Parliamentary Labour Party 'to use all its power and influence through the appropriate channels to achieve … general discussions with leaders of the USSR, China and the People's Democracies'. Zilliacus claimed he had been implementing this Conference decision and pointed out that the Parliamentary Committee and the NEC were not carrying out Conference decisions at the present time.

On 21 February 1961 Zilliacus was called to appear before Party officials at

Transport House to explain why he had written for a Prague-based Communist magazine. The outcome of the meeting was a written warning to Zilliacus that the NEC 'deplored his conduct' and 'would regard any repetition of it as inconsistent with your membership of the Labour Party'. Unlike Brer Rabbit, Zilliacus could not say nothing, and instead of keeping his head down he responded with a lengthy letter of justification for his actions. The NEC reacted by suspending his membership 'until such time as you give assurances about your future conduct satisfactory to the NEC'. Zilliacus wrote back to protest at the NEC's 'drastic' action and asked what further assurances he could give that would satisfy the NEC. He received no reply, the NEC had given its last word on the subject and Zilliacus remained suspended.

In July Zilliacus wrote to A. L. Williams, the Party's National Agent and Deputy General Secretary, asking for his suspension to be lifted, and was informed that this could not be considered at the present time because the NEC was investigating his attendance at a European Disarmament Conference held in Oslo the previous month. The conference had been organised by Ilya Ehrenburg, the Soviet writer; Carl Bonnevie, leader of a Norwegian unilateralist group; and Tom Driberg, the Labour MP for Barking. The Labour MP John Stonehouse and Zilliacus had received invitations and had attended the conference. A *Daily Telegraph* reporter, however, had accused the Oslo Conference of being a Communist 'front', whose main purpose was to halt or, if possible, reverse the rearmament of West Germany.[12] As Zilliacus observed, he managed to get into trouble with Labour's NEC even when he was suspended from the Party and therefore technically not even a member.

Tom Driberg, who was a member of the NEC, interceded on Zilliacus's behalf with a letter to Ray Gunter, Chairman of the NEC's Organisation Sub Committee, which had been deputed to investigate Zilliacus's role in the 'Oslo affair'.[13] Unlike Zilliacus, whose letters to the NEC were usually long and provocative in tone, Driberg knew that the NEC preferred replies to be short and sweet. He explained that Zilliacus had been invited by Carl Bonnevie at very short notice, and Zilliacus had consulted him as a member of the NEC before he had accepted the invitation. 'So I do not see how Zilly can possibly be blamed for something which was largely my responsibility ... In the event, it was fortunate, from the Western point of view, that Zilly was at Oslo. Even those most critical of him will not deny that he has a considerable knowledge of international affairs'. Apparently when the political commission of the conference was discussing the role of the UN, Ehrenburg – following the current Soviet line of coolness towards the UN and criticism of its secretariat – had tried to get the reference to the UN removed or toned down. Zilliacus objected and after a 'prolonged argument' between Zilliacus and Ehrenburg Zilliacus's draft had been accepted.

Driberg concluded:

It seems to me that [this] point illustrates what I believe to be the truth about Zilly – that he is not in the least a Soviet stooge or a fellow traveller (though there are, of course, some points of Soviet policy which he approves and which coincide pretty closely with our own Labour Party policy). He is primarily, and passionately, a United Nations man.

I am also, personally, convinced that, whatever his errors of judgement or indiscretions in the past, he will now make a genuine effort to be amenable to reasonable discipline – that he will, as I think he said, "count a hundred before speaking" (and will not think it necessary to speak at inordinate length and in a way offensive to his colleagues).

This letter must have helped considerably to clear Zilliacus with the NEC and on 29 September 1961 his suspension was lifted, restoring his status as a Labour MP, thus enabling him to attend in an *ex officio* capacity the Labour Party Annual Conference at Blackpool the following week.

In middle August 1961, Zilliacus accompanied by Jan and Linden holidayed in the Crimea. They had booked a villa not far from Khrushchev's summer residence at Gagri on Cape Pitsunda and when he learned of this the Soviet leader invited the Zilliacus family to pay him a visit. With Khrushchev's agreement Zilliacus used the occasion to interview him on the international situation with a view to publication, and in this way Khrushchev gave Zilliacus a minor scoop by informing him that the USSR would soon be resuming nuclear tests.

'I know that is going to hurt and grieve our friends in the West, particularly the intellectuals, and we have done it only very reluctantly but we cannot help ourselves'.[14]

Khrushchev went on to explain that Soviet attempts to resolve the German question, including the position of Berlin, had been rejected by the West and meanwhile West German military strength had been built up. The West German Government's policy was to regain the territories lost in the Second World War and some German generals were pressing for nuclear weapons. Khrushchev said he had little confidence in the political judgement of the German leaders, Adenauer and Strauss, and he feared Europe could stumble into war. There should be joint military disengagement from German territory as part of a European settlement, and perhaps the resumption of nuclear tests by the USSR would shock the Western governments out of their complacency and bring them to the negotiating table.

Zilliacus agreed this was possible but it was more likely, in his opinion, to accelerate the arms race, and it would also undermine the efforts of those in the West who were working for peace.

The conversation moved on to a discussion of the United Nations with Khrushchev arguing that at present the UN was dominated by the USA and he wondered whether it might not be better to move its location to either Austria or Switzerland. Zilliacus agreed that Red China should become a member of the Security Council, but he thought the growing influence of the Third World countries inside the UN was giving it a better balance and he considered that the Afro-Asian states should be represented on the Security Council.

Konni and Jan Zilliacus also took the opportunity of visiting Paul Robeson, then convalescing at the Barveekha Sanatorium after being treated by Soviet doctors for 'depressive paranoiac psychosis generated by an involutional form of antiosclerosis',[15] and were deeply shocked at his poor mental and physical condition. They also arranged to meet Rockwell Kent, the artist and veteran American leftist, who was enjoying a summer holiday in the Crimea.

In September Zilliacus attended the East-West Round Table Conference held that year in Rome, where the main topics under discussion were the resumption of nuclear tests and the future of the UN. The Soviet delegation included A. T. Adzhebei, editor of *Izvestia*; A. E. Korneichuk the playwright; and Ilya Ehrenburg.[16]

The East-West Round Table Conferences had been started in 1959 by groups of intellectuals from both sides of the Iron Curtain, with Sweden playing a prominent role, in an attempt to bridge the divisions of the Cold War. Zilliacus was a leading member of the Round Table's Organising Committee and rarely missed a meeting. He was often accompanied by John Mendelson, who was fluent in German and French and could communicate in several other languages. Others who attended over the years were the Labour MPs Bob Edwards, Eric Heffer, Ian Mikardo, Philip Noel-Baker, Reg Prentice, Julian Snow, George Thomson and William Warbey; the Conservative MPs Christopher Chataway, Anthony Courtney, Douglas Dodds-Parker and Sir Cyril Osborne; the Liberal MPs Eric Lubbock and Jeremy Thorpe; the economist Joan Robinson, and the historians Edward and Dorothy Thompson. Participants were encouraged to pay their own travelling expenses, while the costs of the venue and hotel accommodation were met by the Round Table. The finances of the Round Table were covered by equal contributions from East and West. The money from the Eastern Bloc was provided by state agencies, and Western financial support came from trusts and philanthropic businessmen. Sir Jock Campbell, Chairman of Booker Brothers, and Alec Horsley, Chairman of Northern Dairies, were the Round Table's main British backers. Zilliacus was heavily involved in raising money to support the Round Table's work – 'passing round the hat' he called it – and it was a task he did not relish. However he thoroughly enjoyed the Round Table conferences and considered them a useful means of exchanging views and gathering information.

At the Labour Party's Blackpool Conference held in October, the NEC's defence policy was carried by almost three to one, and a unilateralist resolution moved by Frank Cousins of the TGWU was also defeated by a large majority. Gaitskell had campaigned hard for this result, assisted by the Campaign for

Democratic Socialism working on his behalf in the constituencies, together with several of the big unions being persuaded to reverse their previous support for unilateralism.[17] Zilliacus was disappointed by this setback and he continued to work for nuclear disarmament through CND and VFS, although a new issue had come to the fore to engage the attention of the Labour Party: the question of British membership of the Common Market.

In July 1961 Harold Macmillan launched Britain's bid for entry to the Common Market. Gaitskell's initial response to Britain's application was one of caution. He accepted the principle of membership provided the conditions of entry were not too onerous and were tailored to meet Britain's special requirements, although he believed that however successful the negotiations the French would veto British membership. As the months went by Gaitskell began to adopt a more anti-Common Market position, and at the Labour Party's Annual Conference held at Brighton in October 1961 his speech on the subject was strongly opposed to entry.[18] He regarded the economic arguments for and against entry as 'evenly balanced'; it was the political implications that disturbed Gaitskell. He pointed out that membership of the Common Market would mean the end of Britain as an independent state and would involve a serious weakening of Britain's links with the Commonwealth. There were also the effects on our partners in the European Free Trade Association to be considered, and he attacked the protectionism inherent in the Common Agricultural Policy. Gaitskell spoke with passion and conviction. It was not only what he said but how he said it that impressed the delegates in the hall, who gave him a standing ovation.

Zilliacus was pleased that Gaitskell had come out against British membership of the Common Market and had carried the bulk of the Labour Party with him. Yet Zilliacus's reasons for opposing British entry were very different to Gaitskell's.

Zilliacus believed that:

> not only was the EEC launched as part of the cold war policy that had produced NATO. Its constitution, the Rome Treaty, was framed under the influence of the great cartels, combines, monopolies and holding companies which have dominated the life of the Six since the war ... The Rome Treaty allows planning and even nationalisation for greater economic efficiency, provided there is no interference with free competition, but rules out planning and public ownership geared to social purposes ... In short, that in the EEC it is 'yes' to State capitalism and 'no' to Socialism.[19]

Gaitskell with his references to the end of 'a thousand years of history' and reminders of Commonwealth troops fighting alongside British forces at Gallipoli and Vimy Ridge, not to mention the supposed threat to the British cup of tea, was appealing to the past. Zilliacus's opposition was based on a Marxist analysis of the Common Market and the economic forces that had brought it into existence and continued to shape its development. The fact was that opposition to British entry cut across the left-right divisions inside the Labour Party and Gaitskell was successful in rallying those disparate elements behind his banner.

In the summer of 1961 Zilliacus had vacationed at the Romanian coastal resort of Mamaia, where he met Nicolas Guillen. Guillen was a poet and the President of the Cuban Writers' Union. The two men got on extremely well and in the course of conversation Guillen asked Zilliacus if he would be interested in visiting Cuba, and Zilliacus replied that he would like to very much. Hence, when Guillen returned to Cuba, he had arranged for Zilliacus to take a small study group to Cuba in the first two weeks of January 1963, as guests of the Cuban Writers' Union. Zilliacus was accompanied by his wife Jan, daughter Linden, and the Labour MPs Ian Mikardo and Renée Short. When the British party arrived in Havana they were joined by the French film director, Agnes Varda, the Canadian Cedric Cox – a National Democratic Party member of British Columbia's legislative assembly – and the writer and documentary film maker, Felix Greene. At the beginning of their visit the group had lunch with Fidel Castro and Che Guevara, they then toured the country's schools, hospitals and agricultural co-operatives, and enjoyed several cultural evenings of Cuban music, dance and drama. Zilliacus had been sympathetic to Castro's revolution before he toured the country and the visit confirmed him in his views. He came back convinced that Castro enjoyed the support of the vast majority of Cubans.[20]

On his return to London Zilliacus heard the announcement that Hugh Gaitskell had died. In the previous December Gaitskell had been admitted to Manor House Hospital for a medical examination. He was discharged and then readmitted to the Middlesex Hospital, where he died of the rare disease *lupus erythematosus* on 18 January 1963. Zilliacus was shocked by the news. He was a compassionate man and took no pleasure in the death of a leader he had often opposed, and it was not just a case of disagreeing with Gaitskell's policies: Zilliacus had never warmed to Gaitskell as a person. Even so, to be struck down when at the peak of one's powers with the Prime Ministership almost within one's grasp was a cruel fate and Zilliacus recognised it as such. He also thought of Dora Gaitskell's loss and the grief being suffered by the Gaitskell daughters, Julia and Cressida.[21] Nevertheless there was no overlooking the fact that the premature death of Hugh Gaitskell had closed a chapter in the history of the Labour Party, and many on the left were not sorry to have the opportunity of turning to a new page.[22]

Chapter 26

Guns or Butter?

The death of Hugh Gaitskell meant that the PLP would have to elect a new leader. George Brown, the Party's Deputy Leader, was an obvious candidate for the post. Harold Wilson, the former Bevanite who had challenged Gaitskell for the leadership in 1960, was also expected to stand for election. Brown, a trade union sponsored MP, was on the right wing of the Party, and he expected to receive the votes of the centre-right MPs who had supported Gaitskell. Unfortunately for Brown this was not the case. Brown was a man with a volatile temperament made worse by a weakness for alcohol, and a group of centre-right MPs encouraged James Callaghan to stand for the leadership. Hence the centre-right vote was split on the first ballot. When the result of this ballot was declared at the weekly PLP meeting on 7 February Wilson had 115 votes, Brown 88 and Callaghan 41. On the second ballot a week later the result was Wilson 144 and Brown 103.[1]

Zilliacus supported Wilson in both ballots as he had done when Wilson had challenged Gaitskell for the leadership two years before. Zilliacus supported Wilson in the full knowledge that Wilson was a centre-left figure who would lead from this position. However, he regarded this as preferable to continued right-wing dominance of the Party. Furthermore, he knew Wilson to be an adroit politician capable of leading the Labour Party to victory at the next election. Zilliacus, therefore, was reasonably happy with the outcome of the leadership election and over the next nineteen months Wilson did not disappoint him.

First, Harold Wilson went out of his way to conciliate the Gaitskellites in the interests of party unity and he was successful in achieving this. He did not attempt a radical revision of Labour policy but he gave it a new twist by successfully linking the Labour Party's socialism with the 'scientific revolution'. When the Profumo affair broke in the summer of 1963 Wilson handled the sordid revelations with considerable skill, gaining maximum political advantage for the Labour Party. He was also lucky in that his election to the Labour leadership coincided with a downturn in the British economy. The Macmillan boom years were over and in October 1963 Macmillan resigned and was replaced by Sir Alec Douglas-Hume. Sir Alec appeared an old-fashioned tweedy figure in the 'swinging sixties', but nevertheless the Conservative Party recovered ground under his leadership and, in spite of a brilliantly fought election campaign by Harold Wilson, Labour was returned to office with an overall majority of only four.

In Gorton Zilliacus was content to fight his campaign on Labour's manifesto,

The New Britain, which promised the country a programme of modernisation. There was to be a National Plan to boost Britain's flagging economy and so secure a higher rate of growth, the social services were to be improved, more council house building was to be encouraged, secondary education was to be reorganised on comprehensive lines, and higher education was to be expanded. In foreign affairs a new post of Minister of Disarmament was to be created with responsibility for working to halt the spread of nuclear weapons and to curb the international trade in conventional arms; and greater support for the United Nations was promised. Although Zilliacus was not in good health he did not spare himself, and his Conservative opponent, Edwin Hodson, an accountant by profession, was on the defensive for most of the campaign.

The result at Gorton was:

Konni Zilliacus (Labour)	23,895
Edwin Hodson (Conservative)	19,465
Labour majority	4,430 [2]

Zilliacus was delighted with his increased majority. Clearly he had benefited by the national swing to Labour of 3.4 per cent and the higher swing to Labour candidates in the Greater Manchester area of 4.5 per cent. However, in addition, his years of work as an MP for Gorton, dealing with local and personal problems, were beginning to pay off and, as more people in his constituency got to know him better, he was no longer viewed as something of a red ogre, as he had certainly been by some when he had first fought the seat in 1955.[3]

Harold Wilson lost no time in forming a government. George Brown became Deputy Premier and Minister for Economic Affairs, James Callaghan was appointed Chancellor of the Exchequer, Patrick Gordon Walker Foreign Secretary, and Denis Healey took over Defence. In a twenty-three member Cabinet Wilson included four left-wingers: Anthony Greenwood was appointed Secretary of State for Colonial Affairs, Richard Crossman Minister of Housing and Local Government, Barbara Castle Minister for Overseas Development, and Frank Cousins was recruited from the TGWU to serve as Minister of Technology. In the wake of the major appointments came the junior ministers and among these Zilliacus was pleased when his friend Stephen Swingler was appointed Joint Parliamentary Secretary at the Ministry of Transport, and another friend, Harold Davies, became Joint Parliamentary Secretary at the Ministry of Pensions and National Insurance. The non-party Alun Gwynne-Jones, the defence correspondent of *The Times,* was ennobled, becoming Lord Chalfont, and appointed Minister of Disarmament at the Foreign Office. Zilliacus for reasons of age, health, security considerations, and a long record of dissent against official Party policy was never likely to be made a minister, yet if the cards had fallen differently for him or if he had chosen to play them in a different way, he would have been the ideal candidate to serve as a minister responsible for disarmament matters located in the Foreign Office.

The Labour Government inherited a difficult economic situation. The previous Conservative Chancellor, Reginald Maudling, had stoked up a pre-election boom sucking in imports, and the Treasury forecast a balance of payments deficit of £750-800 million for 1964 compared with a figure of £35 million in 1963. An immediate decision was taken by a triumvirate of Wilson, Brown and Callaghan not to devalue the pound and this meant that the new government had to borrow from abroad to cover the looming deficit; it also raised the bank rate to 7 per cent and imposed a temporary surcharge on imports. By these means the immediate crisis was surmounted, giving George Brown at the Department of Economic Affairs time to prepare a National Plan for economic growth and negotiate a voluntary incomes policy with the trade unions and employers' organisations. Increases in old age pensions, and sickness and unemployment benefits were announced, and in a spring budget Callaghan introduced a corporation tax and a capital gains tax. In spite of the economic difficulties facing the newly elected Labour Government and its dependence on a wafer-thin majority in the Commons, Harold Wilson was determined to appear dynamic and press on with the implementation of Labour's programme.

In December 1964 Wilson flew to Washington to meet President Johnson. When in opposition Labour had been critical of the Nassau Agreement under which the USA had agreed to sell Britain the Polaris submarine-launched missile. It was understood that the submarines would normally be under NATO command except when 'supreme national interests were at stake'. Within days of taking office a triumvirate of Wilson, Gordon Walker and Healey decided to keep Polaris and the order for four submarines was confirmed. At his December meeting with the American President, Wilson stated his intention of maintaining Britain's 'world role' and in return Johnson promised American financial support for sterling.

Zilliacus was soon disillusioned by the Wilson Government's foreign and defence policies. In the foreign affairs debate on 23 November 1964, Harold Wilson set out the Labour Government's policy:

I want to make it quite clear that whatever we may do in the field of cost effectiveness, value for money and a stringent review of expenditure, we cannot afford to lose our world role – our role, which, for shorthand purposes is sometimes called our 'East of Suez' role

And in this policy Wilson included the defence of India and Malaysia. He went on:

I was glad to see last week in Washington the full recognition the United States gave to our role as a world peace-keeping power. [4]

Zilliacus saw clearly that the Government could not maintain its existing defence commitments, that underpinned its world role, and at the same time carry out its domestic programme. He summed it up as the dilemma of guns or butter[5] and he developed his critique of government policy when he followed Wilson in the foreign affairs debate.

Zilliacus began by saying that he regarded money spent on armaments as an economic waste and went on:

> It is one of the main factors in the balance of payments crisis. The more we can plough back resources of money, manpower and scientific personnel into productive resources, the better off we shall be economically ... Of course it means organising the economy. It means the kind of plans which have been put forward from this side of the House for greatly developing trade with the underdeveloped countries, East-West trade on mutually planned lines, and so on. This, I believe, is the way to think of the future ... I regard with gloom the prospect of the first international act of the Labour Government being to go off to Washington to sign on as 'Tail-end Charlies' in an American nuclear bomber with a German co-pilot, whether one calls the contraption an Atlantic Nuclear Force or Fred Karno's Nuclear Navy.[6]

He went on to argue that he saw no need to strengthen NATO, on the contrary the emphasis should be on securing disarmament and there should be no 'stepping up the already colossal defence budget until it breaks down our attempts to do what we have promised to do at home. I say all this bluntly because I believe that someone ought to say it from this side of the House and because I know that a great many people feel it'.

The so-called British independent nuclear deterrent, he continued, was made in the USA and will be integrated into NATO under American command. He approved of French policy, which favoured the neutralisation of South East Asia, and said he did not want to see Britain supporting American intervention in Vietnam. In conclusion, he thought we should reopen negotiations with the Russians and try to reach some sort of agreement with them before we considered strengthening NATO.

Zilliacus returned to this theme in the foreign affairs debate the following month:

> Unless we do make radical changes in our international policies, which means foreign policy first and defence policy as a consequence of that, we are going to be on the rocks financially and economically, because this country cannot support anything like the present defence budget and at the same time supply the resources, not only in money but in technicians, and in manpower, and machinery, and the rest, which are needed to modernise our economy, to increase our productivity, to expand out exports, and to fulfil the noble and ambitious social programme to which the Labour Party has set its hand.[7]

He used a Supply Day devoted to Military Expenditure Overseas to warn:

> We need to cut our military coat according to our economic cloth ... I do not think that the urgency and importance of this aspect of the matter has yet to be realised either in the House or, still less, in the country.

He analysed the spending on British forces in Germany, the Middle East and the Far East, and concluded:

> There is an overwhelming feeling that the time has come to call a halt to this mad growth in armaments and military expenditure which threatens to break our economic effort unless we do something drastic to stop it in time.[8]

When the Government's White Paper on defence was presented to the House of Commons in March 1965 he observed:

> So far from cutting defence commitments the Defence White Paper has reaffirmed all existing commitments – NATO, CENTO and SEATO – and added two new ones, a nuclear confrontation with China and an ominous and ill-defined world role. On this basis it will prove impossible to achieve even the very modest aim ... of reducing military expenditure in the next few years to roughly the level in real terms of the present figure.[9]

However, because the Conservatives would do even worse he would support the Government's defence policy in the lobby. He described it as 'a distasteful duty'. This was the dilemma of the Labour Left in the 1964-66 Parliament; with the Labour Government surviving on a slim majority left-wing dissenters could not run the risk of bringing it down by an adverse vote. Michael Foot, John Mendelson, Sydney Silverman, William Warbey and Konni Zilliacus were passionately opposed to American intervention in Vietnam: they could criticise from the back benches but not register their disapproval in the division lobby. Zilliacus was aware they were being denounced by left-wing activists outside Parliament as 'spineless double talkers and time servers', but this was something they had to put up with until the time was ripe to call another general election in the hope of securing a bigger majority.[10] Zilliacus had no problems with the Gorton Labour Party: in 1965 the Party's General Management Committee unanimously passed a resolution of support for him and the stand he was taking on the Vietnam War.

The Victory for Socialism organisation had been dissolved before the 1964 General Election in anticipation of the formation of a Labour Government. Several newly-elected MPs, led by Stan Newens, who had sat in the visitors' gallery of the House of Commons as a teenager and watched Ernest Bevin being savaged by Zilliacus in the foreign affairs debates of the 1940s, felt the need for a similar group in the new Parliament, and so was formed the Tribune Group to act as a focus for left-wing opinion in the PLP.[11] Zilliacus joined the Tribune Group and prepared a number of background papers for its members on such topics as the Common Market and Vietnam.[12]

Zilliacus was very perceptive about the Vietnam War. He foresaw at an early stage of hostilities that American armed intervention would steadily increase but it would not produce an American victory. Together with other left-wing peace horses he criticised American policy, fought to keep Britain out of the war, and tried to get Harold Wilson to condemn US policy on Vietnam. Zilliacus's solution to the conflict was a return to the Geneva Agreement of 1954 involving the withdrawal of all foreign troops from Vietnam, followed by free elections in both North and South Vietnam, with the winners forming a government to rule a reunified Vietnam. If this resulted in a Communist government for the whole of the country it was at least what the Vietnam people had voted for. This outcome was acceptable to Zilliacus and he believed it was preferable to a long drawn-out war with a likely Communist victory at the end of the line.

After eighteen months in office, on 28 February 1966, Harold Wilson announced the dissolution of Parliament, with polling to take place on 31 March. The Labour Government appeared to have mastered the economic crisis it had inherited on taking office and in spite of its small majority had acted decisively on the issues facing the country. Edward Heath, the new Conservative leader, had not had much time to play himself in, whereas Harold Wilson was at the peak of his powers and popularity, and had shown considerable skill in governing with a slender majority. Labour was ahead in the public opinion polls and Harold Wilson judged the time was right to go to the country in the expectation of securing a larger majority.

There was some Parliamentary business to be completed before MPs dispersed to their constituencies and this included a defence debate, allowing Zilliacus to squeeze in a last minute attack on the Government's defence policy:

> This whole defence debate and the Defence White Paper are shot through with nostalgic illusions and nuclear and world military power hankerings and posturings … The most depressing thing about the debate is the assumptions on both sides that we can go on indefinitely for years and years with the greatest, costliest and deadliest arms race in history. It will not work out like that and we must put our energy, will, purpose and policies into transferring the mutual relations of the great powers from the balance of power, as expressed in the rival military alliances, to their obligations, purposes and principles of the UN Charter … We are no longer a first-class military power. But we could be a first-class political power and a first-class force for peace.[13]

Two days after the defence debate Parliament was dissolved, and Zilliacus caught a train to Manchester to begin his three week campaign for re-election.

Chapter 27

The Last Months

When Zilliacus arrived in Gorton to begin his election campaign it was to find that the Gorton Labour Party's election fund amounted to £20.[1] The American millionaire, Corliss Lamont, champion of many left-wing causes, and Franc Joubin, a Canadian mining geologist and financial supporter of the East-West Round Table Conferences, both came to Zilliacus's aid and made generous contributions to his election fund. Even then, Zilliacus had to negotiate an overdraft with his bank manager so that the Gorton Labour Party would have enough money to cover his election expenses.[2]

It was not a good start to his election campaign and a source of worry to him, but things went better after this. Memories of the last jaded years of Conservative rule had not yet faded and Harold Wilson could claim that his government had done a good job in grappling with the economic problems they had inherited from the Conservatives. Labour's campaign slogan was 'You Know Labour Government Works' and Wilson appealed to the electorate to give him a majority to enable him to continue in office. The pipe-smoking, homespun, yet obviously clever Mr Wilson presented an image of competence and classlessness that played well with the electorate.[3]

Zilliacus based his campaign largely on domestic issues. His election address listed Labour's achievements: More Homes; Fairer Rents; Better Schools; Sickness Benefits Up; High Employment. On foreign policy he contented himself with a promise to work to 'subordinate the military alliances, and pursue policies consistent with the principles, purposes and obligations of the Charter of the United Nations'.

Zilliacus's Conservative opponent, Ian Paley, a local youth employment officer, could make little headway against a national swing to Labour of 2.7 per cent, and the result in Gorton was:

Konni Zilliacus (Labour)	24,726
Ian Paley (Conservative)	16,418
Labour majority	8,308

Zilliacus took immense satisfaction from his own result, which showed a 5 per cent swing in his favour, almost twice the national average, and when the national results were counted Labour was found to hold an overall majority of ninety-seven.

The new Parliament was not called to assemble until 18 April and Zilliacus fitted in a meeting of the East-West Round Table held in Paris the weekend before the House of Commons was due to meet. The conference was devoted to discussion of the proliferation of nuclear weapons and among the speakers was the veteran French Socialist, Jules Moch, who delivered a paper on the subject.[4] Zilliacus hurried back from Paris to attend the morning meeting of the newly elected PLP, which included seventy new members and among them was his former campaign organiser Russell Kerr, who had been returned as MP for Feltham. The Labour Left in the PLP was reinforced by a number of left-wingers of a younger generation, who regarded Zilliacus as one of the Left's 'grand old men'. William Warbey, a left-wing stalwart for many years, was missing from the new Parliament. He had become increasingly disenchanted with Labour's foreign policy in the 1964-66 Parliament – especially Wilson's support for American intervention in Vietnam – and in spite of the fact he was only sixty-one years of age and held one of the safest Labour seats in the country, had decided to retire. Retirement was never an option considered by Zilliacus who felt he still had much to contribute in the field of international affairs and, although seventy years old and in poor health, was determined to carry on fighting for what he believed to be right.

Morale among the assembled Labour MPs was high after their decisive victory in the polls and few doubted that the next five years would be a successful period of reform and modernisation comparable to that of the Attlee Government 1945-51. They were soon to be disillusioned on this score. Harold Wilson made few changes in his ministerial team and the Government's legislative programme for the next eighteen months was largely a carry-over from the pre-election period with little thought being given to what would follow.[5] However the Government's Achilles' heel proved to be economic policy.[6] Wilson and Callaghan remained determined not to devalue sterling and when a seamen's strike in May put pressure on the pound the Government was forced to take deflationary measures, including a tightening up of its previously voluntary prices and incomes policy. State control of wages proved too much for Frank Cousins, who resigned from the Cabinet and became a backbench critic of Government policy.

Zilliacus's response to the Government's measures was contained in a pamphlet *Labour's Crisis – Its Nature, Cause and Cure*. In this pamphlet Zilliacus placed most of the blame for the economic crisis on Britain 'spending grotesquely excessive amounts on arms and military commitments'[7] and he traced the problem back to Ernest Bevin's foreign policy in the post-war Labour Government. The solution, according to Zilliacus, was for Britain to replace the Anglo-American alliance by a policy based on support for the United Nations, thus enabling Britain to scale down her overseas commitments, beginning in the Far East, moving on to the removal of British bases in the Middle East, and finally, withdrawing British forces from Germany. The resources released from military purposes could be used to modernise British industry, raise productivity, and boost exports. Freed from the military alliances, Zilliacus argued, Britain could then take the lead, together with France and the Soviet Union, in winding up the Cold War.

The British Government's support for American policy in Vietnam was another sticking point for many Labour MPs. Zilliacus pressed the Prime Minister on several occasions not to send British troops to Vietnam, and when Wilson disassociated the Government from the American bombing of targets in North Vietnam, Zilliacus welcomed the statement but considered it 'inadequate'.[8] In a Commons debate in July 1966, Zilliacus made a long speech on Vietnam.[9] He sketched in the historical background to the conflict at some length and criticised American policy, arguing that the only settlement of interest to the USA was one of unconditional surrender by the North Vietnamese. He wound up by urging the British Government to work closely with the French and Soviet governments in order to get full implementation of the Geneva Agreements of 1954.

In a foreign affairs debate held in December 1966, Zilliacus forecast that de Gaulle would continue to block British entry to the Common Market for as long as Britain maintained its close links with the USA.[10] He put forward his long-held view that economic cooperation in Europe should be brought about by working through the UN's Economic Commission for Europe and not by the creation of trading blocs. He said he was worried at the growth of German nationalism and in particular West German demands for restoration of the former Reich borders of 1937. In conclusion, he urged Britain 'as a member of the Security Council … to wind up the military alliances as part of the evil heritage of the Cold War'.

In the following month Zilliacus's leukaemia suddenly flared up and in turn touched off secondary anaemia, turning a cough into bronchitis and the return of gout. A doctor told him that his spleen was bigger than a rugby football, but after appropriate treatment, involving the taking of eighteen pills a day, was reduced to the size of an orange. By March Zilliacus was feeling much better, although still largely confined to the house.[11] He managed to attend the House of Commons on 7 February 1967, when he questioned the Prime Minister on the results of his recent meeting with President de Gaulle, and the next day he attended a banquet at London's Guildhall as the guest of the Lord Mayor.

The banquet was held in honour of Alexei Kosygin the Soviet Prime Minister, who was paying a week's visit to Britain. Kosygin's stay was a great success. He was given a warm welcome wherever he went and some useful trade talks took place, although Harold Wilson's attempts at using the visit to further a settlement of the Vietnam War ended in failure.

Zilliacus wrote of the visit:

This warm feeling of friendship on the part of the British people is not a thing of yesterday – ultimately it dates back to the revolution for, after all, nearly three-quarters of our population are workers and in spite of all the hostile propaganda and peddling of anti-Communist fanaticism, the feeling has never died that the Soviet Union is a Socialist State, the first in the world and the revolution was carried out by workers and peasants. This feeling came out powerfully in the last war when we were allies and the Soviet Union destroyed 80 per cent of Hitler's Wehrmacht at the cost of the devastation of one-third of European Russia and 20 million casualties. Since then it has been part of this emotional, intellectual resistance to this propaganda of the Cold War and has become stronger as that propaganda loses credibility.[12]

And he welcomed the possible expansion of trade between Britain and the Soviet Union arising out of the visit, not least because he believed that Britain would not gain entry to the Common Market and therefore needed to cultivate alternative trading partners.

Zilliacus's attendances at the House of Commons were now infrequent, and he spoke in the chamber for the last time on 27 February 1967, when he urged the Government to support UN Secretary-General U Thant's proposals aimed at bringing about a negotiated settlement to the Vietnam War.[13]

Zilliacus's illness at least gave him some free time to spend at home and this enabled him to work on his latest book. He had been under contract to the Cresset Press, from as far back as 1959, to write a book called *Challenge to Fear*.[14] The book was intended to be a commentary on international relations since the Russian Revolution and was contracted to be 80,000-100,000 words in length. Unfortunately his hectic political life gave Zilliacus little time to devote to research and writing, and progress on the book proved slow. Furthermore, after completing two-thirds of the book a count revealed that he had already written 300,000 words, and he therefore had to begin paring it down. Nevertheless he still hoped to have it finished in time to be published to coincide with the 50th anniversary of the Russian Revolution for, as he explained to a friend, 'it deals with fifty years of Anglo-Russian relations in terms of my own experiences and reflections'.[15] Zilliacus intended *Challenge to Fear* to be his *magnum opus* and it turned out to be part autobiography, part history and part political analysis. It drew heavily on Zilliacus's previously published books and would have benefited by some rigorous editing of repetitious material. No doubt if he had been allowed the time and enjoyed better health he would have knocked his manuscript into shape. As it was he never completed the work, which remained in the form of a voluminous draft at the time of his death.[16]

Zilliacus also did his best to keep up to date with his correspondence and in the Spring of 1967 his postbag was overwhelmingly concerned with the Abortion Bill, then being steered through the House of Commons as a private member's bill by David Steel. Zilliacus supported the proposed reform of the law concerning abortion, although most of the letters he received were hostile to the change. He believed that the right to have an abortion should be made a statutory right, open to all women, and not just for those who could afford to secure it by a court ruling under civil law.[17]

Most MPs receive odd letters from unusual sources and Zilliacus was no exception. A letter he received in February 1967, however, was not from some crank. It was addressed from Parkhurst Prison and came from Peter Kroger. Kroger and his wife Helen had been found guilty in March 1961 for their part in the Portland spy ring, and both had received a twenty year sentence. The Krogers were professional spies working for the Soviet Union and held American citizenship at the time of their arrest. Peter Kroger had first written to Zilliacus on 9 May 1965 and he followed it up with six other letters, the last dated 21 February 1967. In these letters Kroger asked Zilliacus to arrange for the Polish Consul to visit him on the grounds of his Polish nationality. Although Zilliacus was usually prompt in answering letters and inclined to help people, he had ignored this series of letters from Peter Kroger. Indeed the receipt of the letters irritated him for he had no sympathy for the convicted spy and Kroger was not one of his constituents and therefore he had no obligation to help him. Zilliacus decided to put an end to Kroger's letters by replying that he was unable to assist and hoped Kroger would not write again.[18]

In the summer of 1967 Zilliacus's health continued to deteriorate and it was decided that he would have to be admitted to a hospital to receive treatment. He was no longer well enough to make the journey to Manchester and the weekend before he was due to go into hospital Jan Zilliacus travelled to Gorton to deal with some constituency business on his behalf. When she returned to Maida Vale it was to find that there had been a bonfire in the back garden: in her absence Zilliacus had burned most of his personal papers.

'That will make things easier for you,' he told her, for he had a good idea that he did not have long to live and he spent the last weeks of his life in St Bartholomew's Hospital. Nevertheless he continued to follow international affairs from his hospital bed and when the Six Day War broke out in the Middle East on 5 June 1967 and ended with the Israeli occupation of Egyptian territory in Gaza and Sinai, former Syrian territory on the Golan Heights, and the 'West Bank' formerly held by Jordan, he observed 'They have gone too far', and he was critical of the triumphalism displayed by the Israelis in the wake of their victory over the Arab forces. He died in Barts on 6 July 1967.[19]

Jan Zilliacus was inundated with telegrams, cards and letters of condolence from all over the world. After a private ceremony attended by members of his family and close friends, Zilliacus's body was cremated. In accordance with his last wishes, his ashes were taken to Finland, where they were deposited in the Zilliacus family's vault at the Sandudd cemetery in Helsinki and placed near those of his father Konni Zilliacus Senior and his beloved brother Laurin.

He left no money in his estate, indeed after his death some unpaid bills were presented to Jan Zilliacus for settlement. Zilliacus's good friend, Stephen Swingler, organised a collection among Labour MPs that raised £1260, and this helped to cover immediate expenses. Because Jan was Zilliacus's common law wife she was not eligible to receive the lump sum and pension paid to an MP's widow. Stephen Swingler pursued the matter on Jan's behalf but her application was firmly rejected on legal grounds. The lease on the house in Warrington Crescent had to be renegotiated, leaving Jan with possession of the garden flat, where she lived until her death in 1999.

Several obituaries on Konni Zilliacus appeared in newspapers and journals. Writing in *Tribune*, Philip Noel-Baker paid a warm and generous tribute to Zilliacus, recalling his work for the League of Nations and the Labour Party in the 1920s and 1930s.[20] Palme Dutt in *Labour Monthly* wrote

> Zilliacus had a special place in that generation which, growing up in Britain on the eve of, or during the first World War, was outraged by the revelations which it brought of the nature of British imperialism … In many articles for 'Labour Monthly', starting with 'Appeasement and Armageddon' in April 1939, and in the years 1946-49, he made distinguished contributions to internationalism. They are his particular monument, a source of pride in the midst of sorrow, for us and for all to whom the cause of peace is dear.[21]

When reporting his death the *Daily Mail* referred to Zilliacus as 'an identity-kit lefty',[22] but the obituary writer of *The Times* was much more perceptive in his judgement when he wrote:

> It was impossible to fit Zilliacus easily into any known political category, whether as extreme left winger, fellow traveller or crypto communist. In the eyes of some he appeared to be, at times, one or all of these things, but somehow he managed to elude precise definition as any of them. His immense fecundity of ideas overflowed all over the place, carrying him into excesses of unorthodoxy which he could defend with elaborate logic as being in strictest accord with the true Socialist canon. He was always convinced it was the others that were out of step.[23]

Chapter 28

Valedictories

At the Conway Hall, Red Lion Square, London, on 27 July 1967 at 11.30 a.m. over a hundred people assembled to pay their last respects to Konni Zilliacus. The memorial meeting had been organised by Jo Richardson, Secretary of the Tribune Group in the House of Commons, and among the Labour MPs present in the hall were Frank Allaun, Norman Atkinson, Norman Buchan, Anthony Greenwood, Eric Heffer, Stan Newens, Brian O'Malley and George Thomson. Sir Cyril Osborne, a fairly right-wing Conservative MP, was also present. He had often attended East-West Round Table Conferences with Zilliacus and although their political views were poles apart they had always got on well together and he had come along in remembrance of his old friend.

Zilliacus's first wife, Eugenia, had decided to attend the gathering and she took a seat in the front row. She was accompanied by the children of their marriage, son Dr Joe Zilliacus, and daughter Stella, who since her marriage to Sir Geoffrey Wallinger of the Foreign Office in 1958 had become Lady Wallinger. When Jan Zilliacus and daughter Linden arrived they took their seats in the balcony to avoid any possible embarrassment.

The meeting was to be chaired by Ian Mikardo and there were to be contributions from the journalists James Cameron and Basil Davidson, and the Labour MPs Michael Foot and Russell Kerr.[1]

Ian Mikardo opened the proceedings:

Friends, we who are a handful of the very large number of those who were Zilly's friends, admirers and pupils, are met this morning to pay tribute to and to give thanks for all the things that he was to us and the things that he did for us and for many others. I am sorry, very sorry, Fenner Brockway who was to have been here and to have spoken was taken ill yesterday and can't be here, and another who is omitted from us, because he is in hospital, is Sydney Silverman, and I want to read part of a note I have had from him.
He writes:
I am very sorry that I am not able to be present today. Zilly was in many ways the greatest international Socialist of my time. It is for that reason, and only for that reason, he earned the distinction of being refused a visa to the United States, and being refused a visa to the Soviet Union, and of being expelled from the Labour Party all within the same year. He never gave up fighting for the principles of the United Nations, based on the all-inclusive covenants of the Charter, no matter who opposed him, whether it was Ernest Bevin or Wall Street or Stalin. He was

completely devoted in the best sense to the socialist causes which are the basis of peace.

I want to read part of only one other of the very many messages which have been received and this is from the Speaker of the House of Commons, Horace King, who writes:

I knew Zilly over forty years, first through his books on internationalism and then for the past thirty years the man himself. Through all his writings, all his speeches, and all his actions there burned a clear flame of passionate sincerity and devotion to his fellow men. He was held in high esteem and affection, and loved both by those who shared his opinions and those who profoundly disagreed. I share, as an old friend, your deep sorrow at his passing.

Friends, I call on Jim Cameron'

James Cameron:

'Well I hope it's not an impertinence for an absolute non-politician to ask for a very, very brief moment in this meeting. I am immensely complimented to be here as all over the years I was immensely complimented to be able to share in Zilly's very lavish gift of friendship. Jannie will remember once, long, long ago now, when my family and Zilly's shared holidays together in their cottage by the Orwell. A period that sticks in my mind not as a great time of dialectical discussion and political repining in eleven languages, but as a time of writing ribald songs and eating fish, and chasing our children around the field. The children now grown up who have now begotten their own children, who may one day be glad that their grandparents had the good fortune to know a good man. It always seemed to me that Zilly's conflict with the world was not political opposition or moral indignation but the detailed exasperation of a gifted and experienced man who saw the fallacies of history and who saw all the libraries of human experience unexploited and unused, with power always in the hands of the clumsy people. I often used to wish I had an intelligence like his so much greater would have been my understanding, and then I sometimes was glad I had not, so much deeper would have been my disenchantment. I am grateful, nonetheless, that in that busy, good life he had a little time to include me. Thank you.'

Ian Mikardo:

'Jim, you said you were not a politician. You know, in a way Zilly was a non-politician. Most people who didn't know him personally but knew him only from reading what he wrote and reading about him, would think of him pre-eminently as a politician, but he really wasn't. He was a man of political ideas, but he wasn't very good at politics. The tactics, the ritual dances of parliamentary procedure and the order paper, were in a language that wasn't contained within the eleven he spoke. They were all foreign to him and when it really came to the tough stuff and the in-fighting I sometimes thought of Zilly as a child walking around a jungle of man-eating animals. That's why he was more than once such an easy victim for the hatchet men. Zilly was pre-eminently an analyst, perhaps unparalleled as a political analyst, and perhaps even more than that a teacher, a great teacher, and not only those like myself of his own generation learned at his feet, but the next generation of people in our movement derived a great deal from him and many of the new, younger men we have had in the House of Commons in the last three years know a great deal of what they know because of what they learned from Zilly. One of them is Russell Kerr.'

Russell Kerr:

'Mention has been made in the press, and also here this morning, of the more obvious qualities of the dear friend that we are gathered here to honour on this sad occasion. Tribute has rightly been paid to his vast, not to say encyclopaedic, knowledge of international affairs and to his long and meritorious service between the wars as a senior and highly respected member of the League of Nations Secretariat struggling might and main, week in week out, to combat fascism, to prevent its allies in this country and elsewhere, dragging the world into a second world war. Others in their tribute to Zilly have stressed the quite extraordinary influence he wielded in many parts of Europe, particularly in the difficult and anxious days of the Cold War. They have told of his friendship with Marshal Tito, and of his high standing with many other leaders east and west. Also, regrettably, they have told us how, during the same difficult years, his voice and his warnings about the future went largely unheeded by the majority of his parliamentary colleagues who not only accorded far too little honour to this prophet in his own country, but even to their eternal shame saw fit to remove him from their midst, albeit for a few years only. Other tributes to this very remarkable man have talked of his tremendous fighting spirit, never better exemplified than during the last eight years when he knew he was dying but became even more determined to fill the unforgiving minutes with sixty seconds worth of distance running, to quote a person with whose imperialist notions I have often found myself in violent disagreement. Others, again, have referred to his ever present humour, and to his wit. Remember, for example, his pleading to the then Labour Government, who had just begun surreptitiously to manufacture H-bombs, 'no annihilation without representation'. But for me, at any rate, the Everest and the whole Himalayan range of virtues possessed by this great man was the obvious and almost overwhelming love of mankind.
Inevitably in our memories of a dear friend now gone from us, we shall each of us recall moments of special joy or poignancy, which left impressions more vivid than others. For me, such especially vivid memories of him are mostly centred on the days of our early appointments in the late 1940s. After two years in this country during the war, I had returned to my native Australia for two or three years but had then returned to live here in the second half of 1948. In the autumn of the following, having by this time heard much of Zilly as Gateshead's fighting MP, and also having learned of the failure of his enemies, inside and outside the Party, to silence him, I observed with a sadness, shared I am sure by many others, his expulsion from the party he had served so long and so well for nearly thirty years. A few weeks after his expulsion was confirmed by the Labour Party Conference, I saw in the *New Statesman* an advertisement seeking a campaign organiser for the newly

independent Member for Gateshead East. Even the title had that authentic touch of bigness about it, which I shall always associate with dear Zilly. So I wrote to him listing my qualifications. First, I was totally inexperienced politically, apart from a little student activity pre-war. Secondly, I had been in the country little more than a year, apart from the two years of my wartime service. Thirdly, despite the foregoing I was willing to give it a go if he wanted me. He immediately accepted me for the job and almost from that time Zilly and I became the firmest of friends, and no political stripling ever received from his mentor such encouragement as it was my privilege to receive from him. To Zilly's family, particularly Jan, we express our sorrow and love on this sad occasion, but also our gratitude for their part in making a big man into a great and good man.'

Ian Mikardo then invited Basil Davidson to speak.

Basil Davidson:

'I would like to echo, if I may, the words which Jim Cameron opened with: I too feel immensely complimented as someone merely on the outside periphery of political life at having the opportunity of saying at least a few words. Perhaps one can say them with some confidence in that whether Zilly was a good politician or not he was certainly not only a politician, and he spoke, too, in many languages to people of all sorts. He was for me one of the finest men I have ever known and although this is bound to be a sad occasion yet, in its curious way, it also catches some of the zest for life that Zilly had. His opponents, his enemies, called him all sorts of things when they were angry with him and when they were less angry they used to call him a romantic, a crank, an innocent, not in the sense that Mik rightly meant, and he became extremely unfashionable. He was out of tune with the times. He differed from other prophets of doom in believing that human nature can be changed not only for the worst but also for the better.

I knew him years ago, in my case after war, and he seemed to me to combine erudition, hard headedness, a deep penetration into the springs of human action together with an immense zest for life. This combination came across from the earliest moment that I met him, which happened to be in a wacky old aeroplane going to Yugoslavia at the end of 1945. That was a time when little was known about the Balkans, even less than is known now, and the plane was full of people who wished to learn more. To my amazement Zilly knew it all perfectly well and he could speak the languages of the Balkans and obviously enjoyed watching the unfolding of events. Then I knew him well in the years after the war, which were a curious mixture of the sour and the sweet, when he and Jan were such marvellous hosts in Abbey Road. We used to live along a few hundred yards away, and many a splendid evening was passed in their company.

It seems to me that no matter how eccentric his position often seemed to be to those who disagreed with him, he really stood in the mainstream of our life and not only of our movement's life but of our country's life.

Ian Mikardo then introduced Michael Foot.

Michael Foot:

'There are many in this hall who knew Zilly more intimately than I knew him, and who could speak of him more closely, but I am extremely glad to have been invited to pay my tribute on my own behalf, on behalf of those at *Tribune*, and I believe on behalf of my parliamentary colleagues in the House of Commons. My first knowledge of Zilly was at *Tribune* in the year 1937, when we started to get huge manuscripts poured into us, a considerable part of them written in a handwriting that was distinctly legible, and my task was to sub-edit these outpourings. We were extremely grateful to have them then. The outpourings have continued from that day until very recently. Sometimes he supported us and sustained us, sometimes he cursed us, but time and again he overwhelmed us with his greater knowledge of world affairs and with his unfailing eagerness to understand what was happening and what were the views of other people.

I believe one of the most remarkable articles we have ever published in *Tribune* was the tribute written by Philip Noel-Baker a week or two ago, and no one could say better than Philip Noel-Baker did in that article what Zilly meant to those of us who met him for the first time or knew of his activities in the 1920s and 30s. He fought for the cause of genuine collective security throughout all those years. There was nobody to compare with him. *Inquest on Peace* by Vigilantes was in my opinion the best book of the whole of that time. It was written from his deep knowledge, but it was written by a man who wished to prevent a world war. Long before the Churchills or Edens ever lisped the words collective security, Zilly understood it and was campaigning for it, and if Zilly's advice had been taken there would have been no Second World War, no Auschwitz, no Buchenwald, no Hiroshima or any of the other agonies that we have subsequently endured.

He also had, we should not forget, a marvellous gift of burning invective which he would unleash on the heads of all deserving candidates, and there were many available. Sometimes when I heard him in the House of Commons pouring out his anger, I almost thought there was a streak of aesthetic delight in the way he did it. He wanted the job to be done as well as possible and it was right that it should be so.

I will say no more because reference has already been made to some of the incidents in his conflict with the Labour Party, some incidents which were inevitable but some incidents which are so deplorable that some of us will never forgive them and never forget them. After the world war he had striven to prevent, he became a major exponent of the ideas and mainsprings of policy accepted by the Soviet Union. Sometimes charges were made against him on that account, that he was a spokesman for their policies. This was never the case. Zilly was an independent man the whole of his life, everyone who knew him knew that, but he knew more of Soviet policy than the rest of us. He was the most skilled and experienced interpreter of what made Russian policy and what actuated Russian policy. He set about, in 1945, to stop the third world war. He devoted all his energies to that purpose. Almost the last speech I heard him make was the one he made at a meeting of the foreign affairs group of the PLP about Vietnam and he raised the whole issue to a different plane than the other speakers could do.

I believe his greatest quality was his passion and indomitable zest and gusto which he threw into all the activities in which he engaged. He devoted his whole life to the cause of peace … Sometimes the lines that he reminded me of were those of Wordsworth: 'We live by admiration, hope and love', and I would add in Zilly's case 'comradeship'. I believe that he lived by admiration, hope and love and comradeship and those of us who are here will treasure it for the rest of our days.'

The Chairman, Ian Mikardo, then wound up the meeting with the words:

'Hence there is much more that might be said and many here who are competent to say it, but let it all be said in our hearts and, more importantly, be reflected in our actions. I have been spiritually stimulated this last half hour by the feeling that once again, for the last time, I have been in Zilly's company and I hope you all have too. Perhaps not quite the last time I shall have the feeling, at least the next time I pass a dissident vote, that I will be carrying Zilly's proxy vote in my pocket as well. Thank you all for coming.'

Notes

Chapter 1: Early Life

[1] *The Times,* 21 June 1924.

[2] Most of the material on the Zilliacus family comes from personal interviews with Konni Zilliacus's daughter, Stella Zilliacus (Lady Wallinger) conducted by Kenneth Millen-Penn and quoted in his Ph.D. thesis 'From Liberal to Socialist internationalism: Konni Zilliacus and the League of Nations, 1894 -1939'. State University of New York at Binghampton, 1993, plus my own interviews with his second wife, Janet Zilliacus, 1996-97.

[2] Zilliacus Senior's political activities are well covered in Michael Futrell, *Northern Underground* (New York 1963) pp 41-66.

[3] *The Times,* op.cit.

[4] K. Zilliacus, *A New Birth of Freedom?* (London, 1957) pp.1-2.

[5] J.H.Badley, *Bedales: A Pioneer School* (London, 1923) et seq.

[6] *Bedale Record* 1909-12, et seq.

Chapter 2: War and Revolution

[1] Konni Zilliacus Folder, Yale Alumni Office et seq.

[2] Interview with Jan Zilliacus.

[3] Zilliacus, 'Challenge to Fear' 5/37-38, Zilliacus Papers, National Museum of Labour History, Manchester.

[4] C.H.Sisson (ed), *Autobiographical and other papers by Philip Mairet* (Manchester, 1981) pp 98-102.

[5] Lieutenant K. Zilliacus's Military Service File, Ministry of Defence et seq.

[6] Josiah Wedgwood, *Memoirs of a Fighting Life* (London, 1940) p 136.

[7] Foreign Office File 371, 1472 2 January 1918, 1472/4025 6 January 1918, Public Record Office.

[8] Wedgwood op. cit. p. 126.

[9] Konni Zilliacus's naturalisation papers dated 8 January 1918, held by Jan Zilliacus, describe Zilliacus's nationality as Finnish.

[10] Zilliacus's Military Service File op.cit.

[11] Josiah Wedgwood, *Essays and Adventures of a Labour MP* (London, 1924) pp 17-18.

[12] The literature on intervention is extensive. For a comprehensive account see Richard H.Ullman, *Intervention and the War* (1961), *Britain and the Russian Civil War* (1968), and *The Anglo-Soviet Accord* (1972). The three volumes are published by Princeton University Press, USA.

[13] Zilliacus, 'Challenge to Fear' op. cit. 2/2, Zilliacus Papers.

[14] Ibid., 5/43.

[15] Zilliacus, 'Challenge to Fear' op. cit. 5/54.

[16] Andrew Rothstein, *When Britain invaded the Soviet Union: the Consul who rebelled* (London, 1979) p XII.

[17] Zilliacus, Challenge to Fear, op. cit. 5/54, Zilliacus Papers.

[18] Ibid., 5/74.

Chapter 3: Geneva

[1] K.Zilliacus, *Why I Was Expelled* (London 1949) p. 7.

[2] See Catherine Anne Cline, *Recruits to Labour - the British Labour Party 1914-1931* (New York, 1963) especially Ch IV.

[3] Letter, Zilliacus to C.P. Scott, 2 July 1920, *Manchester Guardian* Papers.

[4] Letters, Zilliacus to C.P.Scott and internal editorial memoranda, July 1920, *Manchester Guardian* Papers.

[5] League Secretariat internal correspondence and memoranda, 1925, League of Nations Archives, Geneva.

[6] Zilliacus, 'Challenge to Fear, op.cit, 6/3-6, Zilliacus Papers.

[7] Zilliacus destroyed his own papers before he entered hospital for the final time, leaving only the manuscript of 'Challenge to Fear' as a kind of last testament to his life and work.

[8] For Zilliacus - Cecil correspondence see Lord Robert Cecil Papers, British Library, London.

[9] For Zilliacus - Angell correspondence see Norman Angell Papers, Ball State University Library, Muncie, Indiana.

[10] Zilliacus, 'Challenge to Fear', op.cit, 6/25. Zilliacus Papers.

[11] For Zilliacus - Noel-Baker correspondence see Noel-Baker Papers, Churchill College, Cambridge.

[12] For full life see David J Whittaker, *Fighter for Peace: Philip Noel-Baker 1889-1982* (York 1989).

[13] For full life see Ben Pimlott, *Hugh Dalton* (London 1985).

[14] Hugh Dalton Diary for September 1925, Hugh Dalton Papers, British Library of Political and Economic Science, London.

[15] Zilliacus, 'Challenge to Fear', op.cit, 6/27, Zilliacus Papers.

[16] For examples of socialising between Zilliacus and Dalton see Hugh Dalton Diary.

[17] Mary Agnes Hamilton, *Remembering My Good Friends* (London, 1944) p.189.

[18] Zilliacus, 'Challenge to Fear', op.cit, 6/35, Zilliacus Papers.

[19] Ibid., 11/36.

[20] Ibid., 6/33.

[21] Hugh Dalton, *Call Back Yesterday* (London 1953) p.259. For a less partisan account see David Carlton, *MacDonald versus Henderson: The Foreign Policy of the Second Labour Government* (London, 1970).

[22] Zilliacus, 'Challenge to Fear', op. cit, 6/38, Zilliacus Papers.

[23] Because of his conditions of service as a League of Nations official both books had to be published under pseudonyms. *The League of Nations Today* was published in 1923 under the authorship of Roth Williams; and *The Origins, Structure and Working of the League of Nations* was published in 1928 under the assumed name of C.Howard-Ellis. The 1923 book contains suggestions on how to make the League more effective, the 1928 publication is more of a textbook.

[24] Perhaps the most authoritative book on the League of Nations remains F.P. Walters, *A History of the League of Nations* (Oxford 1952). Three more recent books are: George Scott, *The Rise and Fall of the League of Nations* (London 1973), James Avery Joyce, *Broken Star: The Story of the League of Nations* (Swansea 1978), and F.S. Northedge *The League of Nations – its life and times 1920-1946* (Leicester, 1986).

[25] For full account of this crisis see James Barros, *The Corfu Incident of 1923: Mussolini and the League of Nations* (Princeton, 1965).

[26] Letter, Zilliacus to Angell, 28 September 1923, Angell Papers.

[27] For account of first Labour Government's foreign policy see Richard W. Lyman, *The First Labour Government 1924* (London, 1957).

[28] Zilliacus, 'Challenge to Fear', op.cit, 6/28-29, Zilliacus Papers.

[29] Ibid., 6/8.

[30] Letter, Zilliacus to C.P.Scott, 20 August 1921, *Manchester Guardian* Papers.

[31] Hugh Dalton, 'British Foreign Policy 1929-1931, *Political Quarterly* Oct-Dec 1931. [32] Hamilton,

op.cit, p.191.

[33] Harold Butler, *The Lost Peace* (London, 1941) p.42.

[34] A phrase used by Leopold Schwarzschild to describe the years of treaty signing and pact making 1925-29 in *World in Trance* (London, 1943).

Chapter 4: The Manchurian Crisis

[1] Zilliacus, 'Challenge to Fear', op.cit., 8/2, Zilliacus Papers.

[2] For full accounts of the crisis see: Sarah R Smith, *The Manchurian Crisis, 1931-32. A tragedy in international relations* (New York, 1948) and R.Bassett, *Democracy and Foreign Policy. A case history: the Sino-Japanese dispute 1931-33* (London, 1952).

[3] League of Nations Official Journal, December 1931, pp. 2453-4.

[4] Zilliacus, 'Challenge to Fear', op.cit., 8/26, Zilliacus Papers.

[5] These are the words of the poet Lin Yuteng quoted in Dick Wilson, *When Tigers Fight: The Story of the Sino-Japanese War 1937-1945* (London, 1982) p. 1.

[6] Zilliacus, 'Challenge to Fear', op.cit., 8/13, Zilliacus Papers.

[7] Zilliacus-E.T.Scott correspondence, *Manchester Guardian* Papers.

[8] Zilliacus-W.P.Crozier correspondence, *Manchester Guardian* Papers.

[9] Zilliacus-Angell correspondence, Angell Papers.

[10] Interview with Lady Wallinger, 1 July 1984 quoted in Millen-Penn thesis op.cit., p.19.

[11] Interview with Jan Zilliacus.

Chapter 5: Disarmament

[1] Vigilantes, Inquest on Peace (London, 1935) p. 45.

[2] Ibid., p.47.

[3] Zilliacus, 'Challenge to Fear', op. cit, 8/40-41, Zilliacus Papers.

[4] Quoted in F.M.Leventhal, *Arthur Henderson* (Manchester, 1989) p.203.

[5] Sir John Simon was often described by his contemporaries as 'shifty' or 'sly' – see David Dutton, *Simon – a political biography of Sir John Simon* (London, 1992) pp. 334-5. Lloyd George spoke of Simon leaving behind him ' the slime of hypocrisy', Hansard 5th series Vol. 254, cols. 1657-8; and Harold Nicolson described him as 'a toad and a worm' in *Diary and Letters 1939-45* (London, 1967) p. 407.

[6] Leventhal, op.cit., p. 213.

[7] Zilliacus, 'Challenge to Fear', op. cit., 11/4, Zilliacus Papers.

[8] Ibid., 11/3.

[9] Henderson spoke to Hugh Dalton about the warning he had received from an unnamed source and Dalton recorded the conversation in his diary for 12 January 1932.

[10] Zilliacus, 'Challenge to Fear', op. cit., 11/3, Zilliacus Papers.

[11] The evolution of Labour's foreign policy in the 1930s is well covered in John F. Naylor, *Labour's International Policy – the Labour Party in the 1930s* (London, 1969).

[12] Zilliacus, 'Challenge to Fear', op. cit.,11/8-9.

[13] Ibid., 11/9.

[14] Loc. cit.

[15] Zilliacus refers to these documents in 'Challenge to Fear' 11/2 and some copies survive among the Attlee Papers at the Bodleian Library, Oxford and the Noel-Baker Papers at the Churchill Archives Centre, Churchill College, Cambridge.

[16] Zilliacus, 'Challenge to Fear', op. cit., 11/20-21, Zilliacus Papers.

[17] Ibid. 11/27 and Pimlott, *Hugh Dalton* pp. 214-5.

[18] Letter, Zilliacus to Noel-Baker, 29 November 1937, Noel-Baker Papers.

[19] Zilliacus, 'Challenge to Fear', op. cit., 11/42.

[20] Ibid., 11/ 22-23.

[21] Philip M. Williams, *Hugh Gaitskell – a political biography* (London, 1979) p.63 and Michael

Stewart, *Life and Labour – an autobiography* (London, 1990) p.36. Michael Stewart mistakenly credits Hugh Dalton as the person responsible for organising the summer school. Zilliacus was undoubtedly director of studies and Dalton most probably played a key role in selecting who should be awarded places on the course.

[22] Zilliacus, 'Challenge to Fear', op. cit., 11/ 5-6, Zilliacus Papers.

Chapter 6: The Italo-Abyssinian War

[1] The country now known as Ethiopia was more usually referred to as Abyssinia in the 1930s and I have therefore used this name throughout the narrative.

[2] The diplomatic background and military campaigns are well covered in A.J Barker, *The Civilising Mission: the Italo-Ethiopian War 1935-36* (London, 1968).

[3] Zilliacus outlined his views in letters to Norman Angell (Angell Papers) and H.R. Cummings, a League official based in London, see Correspondence Files in League of Nations Archives, Geneva, 1934-35. His published comments are contained in his pamphlet *Abyssinia* and the book *Inquest on Peace*, both published in 1935.

[4] Zilliacus's correspondence with Attlee and other members of the Labour Party covering the Italo-Abyssinia dispute are contained in a file in the Noel-Baker Papers.

[5] Zilliacus , 'Challenge to Fear', op. cit., 11/26-27, Zilliacus Papers.

[6] Ibid. 11/ 29-30.

[7] Zilliacus – Noel-Baker correspondence, July 1935, Noel-Baker Papers.

[8] 'Vigilantes', *Inquest on Peace* (London, 1935) p.5.

[9] Zilliacus, 'Challenge to Fear', op. cit, 8/13-15, Zilliacus Papers.

[10] 'Vigilantes', *The Road to War* (London, 1937) see title page.

[11] 'Vigilantes', *Abyssinia, the essential facts in the dispute and an answer to the question: ought we to support sanctions?* (London, 1935).

[12] *New Statesman and Nation*, 2 November 1935.

[13] Letter Zilliacus to H.R.Cummings, 14 October 1935, League of Nations Correspondence Files.

[14] For full account of the 1935 general election see Tom Stannage, *Baldwin Thwarts the Opposition* (London, 1980).

[15] Zilliacus, 'Challenge to Fear', op. cit., 9/27, Zilliacus Papers.

[16] Letter, Zilliacus to W.P.Crozier, 3 July 1936, *Manchester Guardian* Papers.

Chspter 7: Angell Plus Marx

[1] 'Vigilantes', *Between Two Wars?* (Penguin Special, London 1939) p. 29.

[2] Zilliacus , 'Challenge to Fear' ,7/21-22, Zilliacus Papers.

[3] Norman Angell was a prolific writer and his life and ideas have been the subject of several books and theses: these are usefully brought together in J.D.B.Miller, *Norman Angell and the Futility of War* (London 1986).

[4] Zilliacus, 'Challenge to Fear' ,7/27, Zilliacus Papers.

[5] Ibid. 7/22.

[6] K. Zilliacus, *Mirror of the Present: the way the world is going* (London, 1947) p.10.

[7] Zilliacus, 'Challenge to Fear', 7/28-29, Zilliacus Papers.

[8] A.J.P.Taylor, *The Troublemakers* (London, 1987) p.182.

[9] 'Vigilantes', *Why the League Failed* (Left Book Club, London, 1938) p. 82.

[10] John Lewis, *The Left Book Club – An Historical Record* (London, 1970) p. 23.

[11] A.J.P.Taylor, *English History 1914-1945* (Oxford 1967 ed.) p. 627.

[12] The general background to the publication of *Guilty Men* is well covered in Paul Addison, *The Road to 1945* (London, 1975) p. 110.

[13] 'Vigilantes', *The Road to War* (Left Book Club, London, 1937) p. 66.

[14] Zilliacus, 'Challenge to Fear', 10/1-2, Zilliacus Papers.

[15] Letter, Zilliacus to W.P.Crozier, 11 August 1936, *Manchester Guardian* Papers.

[16] The book was provisionally titled 'Peace and the conflict of ideologies' – see Norman Angell, *After All* (London, 1951) p. 270.

[17] Letter, Zilliacus to Norman Angell, 3 April 1937, Angell Papers.

[18] The changes in Labour's foreign and defence policies are well covered in G.D.H. Cole, *A History of the Labour Party from 1914* (London, 1978 ed.) pp. 330-3, and for a more personal account see Hugh Dalton, *The Fateful Years* (London, 1957) pp. 132-140.

Chapter 8: Annus Miserabilis

[1] Anthony Eden's account of these events can be found in: Earl of Avon, *The Eden Memoirs – Facing the Dictators* (London, 1962).

[2] 'Vigilantes', *Why the League Has Failed* p.95.

[3] 'Vigilantes', *Why We are Losing the Peace* (Left Book Club, London, 1939) p.98.

[4] Winston Churchill, *The Gathering Storm* (London 1948) p. 201.

[5] Zilliacus, 'Challenge to Fear', 10/22-23, Zilliacus Papers.

[6] Ibid. 10/23-24.

[7] Ibid. 10/25-26.

[8] The literature on Appeasement is voluminous: for a well-researched, critical view see M.Gilbert and R.Gott, *The Appeasers* (London, 1962) and for a subtle defence of the policy see John Charmley, *Chamberlain and the Lost Peace* (London, 1989).

[9] These events are covered in some detail in Gordon Brook-Shepherd, *Anschluss – the Rape of Austria* (London, 1963).

[10] The incident is described in Scott, *The Rise and Fall of the League of Nations* pp.387-392.

[11] 'Munich' continues to fascinate historians: the subject is comprehensively covered in Telford Taylor, *Munich: the Price of Peace* (London, 1979), and on the fiftieth anniversary of the Munich Conference there appeared Robert Kee, *Munich: the Eleventh Hour* (London, 1988) to attempt another assessment of the event.

[12] Zilliacus's resignation letter is quoted in James Barros, *Betrayal from Within – Joseph Avenol, Secretary-General of the League of Nations 1933-1940* (Yale, 1969) pp. 173-4. This book provides an interesting account of the career of the League's last Secretary-General.

[13] Zilliacus, 'Challenge to Fear', 11/43, Zilliacus Papers.

[14] Interviews with Mrs Jan Zilliacus, Mrs Dawn Harris Stanford and Mrs Linden Empson, (neé Zilliacus) 1996-99 plus a set of diaries covering the period 1939-67 used by K. Zilliacus to record appointments, addresses and telephone numbers etc in the possession of Mrs Empson.

Chapter 9: Raising Hell

[1] Zilliacus, 'Challenge to Fear' 11/44-45, Zilliacus Papers.

[2] Letter, Zilliacus to W.P.Crozier, 3 March 1939, *Manchester Guardian* Papers.

[3] *Tribune*, 31 March 1939.

[4] Ibid., 23 July and 4 August 1939.

[5] Ibid., 6 April 1939.

[6] Ibid., 14 July 1939.

[7] Ibid., 26 April 1939.

[8] Ibid., 5 May 1939.

[9] Ibid., 12 May 1939.

[10] Ibid., 1 September 1939.

[11] Ibid., 22 September and 29 September 1939.

[12] K. Zilliacus, 'Appeasement and Armageddon', *Labour Monthly*, April 1939.

[13] 'Vigilantes' (K.Zilliacus) *Between Two Wars*, p.16.

[14] Zilliacus 'Challenge to Fear' 11/44, Zilliacus Papers.

[15] Labour Party Conference Report 1939 pp. 240-1.
[16] For Bevin's contribution to the debate see *The Life and Times of Ernest Bevin Vol.1: Trade Union Leader 1881-1940*. London, 1960.
[17] Labour Party Conference Report 1939 pp. 246-7.
[18] Ibid., p. 247.
[19] Zilliacus, 'Challenge to Fear' 11/44, Zilliacus Papers.
[20] Ibid., 11/45.
[21] Ibid., 11/46.
[22] Ibid.
[23] Ibid., 11/47.

Chapter 10: Gateshead

[1] Annual Report of the Gateshead Public Health Department 1941.
[2] J.B.Priestley, *English Journey* (Collected Edition, London, 1949) p.301.
[3] For historical background on Gateshead see F.W.D.Manders, *A History of Gateshead* (Gateshead 1973)
[4] 'Ruth Dodds' by Maureen Callcott and Margaret Espinasse, *Dictionary of Labour Biography* ed. J.M. Bellamy and J. Saville, Vol.7 (London 1974) pp. 63-70. And Maureen Callcott (Ed.) *A Pilgrimage of Grace: the diaries of Ruth Dodds 1905-1974* (Whitley Bay, 1995).
[5] See Don Watson and John Corcoran, '*An Inspiring Example': the North East of England and the Spanish Civil War 1936-39*. (London, 1996) and for a wider view of the Aid to Spain organisations John Fyrth, *The Signal was Spain – the Spanish Aid Movement in Britain* (London 1986).
[6] *Newcastle Journal*, 22 May 1939.
[7] Interview with Len Edmondson, 29 October 1999. Len Edmondson was a member of the Gateshead ILP 1935-50, and one of the Friends of the Soviet Union and the India League in the 1930s.
[8] This point is well argued in Sharon Ferguson, 'Labour Party Politics 1935-45: a case study of Konni Zilliacus and Gateshead Labour Party and Trades Council,' a dissertation submitted in partial fulfilment of the requirements of the degree of BA with Honours in History at the University of Cambridge, 1988.
[9] *Newcastle Journal* and *North Mail*, 19 July 1939.
[10] Ibid., 1 September 1938.
[11] Zilliacus, 'Challenge to Fear' 11/47-48, Zilliacus Papers.
[12] Interview with Len Edmondson, 29 October 1999. Len Edmondson spoke to several of those who had attended the selection meeting.
[13] *Gateshead Herald*, September 1939.
[14] Priestley, op. cit., p. 311.
[15] The first story was recounted by Jan Zilliacus in an interview on 23 February 1996 and the second recalled by Len Edmondson in an interview on 29 October 1999.
[16] *Tribune*, 8 September 1939.

Chapter 11: The War Years

[1] Useful background on the work of the Ministry of Information can be found in Ian MacLaine, *Ministry of Morale – Home Front Morale and the Ministry of Information in World War Two* (London 1979), and an irreverent look at the early months of the Ministry in Malcolm Muggeridge, *Chronicles of a Wasted Time 2 – The Infernal Grove* (London, 1973) pp. 77-83.
[2] Interviews with Mrs Jan Zilliacus and family.
[3] Zilliacus diaries for appointments.
[4] Labour Party Conference Report for 1941 pp. 163-4. For background on Labour's approach to foreign policy during the war years see T.D. Burridge, *British Labour and Hitler's War* (London,

1976).

[5] Labour Party Conference Report 1943 pp. 149-50.

[6] *Gateshead Herald,* December 1944.

[7] Labour Party Conference Report 1945 p. 82

[8] Ibid., p. 132

[9] *Tribune,* 29 September 1939.

[10] Bill Jones, *The Russia Complex – the British Labour Party and the Soviet Union* (Manchester, 1977) pp. 56-7.

[11] *Tribune,* 8 December 1939.

[12] Ibid., 22 December 1939.

[13] Ibid., 29 December 1939.

[14] Ibid., 17 January 1940.

[15] Victor Gollancz (Editor), *The Betrayal of the Left* (London, 1941) p.186.

[16] Arthur Koestler's *Darkness at Noon* was published in the spring of 1941. After the Nazi-Soviet pact, the Soviet attack on Finland, and Communist opposition to the British war effort, John Strachey could still describe his reading of the book as making a 'stunning impression' on him – see John Strachey, *The Strangled Cry* (London, 1962) p.13.

[17] *Tribune,* 27 September 1940.

[18] Ibid., 11 July 1941.

[19] Ibid., 19 August 1941.

[20] Ibid., 12 December 1941.

[21] Ibid.,19 December 1941.

[22] John Campbell, *Nye Bevan and the Mirage of British Socialism* (London, 1987) p. 106.

[23] The UDC held its last meeting in October 1966 under the chairmanship of J.E.Mortimer. It was wound up because of poor attendance at meetings and falling subscriptions from trade unions. The UDC Records are held at the University of Hull Library, and I am grateful to Jim Mortimer for providing additional information.

[24] Judith Cook, *Priestley* (London 1997) pp. 181-9.

[25] Paul Addison, *The Road to 1945* (London 1975) p.159.

[26] Letter from K.Zilliacus to Raymond Gauntlett, 18 June 1942, Kingsley Martin Papers, University of Sussex.

[27] Letter from K.Zilliacus to Kingsley Martin, 2 December 1944, Kingsley Martin Papers.

[28] Letter from Lord Cecil to Konni Zilliacus, 17 November 1944, Kingsley Martin Papers.

[29] Douglas Jay, *Change and Fortune* (London 1980) pp. 123-4.

[30] Letter from K.Zilliacus to C.D.Kimber, Secretary of Federal Union Movement, 21 April 1939, Lionel Curtis Papers, Bodleian Library, Oxford.

[31] K.Zilliacus, Letter in *New Statesman and Nation,* 28 October 1944.

[32] Zilliacus, 'Challenge to Fear' 12/79, Zilliacus Papers.

[33] Ibid., 12/77.

[34] Ibid.,12/79.

[35] On page 165 of his book *Stalin's Secret War* (London, 1981) Nikolai Tolstoy describes how in 1940 Zilliacus, dressed in the uniform of a British officer, visited General Weygard's Headquarters in Beirut, where he examined maps and photographs that formed part of a French plan to strike at the Soviet Union in the Caucasus. Tolstoy speculates that Zilliacus might have passed on the information gained in this way to Soviet intelligence. In fact, as this chapter shows, Zilliacus spent the war working for the Ministry of Information in London and the only uniform he wore was that of a private in the Home Guard.

Chapter 12: Jan

[1] Interviews with Mrs Jan Zilliacus et seq. See also obituaries on Jan Zilliacus by Jim Walker in *The Guardian* 6 May 1999 and by Kevin Brownlow in *The Independent* 1 June 1999.

[2] See Ephraim Katz, *The International Film Encyclopedia* (London, 1980 edition) for entry on Laurence Trimble p.1148.

[3] Letter from Harold Laski to Leonard Woolf, 11 November 1943, Leonard Woolf Papers, University of Sussex. In this letter Laski informed Woolf that Zilliacus had told him of the attempt to recruit him into concealed membership of the Communist Party. Although Laski sometimes embroidered the truth to make himself appear more important there is no reason why he should not have told the unvarnished truth on this occasion.

[4] In the *Partisan Review* for Summer 1946, George Orwell accused Zilliacus of being an 'underground Communist'. In a letter of reply to this accusation, which appeared in *Tribune* on 17 January 1947, Zilliacus wrote:

I am not a member of the CP, never have been a member of the CP, and would consider it a disgraceful thing to do, to be secretly a member of any party or organisation which was not compatible with membership of the Labour Party. I am proud of the fact that I joined the Labour Party when I was demobilised after the first world war nearly 28 years ago, and have stuck to it and worked for it ever since, in good times and bad.

N.B. The Federal Bureau of Investigation in Washington holds files on both Konni and Jan Zilliacus in their Archives but in spite of lengthy correspondence with the FBI, followed by an appeal to the US Department of Justice, these records remained closed to the author.

Chapter 13: The 1945 General Election

[1] For background on the 1945 general election see R.B. McCallum and Alison Readman, *The British General Election of 1945* (Oxford, 1947) and for local coverage *Newcastle Journal*.

[2] Zilliacus, 'Challenge to Fear' 12/85, Zilliacus Papers.

[3] Interview with Len Edmondson.

[4] Interview with Jan Zilliacus.

[5] McCallum and Readman, op. cit., p.166.

[6] *Newcastle Journal*, 6 July 1945.

[7] Zilliacus, 'Challenge to Fear' 14/4, Zilliacus Papers.

[8] Zilliacus expressed his unease at these developments in a series of articles in the *Gateshead Herald* 1943-44.

[9] Zilliacus, 'Challenge to Fear' 12/84, Zilliacus Papers.

Chapter 14: Into Parliament

[1] Zilliacus, 'Challenge to Fear' 14/4, Zilliacus Papers.

[2] James Callaghan, *Time and Chance* (London, 1987) p. 65.

[3] Barbara Castle, *Fighting All the Way* (London, 1993) p. 126.

[4] Christopher Mayhew, *Time to Explain* (London, 1987) p. 86.

[5] Woodrow Wyatt, *Confessions of an Optimist* (London, 1985) pp. 115-6.

[6] The incident is fully covered in Kenneth Harris, *Attlee* (London, 1982) pp. 262-6.

[7] Zilliacus, 'Challenge to Fear' 14/22, Zilliacus Papers.

[8] Ibid., 14/23.

[9] Ibid., 14/22.

[10] Ibid., 14/5.

[11] Hansard, 23 August 1945.

[12] Ibid.

[13] Ernest Bevin's role as Foreign Secretary is thoroughly covered in Alan Bullock, *Ernest Bevin – Foreign Secretary 1945-51* (London 1983) and more critically by John Saville in *The Politics of Continuity – British Foreign Policy and the Labour Government 1945-46* (London, 1993).

[14] Hansard, 23 August 1945.

[15] Zilliacus, 'Challenge to Fear' 14/6-14, Zilliacus Papers.

[16] Memorandum, Zilliacus to Attlee, 11 February 1946, Attlee Papers, Bodleian.

[17] Reply, Attlee to Zilliacus, 17 February 1946, Attlee Papers, Bodleian.

[18] These events are covered in Bullock's *Ernest Bevin - Foreign Secretary 1945-51* pp. 348-354 and for discussion of 'Attlee's heresy' see R.Smith and J.Zametica, 'The Cold War: Clement Attlee Reconsidered 1945-7', *International Affairs* Spring 1985.

[19] Zilliacus, *Why I was Expelled* p. 12.

Chapter 15: The Rebel

[1] *Tribune,* 24 August 1951.

[2] Zilliacus 'Challenge to Fear' 11/48, Zilliacus Papers.

[3] The incident is referred to in the Shaw-Zilliacus correspondence of 1949.
Photocopies of these letters are in the Zilliacus Papers. The originals are held by Linden Empson.

[4] Denis Healey, *The Time of My Life* (London, 1989) p.105.

[5] In his *History of the Second World War* (London, 1970) p.105 Liddell Hart observes: 'Morally even more than materially, the disaster to that army at Stalingrad had an effect from which the German army never recovered.'

[6] Hansard,4 March 1946.

[7] Ibid., 5 March 1946.

[8] Labour Party Conference Report, 13 June 1946.

[9] *Tribune,* 14 June 1946.

[10] Hansard, 23 October 1946.

[11] Ibid.

[12] A copy of the letter can be found in the Benn Levy Papers at the House of Lords Records Office.

[13] The background to the tabling of the Amendment is well covered in Anthony Howard, *Crossman – the pursuit of power* (London, 1990) pp. 130-3.

[14] Hansard, 18 November 1946.

[15] K.Zilliacus, *I Choose Peace* (Penguin Special, London, 1949) p. 336.

[16] The origins of the Cold War have long been the subject of controversy among historians. In 1968 the *Journal of Contemporary History* published separate articles by Paul Seabury and Brian Thomas that attempted to review the existing literature on the subject. In his review Brian Thomas credited Zilliacus with being a pioneer of the revisionist approach. Many books have been published on the Cold War since the Seabury and Thomas reviews, and two of the most useful in providing background for this book have been: Victor Rothwell, *Britain and the Cold War 1941-47* (London, 1982) and Peter Weiler, *British Labour and the Cold War* (Stamford, 1988).

[17] Hansard, 31 March 1947.

[18] See Howard, op. cit., pp.134-5.

[19] For background on the Keep Left group see Jonathan Schneer, *Labour's Conscience – the Labour Left 1945-51* (London, 1988) pp. 60-63.

[20] Zilliacus, *Why I was Expelled* p.19.

[21] *Tribune,* 9 May 1947.

Chapter 16: Margate and After

[1] For an analysis of the relationship between the Labour Government and the constituent parts of the Labour Party under Attlee's premiership see Chapter 2, 'The Framework of Politics 1945-1951, in Kenneth O. Morgan, *Labour in Power 1945-1951* (Oxford, 1984) pp. 45-93.

[2] See Robert Griffiths, *S.O. Davies – a Socialist Faith* (Llandysul, 1983).

[3] For detailed analysis of various left-wing groups inside the Labour Party see Mark Jenkins,

Bevanism – Labour's High Tide (Nottingham, 1979).

[4] Bullock, *Ernest Bevin – Foreign Secretary* pp. 396-8.

[5] Geoffrey Williams and Bruce Reed, *Denis Healey and the Politics of Power* (London, 1971) pp. 60-2.

[6] Labour Party Conference Report 26 May 1947.

[7] Ibid.

[8] Ibid.

[9] Ibid.,24 May 1947.

[10] Harris, op. cit, p. 308.

[11] Labour Party Conference Report, 29 May 1947.

[12] *New Statesman and Nation,* 7 June 1947.

[13] *Tribune,* 20 June 1947.

[14] *New Statesman and Nation,* 14 June 1947.

[15] Ibid.,28 June 1947.

[16] Ibid., 26 July 1947.

[17] Ibid., 20 September 1947.

[18] Zilliacus, *A New Birth of Freedom* pp. 143-4.

[19] Hansard, 10 July 1947.

[20] Vladislav Zubok and Constantine Pleshkov, *Inside the Kremlin's Cold War* (Harvard, 1996) pp. 129-33.

[21] The Manifesto of the Cominform, drafted by Zhadanov, is re-printed in Julius Brauthal, *A History of the International 1943-1968* (London, 1980) Appendix Seven pp. 549-51.

[22] Vladimir Dedijer, *Tito Speaks* (London, 1953) p. 304.

[23] K.Zilliacus, *Tito of Yugoslavia* (London, 1952) p. 211.

[24] The Communist takeover of eastern Europe is covered in Hugh Seton-Watson, *The Pattern of Communist Revolution* (London, 1953) and the demise of the Social Democratic parties in Denis Healey, *The Curtain Falls* (London, 1951).

[25] Pavel Tigrid, 'The Prague Coup of 1948: the Elegant Takeover', in Thomas T.Hammond, ed., *The Anatomy of Communist Takeovers* (Yale, 1975) is a good study of the coup.

[26] Isaac Kramnick and Barry Sheeerman, *Harold Laski – a Life on the Left* (London, 1993) pp. 562-4.

[27] *Tribune,* 19 March 1948.

[28] Howard, op. cit., p. 142, see also Lord Wigg, *George Wigg* (London, 1972) pp. 147-8.

[29] *Tribune,* 14 May 1948.

[30] Schneer, op. cit., p. 38.

Chapter 17: The Titoist

[1] Leah Manning was one of the Labour MPs in the visiting party and she gives an interesting account of the trip in her autobiography: Leah Manning, *A Life for Education* (London, 1970) pp. 210-1.

[2] Zilliacus, *A New Birth of Freedom* p. 114.

[3] Ibid., pp.141-3.

[4] Ibid., pp. 169-72.

[5] Correspondence relating to the visit in Zilliacus Papers.

[6] Zilliacus, *A New Birth of Freedom* p. 13.

[7] Ibid., p. 96.

[8] George Thomas mentions the tour in his autobiography George Thomas, *Mr. Speaker* (London, 1985) p. 67, although he gives the wrong year for the visit. See also Hansard 22 October 1947 for a speech in which he referred to the trip.

[9] Interview with Jan Zilliacus.

[10] Zilliacus gave an account of the interview in his article 'Stalin and all that' in the *New Statesman and Nation,* 1 November 1947.

[11] Zilliacus's views on the early post-war years were largely in line with those of the famous American journalist John Gunther in his *Behind Europe's Curtain* (London, 1949).

[12] The Soviet-Yugoslav dispute is well covered in Adam B. Ulam, *Titoism and the Cominform* (Cambridge, Mass. 1952).

[13] Zilliacus, *A New Birth of Freedom* p.114.

[14] Interview with Jan Zilliacus.

[15] Zilliacus, *Tito of Yugoslavia* pp. 227-8.

[16] Zilliacus, *A New Birth of Freedom* pp. 115-6.

[17] Ibid., pp. 116-7.

[18] *Tribune,* 9 September 1949.

[19] K.Zilliacus, *Tito v Stalin: Yugoslavia and the Cold War* (London, 1951) p. 39.

[20] The author had a long discussion with Jan Zilliacus on this point. She said that, to her knowledge, Konni Zilliacus did intervene on behalf of certain individuals but she doubted if it did much good because everyone in authority was afraid of being caught up in the purges.

[21] Interview with Jan Zilliacus and with Jean Mortimer Molloy. Mrs Molloy was a close friend of Jan Zilliacus and she visited Jovan Obican at his pottery in Dubrovnik, where he recounted the part played by Konni Zilliacus in obtaining his release from prison. See also Bernard Newman, *Tito's Yugoslavia* (London, 1951) p. 200.

[22] Minutes of the British-Yugoslav Association, Papers of the Rev. Canon Stanley G.Evans, Hull University Library, et. seq.

[23] *Yugoslavia Faces the Future,* a report prepared by James Klugman, Betty Wallace, Doreen Warriner and K. Zilliacus (published by the British-Yugoslav Association, London, 1947).

[24] *For a Lasting Peace, For a People's Democracy* No. 28 (55) November 1949.

[25] Ibid., No. 33(60) December 1949).

[26] Newman, op. cit., p.141.

Chapter 18: The Road to NATO

[1] Bullock, *Ernest Bevin – Foreign Secretary* pp. 513-8.

[2] Hansard, 22 January 1948.

[3] Ibid.

[4] Labour Party, NEC Minutes, 13 April 1948.

[5] John Platts-Mills in his unpublished autobiography wrote that the idea came from 'some young Italian left-wing journalist in London' (9/2), and D.N.Pritt stated 'the telegram was sent at the suggestion of a non-Communist student of Italian affairs' in D.N.Pritt, *Brasshats and Bureaucrats* (London, 1966) p. 146. However, in the Zilliacus papers (Nenni Telegram File) there is a letter from Pritt to Zilliacus dated 18 March 1948 saying he had received a suggestion from a Mr L.J. Carruthers of Finchley that a message of support be sent to Nenni. Pritt thought it a good idea but he believed he was not the appropriate person to initiate such a move. 'But do you think you could do it?' he wrote to Zilliacus. A letter from Platts-Mills to Zilliacus dated 19 March 1948 stated he had received a letter suggesting the sending of a message to Nenni. 'I think you had such a thing in mind, but it must be timed'. The suggestion, of course, may have come from more than one source but Zilliacus, who corresponded with Nenni before and after the sending of the telegram, was certainly one of the prime movers in the enterprise.

[6] Robert Jackson, *Rebels and Whips* (London, 1968) p. 68.

[7] Jenkins, *Bevanism* p. 52.

[8] Platts-Mills unpublished autobiography 9/3-4 and interview 4 May 1999.

[9] Hansard, 19 April 1948.

[10] Nenni Telegram File, Zilliacus Papers.

[11] For an account of the Berlin crisis see Richard Collier, *Bridge Across the Sky* (London, 1978).

[12] Hansard, 9 December 1948.

[13] Francis Williams, *Ernest Bevin: Portrait of a Great Englishman* (London, 1952) p. 267.

[14] Hansard, 12 May 1949.

[15] Harold Macmillan, *Tides of Fortune 1945-1955* (London, 1969) p. 134.

Chapter 19: Alarums and Excursions

[1] The speech is printed in full in Zilliacus, *Why I was Expelled* pp. 68-72.

[2] *Sunday Times,* 2 May 1948.

[3] Morgan Phillips' 'Lost Sheep' File, Labour Party Records.

[4] Labour Party Conference Report, 20 May 1948.

[5] Griffiths-Zilliacus correspondence in Morgan Phillips' 'Lost Sheep' File.

[6] *Daily Herald,* 7 June 1948.

[7] *News Chronicle,* 8 June 1948.

[8] *Robotnik,* 6 June 1948.

[9] Letter, Dalton to Phillips, 1 November 1948, 'Lost Sheep' File.

[10] *Kravchenko versus Moscow – the report of the famous Paris case with an introduction by Sir Travers Humphrey* (London, 1950) p. 121. Kravchenko's own account of the trial is given in *I Chose Justice.* For additional background to the case see Alexander Werth, *France 1940-55* (London, 1956) p. 46.

[11] *Kravchenko versus Moscow,* op. cit., pp. 118-121.
Whether Stalin's collectivisation policy was 'economically necessary' is debatable. Alec Nove in his *Economic History of the USSR 1917-91* (Penguin, 1992) p. 188 concludes that more research is required before a final judgement can be made. It is easier to settle the question as to whether the people caught up in the purges of the 1930s were guilty of the charges made against them: the answer is that almost certainly they were not. Robert Conquest's *The Great Terror – a reassessment* (London, 1990) assembles the evidence with impressive thoroughness and concludes that there was no vast internal conspiracy requiring the taking of such drastic measures. Furthermore, the purges did not eliminate a potential fifth column inside the USSR. Large numbers of Soviet citizens are known to have fought for the Germans: the Baltic states provided many recruits for Waffen SS units, thousands of Cossacks served with the German army, and General Vlasov recruited an army of 800,000 Russians to fight alongside the Germans. Many other Soviet citizens served in a non-combat role with German forces. Most of these facts, however, were not known at the time and Zilliacus, at work in the Ministry of Information, perhaps too readily accepted the claims of war-time propaganda. That the German onslaught on the Soviet Union in June 1941 took Stalin by surprise is well established, but whether he had made best use of the eighteen months 'breathing space' given him by the signing of the Nazi-Soviet Pact is more controversial. Military historians and Soviet officers who served through those testing times have varying views on the matter, and study of the fresh evidence coming out of the newly opened Soviet archives should, in time, clarify many points of issue.

[12] Interview with Jan Zilliacus.

[13] *Kravchenko versus Moscow,* op. cit., p. 125.

[14] M. Adereth, *The French Communist Party – a critical history 1920-84* (Manchester, 1984) pp.152-3.

[15] Werth, op. cit., p. 430.

[16] An open letter from K. Zilliacus to the delegates at the Sheffield Peace Congress, 12 November 1950, Zilliacus Papers.

[17] Quoted in Martin Bauml Duberman, *Paul Robeson* (London, 1989) p. 341.

[18] Ron Randin, *Paul Robeson – the man and his mission* (London, 1989) p. 156.

[19] *Gateshead Times,* 6 and 13 May 1949 and *Newcastle Journal,* 7 May 1949.

Chapter 20: The Lost Sheep

[1] *Gateshead Post*, 4 February 1949.

[2] The 'charge sheet' and other relevant correspondence can be found in Morgan Phillips' 'Lost Sheep' File, Labour Party Records.

[3] Memorandum from K. Zilliacus to the members of the Election Sub-Committee, 'Lost Sheep' File et.seq.

[4] Minutes of the Election Sub-Committee, 17 January 1949, Labour Party Records, and Zilliacus, *Why I was Expelled* pp. 37-39.

[5] Zilliacus, *Why I Was Expelled* p. 40.

[6] Obituaries on Sam Watson appeared in *The Times* and *Daily Telegraph*, 8 May 1967 and there is a useful article in *Voice of North East Industry*, July 1966 pp. 37-39. Watson's personal papers are deposited in an archive in the USA.

[7] Zilliacus, *Why I Was Expelled* pp. 40-41.

[8] C. V. Wedgwood, *The Last of the Radicals: The Life of Josiah Wedgwood MP* (London, 1974 ed.), p.139.

[9] Ibid., p. 151.

[10] *Gateshead Times*, 19 September 1947.

[11] Ibid. 30 January 1948.

[12] *Gateshead Herald*, May 1946.

[13] *Gateshead Times*, 23 January and 13 February 1948.

[14] Letter, Sam Watson to Morgan Phillips 22 February 1949, Labour Party Records.

[15] *Gateshead Post*, 11 March 1949.

[16] Zilliacus, *Why I Was Expelled* p. 48.

[17] Minutes of the Election Sub-Committee 16 May 1949 and of the NEC of the Labour Party 18 May 1949, and Zilliacus, *Why I Was Expelled* pp. 48-50.

[18] Kramnick and Sheerman, *Harold Laski – A Life on the Left* pp. 548-9.

[19] Labour Party Conference Report 1949 et. seq.

[20] Minutes of NEC of Labour Party, 27 July 1949.

[21] Interviews with Jan Zilliacus and John Platts-Mills.

[22] See D.N.Pritt, *Brasshats and Bureaucrats* (London, 1966) for Pritt's own account of this period.

Chapter 21: Crusade for Peace

[1] The letter is included in the papers on 'Enquiry on the appeal of Ald. G.C.Esther against the refusal of the Gateshead Central Labour Party and Trades Council to accept him into membership', Morgan Phillips Papers, Labour Party Records.

[2] *Gateshead Post*, August-November 1949.

[3] *Newcastle Journal*, 18 June 1949 and *Gateshead Post*, 24 June 1949, contain accounts of the meeting.

[4] *Gateshead Post*, 16 September 1949.

[5] Letter, K.Zilliacus to George Bernard Shaw, 6 July 1949 – photocopies of the Zilliacus- Shaw correspondence can be found in the Zilliacus Papers, the originals are held by Linden Empson.

[6] Letter, Shaw to Zilliacus, 14 July 1949.

[7] The arrangements for the visit are covered in further correspondence October-November 1949.

[8] *New Statesman and Nation*, 26 November 1949.

[9] Russell Kerr was elected Labour MP for Feltham in 1966.

[10] T.R. Fyvel in *Tribune*, 21 October 1949.

[11] Letter, K. Zilliacus to Max Werner, New York, 29 December 1948, Zilliacus Papers.

[12] See Brian Thomas, 'Cold War Origins II' *Journal of Contemporary History*, January 1968.

[13] 'B .P.' in *Irish Times*, 12 November 1949.

[14] *Gateshead Post*, 28 October 1949.

[15] *Northern Echo,* 21 February 1950.

[16] The North Shields playwright, Tom Hadaway, was such a person and I am grateful to him for recounting his memories of the campaign.

[17] For general background on the 1950 general election see H. G. Nicholas, *The British General Election of 1950* (London, 1950).

[18] *Northern Echo,* 20 February 1950.

[19] Ibid.,15 February 1950.

[20] *New Statesman and Nation,* 6 August 1949.

[21] *The Times Houses of Commons 1950* (London, 1950) p. 21.

Chapter 22: Tito and Slansky

[1] Interviews with Jan Zilliacus.

[2] K. Zilliacus, An open letter to the delegates at the Sheffield Peace Congress, 12 November 1950, Zilliacus Papers.

[3] Interviews with Jan Zilliacus.

[4] The Zilliacus family party consisted of Konni and Jan Zilliacus; Joe, Konni's son by his first marriage; Dawn and Laurie Harris, Jan's children by her first marriage; and Konni and Jan's daughter Linden. The sources are interviews with Jan Zilliacus, Dawn Harris Stanford, and Linden Empson 1996-99.

[5] F.M. Leventhal, *The Last Dissenter: H. N. Brailsford and His World* (Oxford, 1985) p. 294.

[6] An MP's parliamentary salary was £600 for the first year of the 1945-50 Parliament, until legislation was passed raising it to £1,000. For a discussion of the inadequacy of the salary at this time see F.T. Willey, *The Honourable Member* (London, 1974) pp. 59-69.

[7] *Daily Telegraph,* 11 September 1952.

[8] *New Statesman and Nation,* 13 Septemebr 1952.

[9] There is an abundance of information on the Slansky Trial mainly as a result of Dubcek's 'Prague Spring' of 1968. See especially Jir Pelikan (ed.) *The Czechoslovakian Political trials 1950-54: The Sup-pressed Report of the Dubcek Government's Commission of Inquiry 1986* (London, 1971), Eugene Loebl, *Sentenced and Tried* (London 1969), Arthur London *On Trial* (London, 1971), and Karel Kaplan, *Report on the Murder of the General Secretary* (London, 1990).

Reports of the trial were carried in the *Daily Worker,* 21-28 November 1952.

[10] Loebl, op. cit., p. 98.

[11] Ibid., p. 153.

[12] Ibid., p. 195.

[13] Zilliacus, *A New Birth of Freedom?* p. 148.

[14] Ibid., p.149.

Chapter 23: Gorton

[1] See Anthony Seldon, *Churchill's Indian Summer – the Conservative Government of 1951-55* (London, 1981).

[2] For study of Bevanism see Jenkins, *Bevanism – Labour's High Tide,* op.cit.,and the succinct yet valuable account by David Howell, *The Rise and Fall of Bevanism* (Leeds, no date).

[3] Interviews with Jan Zilliacus and family, and Anne Swingler.

[4] Ken Lilley, *Gorton Heritage – a brief history of people and places* (Manchester, 1982).

[5] I am grateful for information provided by Coun. Stanley Carter who was Vice-Chairman of the Gorton Labour Party at this time and a witness to these events.

[6] Hugh Dalton records some of these details in his diary for 1 May 1955.

[7] Ian Mikardo gives this account of the meeting in his autobiography *Back-Bencher* (London, 1988), pp. 130-1.

[8] For general background on the 1955 general election see D. E. Butler, *The British General Election*

of 1955 (London 1955), and the *Manchester Evening News* for details of the local campaign.
[9] *Manchester Evening News,* 11 May 1955.
[10] Duberman, op. cit., pp. 388-90.
[11] For details of the Manchester meeting see the Paul Robeson Archive, Working Class Movement Library, Salford.

Chapter 24: Westminster and Beyond

[1] Interview with Jan Zilliacus.
[2] Mikardo, op. cit., p. 91.
[3] An early example of Zilliacus's new thinking can be found in the Co-operative Movement's magazine *The Millgate,* May 1951. In his article 'Tito will not line up', pp. 4-7, he writes approvingly of Tito's policy of non-alignment, whereas John Platts-Mills in the same edition defends Soviet policy in his article 'Does Russia want peace? Yes', pp. 36-38. See also Don Watson, 'From "Fellow Traveller" to "Fascist Spy": Konni Zilliacus MP and the Cold War, *Socialist History* 11, 1997 pp. 59-87.
[4] Interview with Jan Zilliacus .
[5] For Bevan's speech in full see Labour Party Conference Report, 1957, pp. 179-83.
[6] For a narrative history of CND see Christopher Driver, *The Disarmers* (London, 1964) and for a sociological analysis F. Parkin, *Middle Class Radicalism* (London, 1968).
[7] Interview with Jan Zilliacus.
[8] Zilliacus – Cousins correspondence, Frank Cousins Papers, Warwick Modern Record Centre.
[9] There are two biographies of Frank Cousins: Margaret Stewart, *Frank Cousins – a study* (London, 1968) and Geoffrey Goodman, *The Awkward Warrior* (London, 1979).
[10] Minutes of NEC of the Labour Party, 26 February 1958.
[11] *Daily Telegraph,* 5 March 1958.
[12] Zilliacus, *A New Birth of Freedom,* p. 10.
[13] Ibid., p. 11.
[14] Ibid., p. 97.
[15] Ibid., p. 114.
[16] Ibid., p. 165.
[17] Zilliacus devoted three chapters of his book to Poland, pp. 168-216.
[18] Interviews with Jan Zilliacus and Linden Empson.
[19] Ibid.
[20] Letter from Coun. Stanley Carter.
[21] After the death of Jan Zilliacus a locked suitcase was discovered among her possessions containing correspondence between Konni Zilliacus and his constituents covering the years 1955-67. The constituents' letters contained personal problems they were bringing to the attention of their MP. Mrs Empson considered that it would be a breach of trust, for they had been written in confidence to her father, to allow these letters to be read by members of the public, but prior to their destruction she allowed me to examine the correspondence and make some general observations. Most of these letters came from people encountering problems with receipt of their pensions or social security benefits; there were a few letters concerning local schools; some from local businessmen commenting on the effects of legislation; and there was also a large batch of letters protesting at the proposed reform of the abortion laws.
[22] For general background on the 1959 general election see D. E. Butler and R. Rose, *The British General Election of 1959* (London, 1959) and the *Manchester Evening News* for details of the local campaign.
[23] Interviews with Dawn Harris Stanford and Linden Empson.

Chapter 25: Gaitskell and Khrushchev

[1] Philip M. Williams, *Hugh Gaitskell – a political biography* (London, 1979) pp. 537-44 and Brian Brivati, *Hugh Gaitskell* (London, 1996) pp. 330-9.

[2] Labour Party Annual Conference, 1959, p. 111.

[3] Ibid., p. 122.

[4] Ibid., p. 151.

[5] Minutes of NEC of Labour Party, 16 March 1960.

[6] K. Zilliacus, *Anatomy of a Sacred Cow* (London, 1960) p. 3.

[7] K. Zilliacus, 'The Soviet Union and the West' unpublished article, Zilliacus Papers, and interview with Jan Zilliacus.

[8] For the debate in full see Labour Party Conference Annual Report, 1960, pp. 170-202.

[9] *Daily Herald*, 10 October 1960.

[10] Jean Mann, *Woman in Parliament* (London, 1962) p. 206.

[11] Zilliacus – A. L. Williams Correspondence, Zilliacus Papers.

[12] *Daily Telegraph*, 10, 12 and 15 June 1961; *Sunday Telegraph* 11 June 1961; and 'Letters to the Editor' from Tom Driberg, 19 and 30 June 1961.

[13] Zilliacus – Driberg correspondence, Tom Driberg Papers, Christ Church, Oxford and carbon copy of letter from Tom Driberg to Ray Gunter, 31 July 1961, Zilliacus Papers.

[14] Interviews with Jan Zilliacus and Linden Empson, and 'My Talk with Nikita Khrushchev' by K. Zilliacus. Unpublished article, 5 October 1961, Zilliacus Papers.

[15] Duberman, op. cit., p. 498.

[16] East-West Round Table file, Zilliacus Papers.

[17] Brivati, op. cit. pp. 378-403.

[18] For Gaitskell's speech in full see Labour Party Annual Conference Report, 1962, pp. 154 –65.

[19] K. Zilliacus, 'Britain and the European Economic Community', discussion paper prepared for Tribune Group 1967, Zilliacus Papers.

[20] K. Zilliacus, 'Our lives and Cuba', memorandum 1963, Zilliacus Papers, and interviews with Jan Zilliacus and Linden Empson.

[21] Interview with Jan Zilliacus.

[22] See Janet Morgan (ed.) *The Backbench Diaries of Richard Crossman* (London, 1981) pp. 969-73. Crossman records 'The whole situation inside the Party was transformed by Gaitskell's death; Anthony Wedgwood Benn was reported to have said 'At last the Labour Party is an open society, not a closed Gaitskell clique'; and Michael Foot 'had this wonderful sense that the incredible has happened and that all kinds of things which had been impossible before Gaitskell's illness are now possible again'.

Chapter 26: Guns or Butter?

[1] For a generally sympathetic interpretation of Harold Wilson's career see Ben Pimlott, *Harold Wilson* (London, 1992) and there is Harold Wilson's own account of his first Government in *The Labour Government 1964-70* (London, 1971). A more critical approach can be found in Clive Ponting, *Breach of Promise: Labour in Power 1964-70* (London, 1984) and R. Coopey, S. Fielding and N. Tiratsoo (eds.) *The Wilson Governments 1964-70* (London, 1993). A book with some useful 'behind the scenes' material on this period is Edward Short *Whip to Wilson* (London, 1989).

[2] For general background on the 1964 general election see D. E. Butler and Anthony King, *The British General Election of 1964* (London, 1965), and the *Manchester Evening News* for details of the local campaign.

[3] Interview with Jan Zilliacus.

[4] Hansard, 23 November 1964.

[5] The phrase was coined by Hermann Goering in 1936 and used by Zilliacus in a letter to Professor Fritz Baade, 1 February 1966, see East-West Round Table file, Zilliacus Papers.

[6] Hansard, 23 November 1964.

[7] Ibid., 17 December 1964.

[8] Ibid., 19 January 1965.

[9] Ibid., 3 March 1965

[10] K. Zilliacus, 'The Labour Left Today', draft of unpublished article, 1966, Zilliacus Papers.

[11] Interview with Stan Newens.

[12] Copies of these background papers can be found in the Zilliacus Papers.

[13] Hansard, 8 March 1966.

Chapter 27: The Last Months

[1] Letter, K. Zilliacus to A.S. Horsely, 5 March 1966, Zilliacus Papers.

[2] Letter, K. Zilliacus to Franc R. Joubin, 8 May 1966, Zilliacus Papers; Corliss Lamont (ed.) *Dear Corliss – Letters from eminent persons* (New York, 1990) pp. 199-200; and interview with Jan Zilliacus.

[3] For general background on the 1966 general election see D. E. Butler and Anthony King, *The British General Election of 1966* (London, 1966), and the *Manchester Evening News* for details of local campaign.

[4] East-West Round Table file, Zilliacus Papers.

[5] Ponting, *Breach of Promise,* pp. 167-8.

[6] Ibid., pp. 184-203.

[7] K. Zilliacus, *Labour's Crisis – Its Nature, Cause and Cure* (London, 1962) p. 2.

[8] Hansard, 29 June 1966.

[9] Ibid., 7 July 1966.

[10] Ibid., 6 December 1966.

[11] Letter, K. Zilliacus to K. Marks, 27 March 1967, Zilliacus Papers.

[12] K. Zilliacus, 'Anglo-Soviet Relations', unpublished article, Zilliacus Papers.

[13] Hansard, 27 February 1967.

[14] Copy of contract with Cresset Press, Zilliacus Papers.

[15] Letter, K. Zilliacus to E. and R. Perry, 30 March 1967, Zilliacus Papers.

[16] Manuscript of 'Challenge to Fear', Zilliacus Papers.

[17] K. Zilliacus , 'The Question of Abortion', statement of Zilliacus's position on the Abortion Bill, Zilliacus Papers.

[18] Two letters, Peter Kroger to Zilliacus, 17 December 1966 and 21 January 1967, and copy of Zilliacus's reply, 28 March 1967. For background to the Portland spy ring see Arthur Tietjen, *Soviet Spy Ring (London 1967).*

[19] Interviews with Jan Zilliacus and Linden Empson et seq.

[20] *Tribune,* 14 July 1967.

[21] *Labour Monthly,* August 1967.

[22] *Daily Mail,* 7 July 1967.

[23] *The Times,* 7 July 1967.

Chapter 28: Veledictories

[1] Tape of the Conway Hall memorial meeting held by Linden Empson plus an extract from the diary of Stan Newens, who was present and recorded details.

Bibliography

Private Papers

Norman Angell Papers (Ball State University, Indiana).
C. R. Attlee Papers (Bodleian Library, Oxford and Churchill College, Cambridge).
Lord Robert Cecil Papers (British Library, London).
Frank Cousins Papers (Modern Records Centre, University of Warwick).
Lionel Curtis Papers (Bodleian Library, Oxford).
Hugh Dalton Papers (British Library of Political and Economic Science, London).
Tom Driberg Papers (Christ Church, Oxford).
Rev. Stanley G. Evans Papers (Brynmor Jones Library, University of Hull).
Kingsley Martin Papers (University of Sussex).
Philip Noel-Baker Papers (Churchill College, Cambridge).
Leonard Woolf Papers (University of Sussex).
Konni Zilliacus Papers (National Museum of Labour History, Manchester).

Other Archival Material

Foreign Office (Public Records Office, London).
Labour Party (National Museum of Labour History, Manchester).
League of Nations (United Nations Library, Geneva).
Manchester Guardian (John Rylands Library, University of Manchester).
Military Services Files (Ministry of Defence, London).
Paul Robeson Archive (Working Class Movement Library, Salford).
School Records (Bedales School, Petersfield, Hants).
Union of Democratic Control (Brynmor Jones Library, University of Hull).
University of Yale (Alumni Office, New Haven, Connecticut).

Printed Sources

Hansard: House of Commons Debates, Fifth Series.
Labour Party Annual Conference Reports.
Times House of Commons 1945-66.

Works by Konni Zilliacus, including the various pseudonyms used by him.

Books and pamphlets

Roth Williams, *The League of Nations Today* (London, 1923).
Roth Williams, *The League, the Protocol, and Empire* (London, 1925).
C. Howard-Ellis, *The Origin, Structure, and Working of the League of Nations* (New York), 1928).
Vigilantes, *The Dying Peace* (London, 1933).
Vigilantes, *Abyssinia: The Essential Facts in the Dispute and an Answer to the Question – Ought We to Support Sanctions?* (London, 1935).
Vigilantes, *Inquest on Peace* (London, 1935).
Covenanter, *Labour and War Resistance* (London, 1936).

Vigilantes, *The Road to War* (London, 1937)

Vigilantes, *Why the League Has Failed* (London, 1938).

Vigilantes, *Why We Are Losing the Peace* (London, 1939).

Konni Zilliacus, *Between Two Wars?* (London, 1939).

Konni Zilliacus, *Mirror of the Past* (London, 1944).

Diplomaticus, *Can the Tories Win the Peace? And how they lost the last one* (London, 1945)

Konni Zilliacus, *Britain, the USSR and World Peace* (London, 1946).

Konni Zilliacus, *Mirror of the Present: The Way the World is Going* (London, 1947).

Konni Zilliacus, *I Choose Peace* (London, 1949).

Konni Zilliacus, *Why I Was Expelled* (London, 1949).

Konni Zilliacus, *Dragon's Teeth: the background, contents and consequences of the North Atlantic Pact* (London, 1949).

Konni Zilliacus, *Tito versus Stalin: Yugoslavia and the Cold War* (London, 1950).

Konni Zilliacus, *Tito of Yugoslavia* (London, 1952).

Konni Zilliacus, *Four Power Talks: For Peace or War?* (London, 1955).

Konni Zilliacus, *A New Birth of Freedom? World Communism after Stalin* (London, 1957).

Konni Zilliacus, *Mutiny against Madness. H Bombs: The Case for Political Sanity* (London, 1957).

Konni Zilliacus, *Anatomy of a Sacred Cow: Ruthless Realism about NATO Nuclear Weapons* (London, 1960).

Konni Zilliacus, *Labour and the Common Market* (London, 1963).

Konni Zilliacus, *Arms and Labour* (London, 1965).

Konni Zilliacus, *Labour's Crisis: Its Nature, Cause and Cure* (London, 1966).

Articles

Konni Zilliacus was a prolific journalist and published hundreds of articles in newspapers and periodicals. In the 1920s he contributed to the *Manchester Guardian* as an anonymous correspondent of the newspaper, and in the 1930s he used the pseudonyms 'Covenanter', 'A Labour Worker', 'A Socialist', and 'Vigilantes' when writing for the *New Statesman and Nation*, and 'Perspicax' when contributing to *Tribune*. The *New Statesman and Nation* and *Tribune* were the main outlets for his articles after 1945, and he also contributed to other left-wing publications such as *Labour Monthly*, *Reynolds News*, and *Socialist Review*.

Newspapers and periodicals

Daily Worker
Daily Herald
Daily Mail
Daily Telegraph
For a Lasting Peace For a People's Democracy
Gateshead Herald
Gateshead Post
Gateshead Times
Guardian
Independent
Labour Monthly
League of Nations Journal
Manchester Evening News
Manchester Guardian
The Millgate
Newcastle Chronicle
Newcastle Journal

News Chronicle
New Statesman and Nation
Northern Echo
North Mail
Political Quarterly
Robotnik
Socialist History
Sunday Times
The Times
Tribune
Voice of North East Industry

Biography, Diaries, Letters and Memoirs

N. Angell, *After All* (London, 1951).
Earl of Avon, *The Eden Memoirs – Facing the Dictators* (London, 1962).
B. Brivati, *Hugh Gaitskell* (London, 1996).
A. Bullock, *The Life and Times of Ernest Bevin, Volume One, Trade Union Leader 1888-1940* (London, 1960).
A. Bullock, *The Life and Times of Ernest Bevin, Volume Two, Minister of Labour 1940-45* (London, 1967).
A. Bullock, *The Life and Times of Ernest Bevin, Volume Three, Foreign Secretary 1945-51* (London, 1983).
J. Callaghan, *Time and Chance* (London, 1987).
M. Callcott (ed.), *A Pilgrimage of Grace: the diaries of Ruth Dodds 1905-74* (Whitley Bay, 1995).
J. Campbell, *Nye Bevan and the Mirage of British Socialism* (London, 1987).
B. Castle, *Fighting All the Way* (London, 1993).
J. Cook, *Priestley* (London, 1997).
S. Crosland, *Tony Crosland* (London, 1982).
H. Dalton, *Call Back Yesterday* (London, 1953).
H. Dalton, *The Fateful Years* (London, 1957).
V. Dedijer, *Tito Speaks* (London, 1953).
M .B. Duberman, *Paul Robeson* (London, 1989).
D. Dutton, *Simon – a political biography of Sir John Simon* (London, 1992).
M. Foot, *Aneurin Bevan: A Biography, Volume Two, 1945-60* (London, 1973.)
G. Goodman, *The Awkward Warrior. Frank Cousins: His Life and Times* (London, 1979).
R. Griffiths, *S. O. Davies: A Socialist Faith* (Llandysul, 1983).
M. A Hamilton, *Arthur Henderson: A Biography* (London, 1938).
M. A. Hamilton, *Remembering My Good Friends* (London, 1944).
K. Harris, *Attlee* (London, 1982).
D. Healey, *The Time of My Life* (London, 1989).
A. Howard, *Crossman: The Pursuit of Power* (London, 1990).
D. Jay, *Change and Fortune* (London, 1980).
I. Kramnick and B. Sherman, *Harold Laski: A Life on the Left* (London, 1993).
C. Lamont (ed.), *Dear Corliss: Letters from Eminent Persons* (New York, 1990).
F. M. Leventhal, *The Last Dissenter: H. N. Brailsford and His World* (Oxford 1985).
F. M. Leventhal, *Arthur Henderson* (Manchester, 1989).
H. Macmillan, *Tides of Fortune 1945-55* (London, 1969).
J. Mann, *Woman in Parliament* (London, 1962).
L. Manning, *A Life for Education* (London, 1970).
K. Martin, *Harold Laski 1893-1950: A Biographical Memoir* (London, 1953).
C. Mayhew, *Time to Explain* (London, 1987).

I. Mikardo, *Back-Bencher* (London, 1988).

J. Morgan (ed.), *The Backbench Diaries of Richard Crossman* (London, 1981).

M. Muggeridge, *Chronicles of a Wasted Life: The Infernal Grove* (London, 1973).

H. Nicolson, *Diary and Letters 1939-45* (London, 1967).

B. Pimlott, *Hugh Dalton* (London, 1985).

B. Pimlott, *Harold Wilson* (London, 1992).

D.N. Pritt, *Brasshats and Bureaucrats* (London, 1966).

R. Randin, *Paul Robeson: The Man and his Mission* (London, 1989).

W. T. Rodgers (ed.), *Hugh Gaitskell* (London, 1964).

E. Short, *Whip to Wilson* (London, 1989).

C. H. Sisson (ed.), *Autobiographical and other papers by Philip Mairet* (Manchester, 1981).

Margaret Stewart, *Frank Cousins- A Study* (London, 1968).

Michael Stewart, *Life and Labour* (London, 1990).

G. Thomas, *Mr Speaker* (London, 1985).

C.V. Wedgwood, *The Last of the Radicals* (London, 1974 edition).

J. Wedgwood, *Essays and Adventures of a Labour MP* (London, 1924).

J. Wedgwood, *Memoirs of a Fighting Life* (London, 1940).

D. J. Whittaker, *Fighter for Peace: Philip Noel-Baker 1889-1982* (York, 1989).

Lord Wigg, *George Wigg* (London, 1972).

F. Williams, *Ernest Bevin: Portrait of a Great Englishman* (London, 1952).

G. Williams and B. Reed, *Denis Healey and the Politics of Power* (London, 1971).

P. M. Williams, *Hugh Gaitskell: A Political Biography* (London, 1979).

P. M. Williams (ed.), *The Diary of Hugh Gaitskell 1945-56* (London, 1983).

H. Wilson, *The Labour Government 1964-70* (London, 1971).

W. Wyatt, *Confessions of an Optimist* (London, 1985).

Other Books

P. Addison, *The Road to 1945* (London, 1945).

M. Adereth, *The French Communist Party – a critical history 1920-84* (Manchester, 1984).

A.J. Barker, *The Civilizing Mission: the Italo-Ethiopian War 1935-6 (London, 1968).*

J. Barros, *The Corfu Incident of 1923: Mussolini and the League of Nations* (Princeton, 1965).

J. Barros, *Betrayal from Within; Joseph Avenol, Secretary-General of the League of Nations 1933-40* (Yale, 1969).

R. Bassett, *Democracy and Foreign Policy. A case history: the Sino-Japanese War 1937-45* (London, 1952).

J. Brauthal, *A History of the International* (London, 1980).

G. Brook-Shepherd, *Anschluss: The Rape of Austria* (London, 1963).

T. D. Burridge, *British Labour and Hitler's War* (London, 1976).

D. E. Butler, *The British General Election of 1951* (London, 1952).

D. E. Butler, *The British General Election of 1955* (London, 1955).

D. E. Butler and R. Rose, *The British General Election of 1959* (London, 1960).

D. E. Butler and A. King, *The British General Election of 1964* (London, 1965).

D. E. Butler and A. King, *The British General Election of 1966* (London, 1966).

H. Butler, *The Lost Peace* (London, 1941).

D. Carlton, *MacDonald versus Henderson: The Foreign Policy of the Second Labour Government* (London, 1970).

J. Charnley, *Chamberlain and the Lost Peace* (London, 1989).

W. S. Churchill, *The Gathering Storm* (London, 1948).

C. A. Cline, *Recruits to Labour: The British Labour Party 1914-31* (New York, 1963).

G. D. H. Cole, *A History of the Labour Party from 1914* (London, 1978 ed.).

R. Collier, *Bridge Across the Sky* (London, 1978).

R. Conquest, *The Great Terror- A Reassessment* (London, 1990).

R. Coopey, S. Fielding and N. Tiratsoo, *The Wilson Governments 1964-70* (London, 1993).

C. Driver, *The Disarmers* (London, 1964).

M. Futrell, *Northern Underground* (New York, 1963).

J. Fyrth, *The Signal Was Spain: The Spanish Aid Movement in Britain* (London, 1986).

M. Gilbert and R. Gott, *The Appeasers* (London, 1962).

V. Gollancz (ed.), *The Betrayal of the Left* (London, 1941).

J .Gunther, *Behind Europe's Curtain* (London, 1949).

T. T. Hammond (ed.), *The Anatomy of Communist Takeovers* (Yale, 1975).

L. Hart, *History of the Second World War* (London, 1970).

D. Healey, *The Curtain Falls* (London, 1951).

A.   Henderson, *Labour's Way to Peace* (London, 1935).

D. Howell, *The Rise and Fall of Bevanism* (Leeds, no date).

T. Humphreys, *Kravchenko versus Moscow: A Report of the famous Paris case* (London, 1950).

R. Jackson, *Rebels and Whips* (London, 1968).

M. Jenkins, *Bevanism: Labour's High Tide* (Nottingham, 1979).

B. Jones, *The Russian Complex: The British Labour Party and the Soviet Union* (Manchester,1977).

J.A. Joyce, *Broken Star: The Story of the League of Nations* (Swansea, 1978).

E. Katz, *The International Film Encyclopedia* (London, 1980 ed.).

R. Kee, *Munich: The Eleventh Hour* (London, 1988).

A. Koestler, *Darkness at Noon* (London, 1941).

J. Lewis, *The Left Book Club: An Historical Record* (London, 1970).

K. Lilley, *Gorton Heritage: A Brief History of People and Places* (Manchester, 1982).

E. Loebl, *Sentenced and Tried* (London, 1969).

A. London, *On Trial* (London, 1970).

R. W. Lyman, *The First Labour Government 1924* (London, 1957).

F. W. D. Manders, *A History of Gateshead* (Gateshead, 1973).

R. B. McCallum and A. Readman, *The British General Election of 1945* (Oxford, 1947).

I. McLaine, *Ministry of Morale: Home Front Morale and the Ministry of Information in World War Two* (London, 1979).

J.D.B. Miller, *Norman Angell and the Futility of War* (London, 1986).

K. O. Morgan, *Labour in Power 1945-51* (Oxford, 1984).

J.F. Naylor, *Labour's International Policy: The Labour Party in the 1930s* (London, 1969).

B. Newman, *Tito's Yugoslavia* (London, 1951).

H. G. Nicholas, *The British General Election of 1950* (London, 1950).

F. S. Northedge, *The League of Nations: Its Life and Times 1920-46* (Leicester, 1946).

A. Nove, *Economic History of the USSR 1917-91* (London, 1992).

F. Parkin, *Middle Class Radicalism* (London, 1968).

J. Pelikan (ed.), *The Czechoslovak Political Trials 1950-54: The Suppressed Report of the Dubcek Government's Commission of Inquiry, 1968* (London, 1971).

C. Ponting, *Breach of Promise: Labour in Power 1964-70* (London, 1984).

J. B. Priestley, *English Journey* (London, 1949 edition).

A. Rothstein, *When Britain Invaded the Soviet Union: The Consul Who Rebelled* (London, 1979).

V. Rothwell, *Britain and the Cold War 1941-47* (London, 1982).

J. Saville, *The Politics of Continuity: British Foreign Policy and the Labour Government 1945-6* (London, 1993).

J. Schneer, *Labour's Conscience: The Labour Left 1945-51* (London, 1988).

L. Schwarzchild, *World in Trance* (London, 1943).

G. Scott, *The Rise and Fall of the League of Nations* (London, 1973).

A. Seldon, *Churchill's Indian Summer: The Conservative Government of 1951-5* (London, 1981).

H. Seton-Watson, *The Pattern of Communist Revolution* (London, 1953).

S. R. Smith, *The Manchurian Crisis 1931-2: A Tragedy in International Relations* (New York,

1948).

T. Stannage, *Baldwin Thwarts the Opposition* (London, 1980).

J. Strachey, *The Strangled Cry* (London, 1962).

A.J.P. Taylor, *The Troublemakers* (London, 1957).

A.J.P. Taylor, *English History 1914-45* (Oxford, 1967 edition).

T. Taylor, *Munich: The Price of Peace* (London, 1978).

A. Tietjen, *Soviet Spy Ring* (London, 1967).

N. Tolstoy, *Stalin's Secret War* (London, 1981).

A .B. Ulam, *Titoism and the Cominform* (Cambridge, Mass., 1952).

R. H. Ullman, *Intervention and War* (Princeton, 1961).

R. H. Ullman, *Britain and the Civil War* (Princeton, 1968).

R.H. Ullman, *The Anglo-Soviet Accord* (Princeton, 1972).

F. P. Walters, *A History of the League of Nations* (Oxford, 1952).

D. Watson and J. Corcoran, *An Inspiring Example: The North East and the Spanish Civil War 1936-9* (London, 1996).

P. Weiler, *British Labour and the Cold War* (Stanford, 1988).

A. Werth, *France 1940-55* (London, 1956).

F .T. Willey, *The Honourable Member* (London, 1974).

D. Wilson, *When Tigers Fight: The Story of the Sino-Japanese War 1937-45* (London, 1982).

V. Zubok and C. Pleshakov, *Inside the Kremlin's Cold War* (Harvard, 1996).

Articles

Hugh Dalton, 'British Foreign Policy 1929-31', *Political Quarterly* , Oct-Dec, 1931.

R. Smith and J. Zametica, 'The Cold Warrior: Clement Attlee Reconsidered 1945-7', *International Affairs*, Spring 1985.

Brian Thomas, 'Cold War Origins', *Journal of Contemporary History*, January 1968.

Dan Watson, 'From "Fellow Traveller" to "Fascist Spy": Konni Zilliacus MP and the Cold War', *Socialist History* 11, 1997.

Unpublished Thesis and Dissertation

Kenneth Millen-Penn, 'From Liberal to Socialist Internationalism: Konni Zilliacus and the League of Nations, 1894-1939', Ph.D. (State University of New York at Binghampton), 1993.

Sharon Ferguson, 'Labour Party Politics 1935-45: a case study of Konni Zilliacus and the Gateshead Labour Party and Trades Council'.

Dissertation submitted in partial fulfilment of the requirements of the degree of B.A. with Honours in History, University of Cambridge, 1988.

Index

(Note: Individuals are normally listed under the name by which they are best known, or by which they were known at the time of their first significant appearance in the text. Relationships specified are to Konni Zilliacus.)